CHANGING DIRECTIONS

Changing Directions

The Report of The Independent Commission on Transport

CORONET BOOKS
Hodder Paperbacks Ltd., London

Printed and bound in Great Britain for
Coronet Books,
Hodder Paperbacks Ltd.,
St. Paul's House, Warwick Lane,
London, EC4P 4AH
by Hazell Watson & Viney Ltd.,
Aylesbury, Bucks

ISBN 0 340 18765 4

Table of Contents

5

A Personal Statement From The Chairman

I am grateful to my colleagues for permitting me to include a short statement about how this Commission began and why I initiated and chaired it. This is purely a personal statement; it concerns myself alone, and does not necessarily reflect the views of any other member of the Commission. In any case, it is the Report itself that really matters.

So many people have asked why a Church of England bishop should "waste his time" on a Transport Commission that I feel I must explain myself. "Don't you think, Bishop," Lord Beeching commented when I consulted him, "that you would be better employed putting the affairs of the Church in order instead of trying your hand in a secular area where so many experts have failed?"

As a Christian I believe in God, who has disclosed himself through Jesus Christ in flesh and blood. And so matter really matters. As Archbishop Temple said in a memorable sentence, Christianity is the most materialistic of the great world religions. As a Christian I am interested in, and involved in, the secular world.

All Christian ministry (including that of a bishop), inspired by the ministry of Jesus Christ, has three spheres of operation: among individuals, within the Church and to society. This Commission has been part of my ministry to society.

All Christian ministry, following the ministry of Jesus, has two distinct but interconnected functions: to serve and to save. My work on this Commission is part of my service to the community. Since man is called to co-operate in the work of God's salvation—that is, to help to put right or to re-create what man has disordered or destroyed through sin, folly, frailty or thoughtlessness—I hope that, in a very small way, this Report may contribute to our share in working out our salvation.

9

As a Christian I believe that we should be freed from enslavement to what St. Paul called "principalities and powers", which I would paraphrase as the impersonal powers of modern life. Among the principalities and powers which dominate us today, transport is pre-eminent; and we need liberation from enslavement to it.

As a member of the Church of England's Doctrinal Commission, I chair a subgroup which I hope will soon complete a Report on the Theology of Man's Environment. Before literally "pontificating" on a subject like this, I could not refuse an opportunity of studying in depth one particular aspect of it.

How did the opportunity arise? At a Church Leaders' Conference, held in Britain in September 1972, it became clear to members of a Commission on "Man's Stewardship of God's World" that a radical and multidisciplinary examination of our consumer society had become urgently necessary; but how to carry this out was not obvious. Then, out of the blue, a few weeks later, my fellow trustees of the Ecological Foundation approached me to ask whether I would organise and chair a Transport Commission. It seemed sensible to concentrate on one aspect only of our modern technological society; and I knew that I had to accept their invitation. Although I personally was, and remain, convinced that the goal of ever-increasing economic growth, which involves the use of non-renewable resources and which results in their inequitable distribution, is both undesirable and unattainable, I decided that, for the purpose of this inquiry, we should concentrate simply on matters of transport. I remember my feelings as I spent that Christmas holiday writing what seemed like innumerable letters of invitation. To my great surprise, all difficulties fell away. I found myself with an interdisciplinary group comprising persons of eminence from a great variety of walks of life. I had excluded anyone who had a vested interest in a particular mode of transport. I decided to call the Commission "The Independent Commission on Transport", to make quite clear the independence of the Commission from any other body. The responsibility for this report and its recommendations is ours alone.

A Christian as such has no special ability for solving problems, but his concern for human well-being enables

10

him to take an overall view. So he can sometimes take the initiative in a wide-ranging inquiry and invite others to co-operate. We have worked happily together as colleagues, with Stephen Plowden as our Executive Secretary, ever since 15th February 1973, when the first Plenary Session was held and the life of the Commission began.

If our conclusions are accepted at large, the whole way of life of our nation will change—for the better.

21 December 1973   HUGH MONTEFIORE

Independent Commission on Transport

Members

The Right Reverend Hugh Montefiore, *Bishop of Kingston-upon-Thames* (Chairman)

Sir John Betjeman, *Poet Laureate*

Frank Chapple, *General Secretary, EETPU*

Sir James Farquharson, *President, Scottish Association for Public Transport, formerly General Manager, East African Railways and Harbours, etc.*

John Francis, *Director, Society, Religion and Technology Project, Church of Scotland Home Board*

John Garnett, *Director, The Industrial Society*

Michael Graham, *Economic Adviser to Overseas Containers Ltd.*

Mayer Hillman, *Senior Research Officer, Political and Economic Planning*

Dick Jones, *Local Government Planner*

Gerald Leach, *Visiting Fellow, Science Policy Research Unit, Sussex University; formerly Science Correspondent, The Observer*

Norman Lee, *Senior Lecturer in Economics, Manchester University*

Ezra Mishan, *Reader in Economics, London School of Economics*

Jack Parsons, *Lecturer in Social Institutions, Brunel University*

Gabrielle Pike, *Chairman, Women's Group on Public Welfare*

Ronald Preston, *Professor of Social and Pastoral Theology, Manchester University*

Lois Pulling, *Chairman, Working Party on Public Transport, National Council of Women of Great Britain*

David Rubinstein, *Vice-Chairman of the Ramblers' Association; Lecturer in Social History, Hull University*

Graham Searle, *Director, Friends of the Earth*

13

Foreword

We can present this Report only because of practical help received from others. The existence of the Commission was made possible by grants organised by the Ecological Foundation, and we are grateful to Brian Johnson for all the help that he gave as its Director. We have been financed by the generosity of one of its trustees, Jimmy Goldsmith, and by grants from the Ernest Cook Trust, the Hilden Charitable Trust, the Manifold Trust, the Morgan Charitable Trust and the Slater Foundation. Mr. Peyton, when Minister for Transport Industries, on two occasions received the Chairman and Executive Secretary most kindly; and we have had technical assistance from the Department of the Environment and from British Rail. We have been helped by our four Honorary Consultants, all of whom have been active on our behalf; and in addition Denys Munby of Nuffield College, Oxford, has kindly allowed us to consult him. We are especially grateful to the Environmental Consulting Office, which has given us house room in Central London. We acknowledge elsewhere the many individuals and organisations with whom we have been in touch.

We have been most fortunate in the loyalty, enthusiasm and hard work of our staff. Margaret Dixon, and later Pat Quaife, have both been indefatigable, unflappable and seemingly irreplaceable secretaries. Barbara Mostyn (née Williams), of the London School of Economics, and Hugh Saddler, General Secretary of the British Society for Social Responsibility in Science, have been invaluable as Research Assistants. We are grateful to Metra Consulting Group Ltd. for enabling us to have Stephen Plowden as our Executive Secretary. The whole enterprise has rested on his shoulders. It is impossible to speak of what he has done for us except in superlatives, and the whole Commission is

15

united in expressing its gratitude for what he has enabled us to achieve.

Jackie Gillott had to resign at the outset for reasons of health, and later Anthony Storr. Bernard Dixon resigned for reasons of work and Stanley Johnson on his appointment to the EEC, and Des Wilson changed from Commissioner to Consultant when he became involved in party politics. The remaining twenty-three members of the Commission have worked in six committees. Ten plenary sessions have been held, and two residential conferences. The Commission met for the last time on 22 December 1973.

Mr. Graham Searle, who had given much time to the Commission, left for New Zealand before the Report could be finalised. His other duties prevented Mr. Frank Chapple from being present at many plenary sessions, but he has allowed his name to stand with certain reservations recorded later in the Report.

Many people have helped in editing our Report for publication, but the Commission is particularly indebted to Michael Thomson.

CHAPTER 1

The Reason For This Report

1.1 Transport is a subject of growing concern and confusion to a large number of people. Road and air traffic grow continually, and there are predictions of yet further growth. Ordinary people are distressed by the numbers killed and injured as a price for mobility, and, being warned by experts of increasing world shortages, they are worried by transport's seemingly profligate use of resources. Meanwhile bus and rail services deteriorate and fares rise. The expansion of transport as a whole has brought benefits, but most people realise that for some it has caused acute deprivation, and it is increasingly intrusive. People are perplexed by the technicalities of transport issues, and they fear that moral and political choices are being obscured.

1.2 Above all, many people are disturbed by the apparently piecemeal character of transport decisions and the lack of integrated policies. Not only does it seem that wrong decisions are being made, it also seems that the individual and the community are denied any real choice at all in matters of transport. Where we should be taking charge of events, are events taking charge of us?

1.3 We hope that our work on this Commission will show which fears and concerns are justified and which of the many solutions are worth pursuing. We have tried to describe the problems raised by transport and to explain their causes and interactions, hoping in this way to reveal the principles and lines of approach necessary for their solution. In doing this, we have deliberately set ourselves a wide field and a long time perspective.

1.4 We have addressed ourselves to the general educated public on whose understanding of the issues of the day a democracy depends. We have therefore tried to avoid technical language. We hope we have not sacrificed profundity or rigour for the sake of popular intelligibility. Although transport involves many technical problems, the fundamental issues are not technical, but political, social and moral.

1.5 Our aim is to examine the present transport situation in this country, to suggest criteria for national policies and to make recommendations. We can move ourselves, or move goods, by many different modes—foot, bicycle, motor bicycle, car, train, boat or plane. Each mode has its advantages and disadvantages. Part of our task is to contrast the potential of each mode with its present use. We have tried to survey the transport scene as a whole, to place all its main facets in fair perspective and to assess the possibilities for technical and other changes without ignoring economic and financial restraints. We have also tried to recognise the claims of social justice without ignoring the hard facts of political life. We have done our best to represent the interests of the more deprived sections of our own nation, but also to respect our obligations to other nations, including those poorer than our own, and to future generations. Above all, we have tried to appreciate the pervading influence of transport on the quality of life and the character of society itself, judging that many people are ready to question what is meant by "standard of living" when it is plain that the quest for higher material standards often erodes such fundamental values as peace, quiet, beauty, continuity with the past, and a sense of the "fitness of place".

1.6 We have asked some fundamental questions about transport itself. Why do we need it? Why is mobility highly valued? Are we being forced into ways of life we do not like simply by the present structure of society and its institutions? Like Alice, do we have to run a lot faster, simply to keep up with the Red Queen? A solution to our problems depends not so much upon a detailed knowledge of the transport system as upon a fundamental understanding of the ways in which transport, which should be the servant of the community, tends to shape the community geographically, economically, socially and environmentally.

1.7 Before coming to policy recommendations, we consider how transport decisions are made and we contrast this with the way we believe they should be made. We propose criteria and procedures and outline the institutions which we think are required. We believe that radical changes are necessary in the process of decision-making.

1.8 In spite of our wish to be comprehensive, practical reasons of time and resources forced us to limit the scope of our inquiry. It seemed better to cut out some topics altogether than to treat all superficially. We omitted international travel, apart from the direct physical impact on this country caused, for instance, by aircraft noise or port traffic. We regretted having to make this omission, because international travel raises many issues similar to those raised by domestic transport. However, there are many domestic issues, affecting people every day, which have no international counterpart. In any case, we could not include international travel without considering the interests of other countries and without examining some major projects related to international travel, such as Concorde, Maplin and the Channel Tunnel. Neither task was possible within our resources.

1.9 Another topic not included is the role played by the transport industries, particularly the motor industry, within the economy. It is sometimes argued that any policy harmful to the motor industry would have such drastic repercussions on the national economy that it could not be contemplated. We do not attempt to predict the effects of our proposals on the motor industry, but we do not accept that the future of the motor industry need be as crucial to the economy as this theory suggests. Certainly there could be an important short-term problem here, affecting the speed with which policy changes could be introduced. In the long term, however, the value of the motor industry, like that of any other industry, depends on the value of its products to society. There are many other products, e.g. houses, schools and hospitals, to which resources of capital, materials and labour could be diverted in the long run.

1.10 We have said little about new technology, either in transport itself or in substitutes for transport such as telecommunications. Conceivably, new technology might eventually revolutionise transport problems, for instance by obviating the need to make so many journeys. But, having considered papers on the subect, we did not see any prospect of new technology having such a drastic effect in the foreseeable future. Also, we do not believe that new technology is essential to a satisfactory solution of the problems, which are basically organisational and political and, given the right will and attitudes, can be solved within the present technology. We do recommend some technical developments, but these are no more than an extension of existing technology. We recognise that more revolutionary technological change may be achieved within the period for which we should be planning, and our chief inference from this fact is that it increases the uncertainty of long-term planning and hence the risk of investing in costly, long-lasting structures.

1.11 Other questions on which we have not been able to give firm answers include pollution and the longer-term energy situation. This is largely because of the fundamental uncertainty that surrounds these issues: experts disagree and there is no way of choosing between them. But it does not necessarily follow that nothing useful can be said about the policy implications. Where different views lead to different policy implications, it is still necessary to come to a policy, after giving due weight to the unavoidable uncertainty.

1.12 Not all the problems posed by transport are related to transport policy. Some can be tackled by specific measures not requiring policy decisions, e.g. certain safety regulations. In general, we are concerned with transport policy, not with specific measures. But some consideration of specific measures is necessary to ensure that changes in policy are in fact required. We have indeed made some recommendations of a specific kind.

1.13 During the course of our discussions in 1973, new measures or proposals have been introduced or approved by government which otherwise we would have felt bound to propose. We were encouraged by the contents of *Government Observations on the Second Report of the Expenditure Committee on Urban Transport* (Cmnd. 5366). As we complete our Report, we are glad to hear of a Bill to be laid before Parliament to give additional help to British Rail, particularly in respect of freight services, with computer-controlled wagon systems and high capacity wagons, and to keep in being the existing rail network. We have also noted with satisfaction that during the course of our deliberations The Heavy Commercial Vehicles (Controls and Regulations)

Act 1973 (commonly known as the Dykes Act) has become law, and that a new Protection of the Environment Bill has been introduced. We note, however, that many provisions under these measures are permissive and not mandatory.

1.14 With the time and resources at our disposal, we have not tried to conduct original research but have relied on existing information. On some topics which we regard as important, such as pedestrian movement, the information is far from adequate, but we have avoided simply concluding that more research is necessary. We have reached major policy conclusions. We have good grounds for confidence in them, not least because so many important considerations point in the same direction. We have given our reasoning as fully as possible, and we hope that our report will make a useful contribution to the debate on this important subject.

CHAPTER 2

The Scale of Transport Activity

2.1 Before the problems that transport poses for society can be properly understood, it is necessary to have some idea of the scale of the changes that are now taking place. This chapter gives a general picture of recent trends and also attempts to make some projections based on them where official projections are not available. Official projections are given where possible, and others conform as closely as possible with official data where these exist. The projections assume that the policies now officially proposed will be implemented and, more generally, that neither substantial changes in transport policy nor major external events will occur to alter the trends of recent years. Whether present policies *should* be pursued and trends allowed to develop is, of course, the whole point at issue. The purpose of this chapter, however, is to give some idea of the scale of transport activity which would result if that were to happen.

2.2 Even within these assumptions there is a good deal of room for debate about how projections should be made, and in later chapters we raise some questions about official methods. But these questions are not important for the immediate purpose of painting a very general background picture.

Personal travel

2.3 Figure 2.1 shows the changes in personal travel in Great Britain since 1953 (measured in 1,000 millions of passenger-miles), and the development that can be expected if present trends continue up to the year 2001. More detailed figures for past trends and an explanation of the assumptions embodied in the projections of Figure 2.1 are given in Appendix 1.

2.4 The picture is that of a vast increase, almost entirely accounted for by cars and taxis. Whereas in 1953 these were

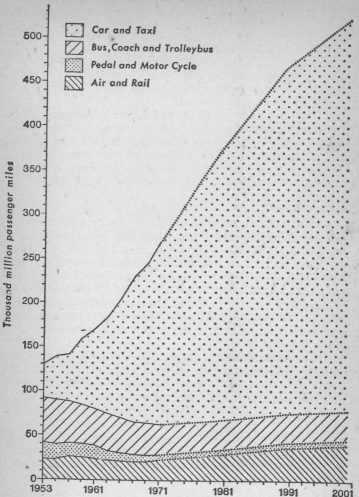

Figure 2.1: Growth of personal travel in Great Britain

Legend:
- Car and Taxi
- Bus, Coach and Trolleybus
- Pedal and Motor Cycle
- Air and Rail

Y-axis: Thousand million passenger miles

X-axis years: 1953, 1961, 1971, 1981, 1991, 2001

Units: thousand million passenger miles.

Years: actual figures from 1953 to 1971; projections for 1981, 1991, 2001.

Modes: air, rail, bus, coach and trolley bus, pedal cycle, motor cycle, car and taxi.

Sources: Passenger Transport in Great Britain, Highway Statistics.
Other assumptions as explained in Appendix 1.

responsible for less than 30% of personal mileage travelled—a smaller share than that held by bus and coach—by 1971 they accounted for 77%. With the trivial exception of domestic air travel, which itself has not grown in the last five years, fewer passenger miles were achieved by each mode of travel other than car and taxi in 1971 than in 1953. Travel by motorcycle and pedal cycle, particularly the latter, has shown the most rapid decline.

2.5 The projections up to the end of the century show that by then there would be roughly four times as much personal travel as in 1953 and twice as much as in 1971, and almost all the increase would be accounted for by cars. Cars and taxis together would account for 85% of all personal travel by 2001, compared with 77% in 1971 and 29% in 1953.

Goods transport

2.6 Figure 2.2 deals with goods transport (measured in thousands of millions of ton-miles) and presents a similar picture. More detailed figures and explanations can be found in Appendix 1. From 1953 to 1971 goods transport increased by 57%, and this increase was entirely accounted for by road goods transport, which increased by 260%. If these trends were to continue, by the end of the century the annual total of ton-miles would be twice that of today and road transport would be carrying 82% of the total, compared with 63% in 1971 and 38% in 1953.

2.7 The dramatic increase in the use of heavy goods vehicles can be seen in Figure 2.3. Between 1962 and 1971 the ton-miles of vehicles above five tons unladen weight increased over three times, while the ton mileage of vehicles over eight tons unladen weight increased nearly six times. There are no official projections corresponding to these figures, and in this case we have not attempted to make our own. Official projections of goods vehicle mileage do, however, rest on the assumption that there will continue to be an increase in the average size and weight of heavy goods vehicles.

Vehicle miles and vehicle numbers

2.8 Figure 2.4 shows what this great increase in travel by road has meant in terms of vehicle miles and what it will mean if present trends are maintained, the broad picture being, of course, much the same as for passenger and

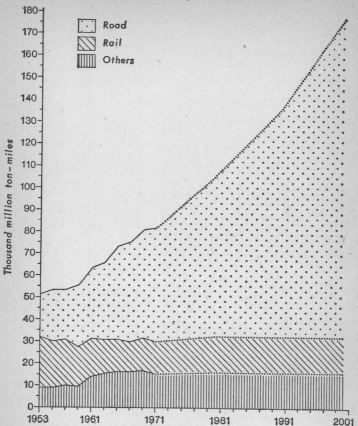

Figure 2.2: Goods transport in Great Britain

Legend:
Road
Rail
Others

Y-axis: Thousand million ton-miles (0 to 180)
X-axis: 1953, 1961, 1971, 1981, 1991, 2001

Units: thousand million ton-miles.

Years: actual figures from 1953 to 1971; projections for 1981, 1991, 2001.

Modes: pipelines, inland waterways, coastal shipping, rail, road.

Sources: Annual Abstracts of Statistics, HMSO.
Transport and Road Research Laboratory Report LR 429, HMSO.
Other assumptions as explained in Appendix 1.

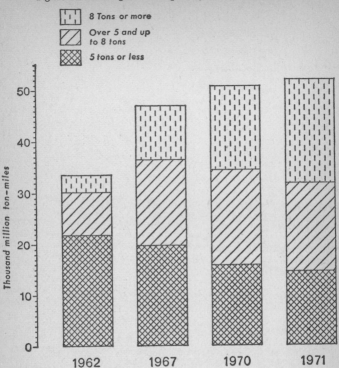

Figure 2.3: Road goods transport by size of vehicle used

Units: thousand million ton-miles.

Years: actual figures for 1962, 1967/68, 1970, 1971.
Sizes: 5 tons or less, over 5 tons and less than 8 tons, 8 tons and over.

Sources: Survey of Road Goods Transport 1962. HMSO, 1963.
Survey of the Transport of Goods by Road 1967–68. HMSO, 1971.
The Transport of Goods by Road 1970–72. HMSO, 1972.

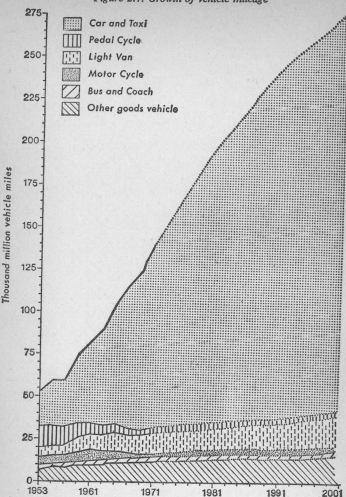

Figure 2.4: Growth of vehicle mileage

Legend:
- Car and Taxi
- Pedal Cycle
- Light Van
- Motor Cycle
- Bus and Coach
- Other goods vehicle

Thousand million vehicle miles (vertical axis, 0 to 275)

Years (horizontal axis): 1953, 1961, 1971, 1981, 1991, 2001

Units: thousand million vehicle miles.

Years: actual figures from 1953 to 1971; projections for 1981, 1991, 2001.

Modes: pedal cycles, motor cycle, car and taxi, bus and coach, light van, other goods vehicles.

Sources: Highway Statistics. HMSO.

Forecasts of Vehicles and Traffic in Great Britain, 1972 Revision, TRRL Report LR 543. HMSO, 1973.

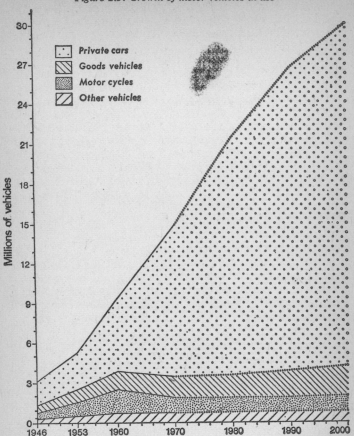

Figure 2.5: Growth of motor vehicles in use

Units: millions of vehicles.

Years: actual figures for 1946, 1953, 1960, 1970; projections for 1980, 1990, 2000.

Types of vehicle: other vehicles, motor cycles, private cars, goods vehicles.

Sources: Basic Road Statistics 1972, British Roads Federation, 1972.
   Forecasts of Vehicles and Traffic in Great Britain, 1972 Revision, TRRL Report LR 543. HMSO, 1973.

28

ton-miles. Vehicle miles increased 2·6 times between 1953 and 1971 and are expected to increase a further 2·1 times by the year 2000. More detailed figures of vehicle miles are given in Appendix 1.

2.9 The number of vehicles in use is shown in Figure 2.5, and once again the story is the same. The increase between 1953 and 1971 was 2·8 times, and by 2000 a further doubling is envisaged. The increase in the numbers of goods vehicles of different sizes is shown in Appendix 1. Heavy goods vehicles have increased particularly fast. Between 1957 and 1971 the number of goods vehicles of all weights increased by a factor of 1·3, whereas those between 5 and 8 tons unladen weight increased 4·8 times and those over 8 tons unladen increased more than 9 times. In 1971 the two last categories together comprised 13% of all goods vehicles, compared with 3% in 1957.

Roads

2.10 The mileage of public roads in Great Britain increased by 12% between 1953 and 1971, as shown in Table 2.1. Mileage is, however, an indifferent guide to total road capacity, since it takes no account of the capacities of different types of roads or of the possible effects of measures such as widening roads, enlarging junctions, and so on.

Table 2.1: Mileage of public roads in Great Britain
Units: thousand miles

	1953	1958	1963	1968	1969	1970	1971
Motorways	—	—	0·2	0·6	0·6	0·7	0·8
Trunk Roads	8·3	8·3	8·3	8·4	8·4	8·3	8·3
Class I or principal roads	19·6	19·7	19·8	20·2	20·2	20·3	20·3
All other roads	158·5	163·1	170·1	174·8	177·2	178·7	179·9
Total	186·4	191·1	198·4	204·0	206·4	207·9	209·3

Source: Highway Statistics, HMSO.

2.11 Present policy statements do not allow projections to be made in the same form as this Table. Current inter-urban road building plans [1] envisage that by the early 1980s there will be roughly 2000 miles of motorway and a further 1500 miles of "high quality strategic trunk routes" in Great

Britain, as compared with about 1000 miles of each at the end of 1972. Most of the 1500 extra miles of non-motorway trunk routes are expected to take the form of improvements to existing roads, but there will also be some new routes. Comparable figures for urban road building are not given, but in terms of cash it is expected that the size of the urban road building programme will overtake that of the inter-urban "by the 1980s" [2].[1] The costs of the road programme are discussed in the next chapter.

Railways

2.12 The decline in British Rail's track mileage between 1955 and 1971 is shown in Table 2.2. The total mileage open to passenger traffic fell by 39%, the number of stations by 56%, the carrying capacity of passenger carriages by 54%, and the capacity of freight wagons by 65%. The British Railways Board now envisages that the size of the network

Table 2.2: *British Railways Assets*

Asset	Unit	1955	1959	1964	1969	1970	1971
Route open for passenger traffic	miles	14,801	14,063	10,884	9,375	9,095	8,980
Other routes	miles	4,260	4,421	4,036	2,723	2,704	2,663
Passenger only stations	number	1,717	1,646	2,270	2,247	2,222	2,213
Passenger and freight stations	number	3,878	3,414	1,304	264	224	218
Total passenger stations	number	5,595	5,060	3,574	2,511	2,446	2,431
Total freight depots	number	?	5,786	2,833	734	646	?
Total seats in passenger carriages	thousands	2,459	2,361	1,546	1,163	1,155	1,135
Total capacity of freight vehicles	thousand tons	15,556	14,265	10,369	7,075	6,420	5,428

Sources: Annual Abstract of Statistics, HMSO.
British Railways Board: *Annual Report and Accounts*.
British Railways Board: *Facts and Figures—British Railways*.

[1] This phrase occurred in the statement of the then Labour Minister of Transport. As far as we know, nothing in the present Government's plans would modify it.

will henceforth remain about the same [3], and the Government has agreed [4].

Conclusion

2.13 The main features of the last twenty years have been the vast increases in personal travel by car, and in goods movements by lorry, in particular by heavy lorries. This trend has been accompanied by a striking decline in competing modes of transport in both relative and absolute terms. Present transport policies are formulated in the belief that these trends will continue. They do not anticipate any potentially disrupting external events or allow scope for any radical changes in policy. They expect that, compared with 1971, by the end of the century the number of miles people travel each year by private car, the ton miles of road freight and the road vehicle mileage, will all double.

2.14 In the next two chapters we discuss the costs and other disadvantages associated with these trends and policies, and in Chapter 5 the benefits they bring in terms of mobility.

REFERENCES

[1] *Hansard*, 23 June 1971, cols. 289 and 290.
[2] *Hansard*, 27 May 1970, col. 1792.
[3] British Railways Board: *Review of Railway Policy*, June 1973.
[4] *Hansard*, 28 November 1973, cols. 397–407.

CHAPTER 3

Resource Costs

3.1 In this chapter and the next we consider the costs of transport—all those factors which must be placed on the debit side in an assessment of the transport system. Here we consider resource costs, that is to say costs which can be measured in physical terms; Chapter 4 deals with the less material, but no less important, disadvantages and side effects of transport.

3.2 The first stage is to assess the costs of transport in monetary terms and the second is to consider certain other resources, particularly energy and land. Of course the monetary cost of transport includes the cost of energy consumed and land acquired. But there are or soon will be constraints on the supply of both energy and land, inadequately reflected in their present costs, which will almost certainly have important effects on future transport policy. It is for this reason that these resources are given special consideration.

MONETARY COSTS

Costs and the national economy

3.3 The total amount spent on domestic transport in the UK in three sample years, and the proportion of the Gross Domestic Product that this represents, are shown in Table 3.1.

3.4 These figures exclude all domestic air travel and also freight movements by coastal shipping and inland waterways, none of which can be separated from international air and sea transport. The costs of such items as garages attached to houses or business premises (including the premises of road haulage operators) are not included, nor is the indirect cost of transport policy in requiring more land to be made available for development (see paragraph 3.77

Table 3.1: Transport expenditure and GDP
Unit: £ million at current prices

Item	1958	1963	1970
Railways	448	551	578
Road passenger transport	268	350	495
Road haulage	437	655	1,212
Capital and running costs of cars and motorcycles (net of tax)	503	872	1,508
Bicycles and prams	48	44	39
Road construction and maintenance	228	362	813
Economic cost of road accidents	140	216	346
Total domestic transport	2,072	3,050	4,991
Gross Domestic Product	20,186	26,881	42,606
Transport expenditure as % of G.D.P.	10·3%	11·3%	11·7%

Source: National Income and Expenditure; Family Expenditure Survey

below). The costs of police traffic control (estimated to be £37 million in 1962[1] are also excluded. Road construction and maintenance costs include lighting, cleaning and car parks. The purely economic costs of road accidents cover medical services, lost production and damage to motor vehicles. They do not include any monetary allowance for the suffering and grief involved. Further explanation of the derivation of these costs is given in Appendix 2.

3.5 It will be seen that the share of GDP accounted for by domestic transport has risen since 1958. In percentage terms the increase seems small; but it must be remembered that the total GDP, the base of the percentage, was very large even at the beginning, and has increased considerably over the years. If the share accounted for by transport had remained at the 1958 level, instead of rising between 1958 and 1970, the saving would have been £269 million in 1963 and £597 million by 1970. These savings are respectively almost a third and almost a half of the total expenditure, public and private, on new homes in those years.

Private costs

3.6 The increasing cost of transport to the nation is matched by the increasing share of family expenditure devoted to

[1] Min. of Transport, 1964, Evidence to Geddes Committee.

33

Table 3.2: Transport expenditure and total expenditure of households
Units: Average annual cost per house in £ at current prices

Item	1958*	1961	1963	1965	1967	1969	1971
Capital cost of cars and motorcycles	8·78	30·66	42·08	52·52	47·79	70·25	80·08
Running costs of cars and motorcycles	25·83	30·77	40·58	49·53	64·61	78·70	89·96
Bicycles and prams	2·91	2·42	2·47	2·34	1·85	2·70	2·60
Travel, except air travel	26·00 (est.)	27·21	29·23	30·96	32·47	33·02	43·16
Total Transport	63·52	91·06	114·36	135·35	146·72	184·67	215·80
Total Household expenditure	766·87	893·63	995·11	1105·18	1212·9	1371·4	1611·5
Transport as % of Total	8·3	10·2	11·5	12·2	13·0	13·4	13·4

* The figures for 1958 are subject to a relatively large sampling error.
Source: Family Expenditure Surveys.

personal travel, as Table 3.2 shows. These costs include tax.
3.7 The figures in the Family Expenditure Survey also raise important questions of social justice. They show, for example, that the average weekly expenditure on cars by the households owning them is greater than the old age pension.

FUEL AND ENERGY

3.8 Until very recently, consideration of energy resources has played little part in shaping transport policy. The rise of the internal combustion engine was accompanied by the expansion of the sources of its fuel oil. The oil industry demonstrated that it had the flexibility to meet all demands at an economic price anywhere in the world.
3.9 Although oil is a non-renewable resource, estimates of

the ultimately recoverable reserves have increased with consumption, and it has seemed reasonable to assume that this would continue until well into the next century. Even though resources are finite, the argument went, supply constraints would come into action gradually, exert pressure on prices to rise in response, and so stimulate research into alternative sources of energy. This philosophy has now been undermined by Arab actions in autumn 1973; these have brought shortage and high prices well before the West was prepared for them, if it ever would have been, but fortunately before the change meant disaster.

3.10 The object of this section is not to go into the general question of energy policy, but to assess the energy problem facing the transport industries and the weight to be accorded to it in considering future transport policies.

PRESENT ENERGY CONSUMPTION BY TRANSPORT

Total energy consumption

3.11 The amount of energy, used directly by domestic transport for the propulsion of vehicles, is shown in Table 3.3. Consumption is shown in two ways: as "end-use" or "useful" consumption and as "primary" consumption. End-use consumption measures the amount of energy actually delivered to the user when he buys a gallon of petrol or a unit of electricity. Primary consumption is greater than this because it includes an allowance for the energy used by the energy industries themselves in extracting, transporting and processing the fuel. The Table also shows the change in the share of energy consumed by transport between 1960 and 1971, and it can be seen that energy consumption in transport has been growing faster than in any other major sector of the economy. Further explanation of this Table is given in Appendix 2.

3.12 It would be useful to know also the energy consumed by transport indirectly, i.e. that used in making vehicles, building roads and carrying out maintenance and repairs etc. No estimates of this indirect energy consumption have been made for the UK, but figures are available from the USA. The American data show that for all transport, direct consumption is 29%, and indirect consumption 11%, of

Table 3.3: Primary and end-use consumption of energy
in the UK 1960 and 1971
Unit: million therms

	Primary consumption 1971	%	End-use consumption 1960	1971	%	Change 1960 –1971, %
Domestic transport:						
Rail	838	1·0	2,858	597	1·0	−79
Road	9,964	12·3	4,586	8,897	16·6	+94
Domestic air (est.)	149	0·2	64	135	0·2	+111
Domestic water	253	0·3	145	204	0·4	+41
All domestic transport	11,204	13·8	7,653	9,833	17·2	+28·3
International air transport	1,734	2·1	734	1,551	2·7	+100
Industry	33,605	41·2	21,351	24,027	42·1	+12·6
Domestic	22,980	28·2	14,425	14,150	24·8	−1·9
Agriculture, public service, miscellaneous	11,978	14·7	6,368	7,615	13·0	+19·6
All consumers	81,501	100·0	50,531	56,994	100·0	+13

national end-use energy consumption [1]. For automobiles only, direct consumption is 27% and indirect consumption 21% of national primary energy consumption [2]. The ratio of indirect to direct consumption, which can only be approximate, is probably about the same in the UK. If so, transport accounts, directly and indirectly, for about 25% of end-use consumption.

Oil consumption

3.13 When just one energy source—oil—is considered, the patterns are rather different. Oil is overwhelmingly the most important fuel for transport, supplying virtually 100% of primary energy for road vehicles and aircraft, 61% for rail and 90% for water transport. Altogether, 98·5% of transport energy is oil.

3.14 Table 3.4 shows that domestic transport accounted for 22½% of all oil consumption and international air transport for a further 3½% in 1971, whereas in 1960 the two together accounted for 29%. Thus, though of course consumption of

Table 3.4: Consumption of oil in the UK
Unit: million tons

	1960	%	1971	%	% change
Domestic transport:					
Rail	0·24	0·6	1·08	1·1	+305
Road	10·09	23·9	19·84	20·7	+97
Air	0·14	0·3	0·30	0·3	
Water	0·33	0·8	0·47	0·5	+42
All domestic transport	10·80	25·6	21·69	22·6	+102
International air transport	1·63	3·9	3·45	3·6	+112
Gas works	1·08	2·6	2·48	2·6	+130
Power stations	5·47	13·0	14·55	15·2	+166
Refineries	3·34	7·9	6·09	6·3	+82
Non-fuel uses	3·54	8·4	9·32	9·7	+163
Industry	9·91	23·5	26·42	27·5	+167
Domestic	1·50	3·6	2·96	3·1	+97
Agriculture, public service, miscellaneous	4·82	11·5	9·05	9·4	+88
All consumers	42·09	100·0	95·98	100·0	+128

Source: Digest of UK Energy Statistics 1972, HMSO, 1973.

oil by transport has increased greatly in absolute terms, it has shown a small *proportionate* decline. The reason is that, while transport has always been heavily dependent on oil, other energy (and non-energy) users have been switching to oil from other fuels (mainly from coal).

3.15 The figures in Chapter 2 suggest that the consumption of oil by transport, which in the past decade has grown faster than both passenger miles and vehicle miles, could increase by one-half by 1980 and double soon after 1990.

3.16 These statistics show that if there is any reason why energy consumption in general, and oil consumption in particular, should be reduced, the transport sector is one where major economies could be made. It is not, of course, the only candidate for cuts. Power stations and industry use very large amounts of oil, and substantial economies could be achieved in a number of ways: for example, by the use of waste heat from power stations for space heating and by improving insulation standards in offices, shops and houses.

3.17 But do future prospects for energy supply suggest that consumption should be reduced? Is there really an energy crisis? If there is, what is its nature?

3.18 The events of autumn 1973 have made it clear that there is an energy crisis of some kind, although there is widespread disagreement as to its nature and gravity. We shall start by considering the future supply of oil, which is the subject of most concern in the short and medium term. No one doubts that eventually there will be no more oil and that alternative sources of energy will have to be found; it is to considerations of these alternatives that we turn in the second part of this section.

Oil reserves

3.19 Since 1950 world energy consumption has been growing by about 5% per annum, while consumption of oil has been growing by over 7% per annum. Oil (petroleum) now provides about half the world's fuel. Estimates of ultimately recoverable reserves of oil vary widely; but there is much less variation in predictions of how long these reserves will last, simply because the volume of production is so great that quite large differences in reserves have only a small effect on timing. The estimates of Mr. H. R. Warman, the Exploration Manager of BP, are widely agreed within the oil industry. He has estimated that world oil production (excluding the USSR and China) will reach a peak by about 1983 and then begin a steady decline [3]. The volume of production at the peak would be about 3,600 million tons a year, compared with the 1972 production of about 2,000 million tons. Other authoritative estimates have been given in a recent publication by the Institute of Fuel [4]. The agreement is remarkably close; the most optimistic differ from Warman by no more than 10 years, placing the peak in production some time between 1990 and 1995.

3.20 How does North Sea oil affect this picture? From the global point of view, very little, since the total estimated reserves in the whole North Sea amount to only 2% of world reserves. However, the North Sea will, of course, make a considerable difference to Britain in the medium term. The precise part it will play cannot be predicted, since none of the factors are known with exactitude. But if we assume that energy consumption in Britain continues to grow at 3% per annum, as it did from 1960 to 1972; adopt a moderately optimistic view of the size of the North Sea reserves; and make the further assumption that all the oil produced in the British part of the North Sea will be used in Britain, then the North Sea could meet all Britain's oil needs in about 1983. Production from the North Sea would then reach a peak some time during the ten years up to 1993; after that it would decline to extinction.

3.21 The next round of licensing agreements may enforce a rather lower rate of exploitation; in that case the North Sea could supply, say, two-thirds of Britain's needs for a rather longer period. However, there is still uncertainty about whether we in Britain will be required by the EEC to sell some of our oil to other member countries. In the long run, Britain with all the North Sea oil to itself will be scarcely better placed than the world as a whole. If, as seems probable, it has to be shared with other members of the EEC, the advantage to Britain will be even smaller and of shorter duration.

Political control of oil supply

3.22 Striking as the implications of these figures are, they are grossly optimistic in assuming that oil will ever again be freely available at prices similar to those of early 1973. This is no longer true and will never again be true. Sixty per cent of estimated world oil reserves are in the Persian Gulf region. Over half the remainder are in the USA, the Soviet Union and China; all these countries have a large, or potentially large, domestic demand for oil, and are unlikely to contribute much for the rest of the world. Thus the Arab states exercise a preponderance of control over the world's oil supplies.

3.23 Much more significantly, it is not in their medium and long-term economic interest to exploit their reserves as rapidly as the rich nations of Europe, Japan and the USA desire, or as the predictions listed earlier assume. They can maintain the level and prolong the duration of their income from oil by further increasing the price and holding down production, as they are now doing. A country like Britain, with its chronic balance of payments problem, will be severely affected by the rise in price even if it escapes severe limitations of supply. Indeed, price rises may be so great that the country may itself need to limit oil imports.

3.24 The control which the industrialised countries exercise over their sources of oil is being weakened by other means as well. The discussion so far has assumed that the limited world oil supplies will be available mainly to the rich countries. Over the period 1967–72 the rate of increase of oil consumption of many poorer countries in Asia, Africa and Latin America has been as great as the rate of increase in the rich countries, though from a much lower base. In Europe and Japan, much of the growth in oil consumption has occurred as oil replaced other fuels; and this replacement is now almost complete. Thus, even without restraints on supply, growth in oil consumption would have slowed down as it became consonant with growth in energy consumption as a whole. But, given enough oil, the consumption of the poorer countries could continue to increase for a long time, and it seems certain that by 1980–85 they will have a stronger voice in the world oil market. It is also quite possible that the oil producing countries might give them preferential treatment.

3.25 At the time of writing, the Arab oil export embargoes and the OPEC price rises of October–December 1973 have only just been implemented, and there is no telling how far or fast the changes will go. However, it is important to stress that the arguments we have put forward do not depend on the resulting short-term shortages of supply. The significance of the Arab actions is that they expose and bring forward in time problems latent in the geographical imbalance which has been building up over the last two decades. Before the embargoes and price increases a prudent attitude to the depletion of oil reserves (which no country showed) would have been merely wise. It has now become a compelling necessity, and will remain so if and when the short-term crisis is past and the embargoes are relaxed.

3.26 Spokesmen for the oil industry in this country believe that the situation calls for restraint, "the tempering of the rate of increase in demand" and a reduction in the "inefficiency and wastage inherent in energy use today". These phrases are taken from an address given by Mr. Geoffrey Chandler, President of the Institute of Petroleum, at a meeting of the Institute in June 1973. He went on to say that, although rising prices would themselves help to bring about these reductions, they would probably not be a sufficient spur, and that "more systematic measures may have to be

40

taken to reduce the rate of growth of demand, for example by rationalising transport, by improving insulation standards, by the selective use of fuels in their more efficient applications. There is a long lead time to the fulfilment of all these aims, and action therefore requires to be initiated with the utmost urgency."

Lead time for new energy sources

3.27 The question of lead time is of crucial importance, and has been largely ignored in popular discussions of energy. Europe, North America and Japan are now faced with a reduction in oil supplies for which they are completely unprepared. Oil supply from now on will be subject to intermittent disruption and chronic uncertainty. Considerations of the oil reserves alone would suggest that there are at most 10–20 years before large scale alternatives are needed. In fact the need is far more urgent than even these figures suggest.

3.28 New untried sources of energy cannot be quickly developed and installed on a large scale. Nor can the existing non-oil energy industries be immediately expanded to meet the massive demand imposed by a switch away from oil. It seems that the restraint suggested by Mr. Chandler will be essential for some years. This does not necessarily mean restraint on the use of oil for transport. Some other oil users, most notably electricity generation, can switch to other energy sources without much difficulty. Oil-derived liquid fuels, on the other hand, are particularly suitable for powering transport, and it could be decided to give transport priority in the use of oil. The extent to which this will occur depends in part on economic and political factors and in part on the technical limitations of alternative energy sources.

Alternatives to oil

3.29 The alternative primary sources of energy are natural gas, hydro-power, geothermal power, tidal power, wind power, coal, oil shales and tar sands, nuclear fission, nuclear fusion and solar power. Of these, natural gas is expected to become exhausted at about the same rate as oil and is already included in the forecasts of oil and energy consumption. Hydro, geothermal, wind and tidal power are small in

41

amount or geographically restricted, or both. The remaining five sources are the important ones. Of the primary fuels, only oil from shales and tar sands (plus some gas and coal) could be directly used for transport.

3.30 The important secondary sources are electricity, used directly for rail transport or indirectly (via batteries) for road vehicles; oil and gas from coal; and other fuels, such as hydrogen and methanol, derived from abundant raw materials using electricity. The ways in which these fuels might be used to power transport, either directly or via fuel cells, are discussed briefly below. Other secondary fuels can be derived from organic wastes or standing crops; these, mostly derived ultimately from solar energy, are also discussed below.

Coal, oil shales and tar sands

3.31 Reserves of the fossil fuels (coal, oil shales and tar sands) may be equivalent to about ten times the present oil reserves—sufficient to last for several centuries, even at increased rates of consumption. However, there are great problems of geographical distribution, environmental disruption and economic feasibility associated with each of them.

3.32 Their geographical distribution is very uneven. Coal is the most plentiful: some 56% of coal is in the USSR, 28% in the USA and Canada, 9% in China, 5% in Europe and 2% in the rest of the world. Most of the known oil shale reserves are in the USA, and tar sand reserves are in Canada. It is unlikely that fuel from any of these sources will be freely available at a low price on the world market, although it may be assumed, from the point of view of narrow self-interest, that Britain with its large coal reserves is quite well placed.

3.33 The winning of many of these reserves will produce massive environmental destruction. Much coal will have to be mined by strip (open-cut) methods (underground mining of coal in the quantities required would be vastly expensive, quite apart from the human implications of getting men to work in the severe conditions of underground coal mines). Strip mining on the scale needed would mean moving thousands of millions of tons of rock and sterilising hundreds of square miles of countryside, and local opposition to

42

such developments would be very great. In any case, the present generation surely has no moral right to exhaust these resources and leave such dereliction for future generations.

3.34 In addition to environmental havoc, the capital cost would be enormous. Extraction of oil from shale would probably involve crushing and processing many billions of tons of rock, and there are still some considerable technical problems to be overcome. The National Petroleum Council of the United States has recently calculated that not more than 5% of the US oil consumption in 1985 could be met by oil from tar sands, shale or coal. Even Herman Kahn, well known for his optimism, has said that meeting the energy requirement of the USA from these sources by about 1985 would require a massive mobilisation of money, material resources and manpower comparable with that undertaken during World War Two, starting now. The recent announcement of a process for extracting oil from shale *in situ* appears to offer the possibility of cheaper oil with less environmental destruction, but the capital cost is still vast [5].

3.35 It seems unlikely that oil from coal, oil shale or tar sands can replace conventional oil in the medium term (up to 1990) or that it will be adequate to meet massive long-term energy demands.

Nuclear fission

3.36 Of all the alternatives to oil now being canvassed, nuclear fission is the one most favoured in the medium term by official planning. Reserves of uranium are of limited if uncertain size, but they are sufficient for fission to contribute very greatly to the world's energy consumption during the next 100 to 200 years. Nuclear fission is used to generate electricity in nuclear power stations, so a fission-powered economy is an electric economy. The proponents of fission see it supplying energy in the years between the decline of oil and the harnessing of nuclear fusion and/or solar energy. Before considering how transport would be powered in these circumstances, it is necessary to discuss the grave problems and dangers associated with nuclear fission itself.

3.37 The dangers are of two kinds. Firstly, the "conventional" environmental problems are formidable. Nuclear power stations require enormous quantities of cooling water, and must therefore be located near large rivers or lakes or by the sea. One estimate of British nuclear power requirements by the year 2000 [6] envisages 200,000 MW of capacity. This could be provided by 100 stations of the size of the largest currently being built, or perhaps 10 enormous complexes of 20,000 MW. Continuation of the present policy of siting nuclear power stations away from large centres of population would mean using very many of the best coastal areas in Britain. The high voltage distribution grid required by such a system would itself be an environmental intrusion far greater than the present network of pylons and cables. Society may not wish to incur even this aesthetic price for nuclear power, let alone the health hazards.

3.38 Yet there is an even higher price to be paid. This is the danger of radioactive contamination. This may occur in a great number of ways, but there are three which give rise to particular concern.

3.39 Firstly, the so called high-level wastes are very hot and so dangerously radioactive that they must be kept isolated from living organisms for several thousand years. They are produced in quantities of about 2 to 3 cubic metres per annum per 1000 MW reactor [7] and are stored in refrigerated stainless steel and concrete tanks. A number of far-fetched suggestions have been made about how to dispose of this waste; a more reasonable proposal, now the subject of research, is to solidify the waste in glass and bury it in salt mines. But this has not so far been shown to be safe, and at present the waste is still in the tanks. It would be prudent to moderate energy consumption now, so that no more nuclear fission power stations need be built until this problem is solved to the satisfaction, not only of the nuclear industry, but also of the public. However, the proponents of nuclear energy assume that somehow, quite soon, a completely safe solution will be found, and that in the meanwhile the building of new stations should proceed as fast as possible. To most of the Commission this is an attitude born not of scientific scepticism but of *hubris* and a blind faith in the power of technology to solve every problem it creates.

3.40 The second problem is what to do with reactors when, after 25 to 35 years, they reach the end of their life. The reactor core will be intensely radioactive; it may be technically feasible to dismantle it, but some of it would then have to be stored in the same way as high-level liquid wastes. If the reactor core has been accidentally damaged, dismantling may be impossible, so that the decommissioned reactor will have to be left in situ, isolated from the biosphere, for hundreds of years. Present knowledge of dispersal techniques for liquid waste and decommissioned reactors requires that a protection system of great technical organisational complexity be maintained intact for a thousand years or more. This is the legacy of the present nuclear power programme.

3.41 Thirdly, there is the risk of accidental leakage of radio-active material from an operating nuclear power station, from a waste transporter in transit, or from a fuel repro-cessing plant. The design of all nuclear power installations incorporates numerous highly complex safety features designed to prevent accidents in the first place and to prevent the escape of radioactivity if an accident should nevertheless occur. Even so, there have been some small but unpleasant accidents, such as that at Windscale in 1957.

3.42 We have to ask two questions: what would be the con-sequences of a major accident, and what is the probability of such an accident occurring? The first question was the subject of a study commissioned by the United States Atomic Energy Commission in 1957, which estimated that there would be a possibility of 3,400 deaths, 43,000 injuries and damage to property worth £7,000 millions [7]. A 1965 AEC study put the possible casualty toll at 45,000 [8]. Both these studies were concerned with American light water reactors, none of which have so far been built in Britain. The British nuclear power programme uses gas cooled reactors, and the consequences of the most severe accident to one of these would be considerably less disastrous. The second question cannot be answered positively. Advocates of nuclear power often quote odds, but these are not and cannot be technical estimates. They are entirely speculative, and the question whether or not they should be accepted involves an ethical judgment. There are unknown technical problems concerning the effects of prolonged irradiation on the strength of materials in the reactor; there is the possibility of a chain of human error and simple bad luck; and there is the danger of attack in war or by a suicidal saboteur.

3.43 If nuclear fission is to be an important source of energy for several hundred years, it is thought that fast breeder reactors will be essential. An accident at a breeder reactor is just as likely (or unlikely) as at a conventional reactor. But breeders produce plutonium, which is used to fuel other reactors and must therefore be transported from one to the other. Plutonium is perhaps the most toxic material known; it is also an ideal material for making nuclear weapons. The potentially horrific consequences of accidental escape or theft of plutonium in transit require little emphasis. Can loss or theft be guaranteed never to happen?

3.44 The question for humanity is whether it is prepared to commit itself to massive reliance on nuclear fission before any of these questions are settled. There is no doubt that the consequences of errors—of a high-level waste store leaking, of a major reactor accident, of the accidental escape or theft of plutonium—could be extremely severe. Yet there is considerable doubt about the likelihood of these events; no scientist can put a definite figure on them. The hazards of massive reliance on nuclear power are therefore not technical questions; they transcend technology. These are ethical questions which must in the last resort inform political action. We believe that this must be recognised and the issues discussed through the normal political process, in front of a properly informed public, before it is decided whether to place substantially greater reliance on nuclear fission.[1]

Nuclear fusion

3.45 The sources of energy discussed so far—coal, oil shale, tar sands and nuclear fission—are medium-term alternatives. Many people believe that they could be gradually scaled up towards a massive development after 1985, when they would be a substitute for the diminishing flow of oil. However, they are all dependent on finite resources and are unlikely to last longer than a few hundred years. In the long term, the only possibilities are nuclear fusion and solar energy.

3.46 Nuclear fusion uses deuterium (heavy hydrogen) as fuel; abundant supplies of this are found in sea water. No one expects a prototype fusion (or thermonuclear) reactor to be operating before the year 2000 [9]. Although it is certain in principle that the process could work, there can be no certainty in practice until a fusion reactor is actually

[1] See Note of Reservation on p. 279.

built. Nor can the economic costs be known. The fusion process produces radioactive wastes, but it is believed that these will be much less dangerous and easier to control than the wastes from fission reactors. Once again, however, there can be no certainty until prototypes have been in operation for some time.

Solar energy

3.47 All the energy sources discussed so far depend on non-renewable resources (though fusion may, for practical purposes, be excluded from this category). Our only truly non-exhaustible source of energy is the sun; but solar energy has been a much neglected topic of research. There are signs that this neglect is about to be ended, and it is already clear that there are two broadly distinct ways in which solar energy could be used.

3.48 First, it could be used to produce large quantities of electricity in huge centralised installations covering hundreds of square miles of the desert areas of the world. If such schemes are feasible and can be made sufficiently cheap, they may contribute to large-scale energy production some time after the year 2000; but there can be no certainty about this.

3.49 The other way of using solar energy is by relatively small-scale and localised techniques. Liquid or gaseous fuels for transport, such as methane, could be produced on this scale from standing crops or organic wastes (urban and agricultural) by pyrolysis, fermentation, or other methods of bacterial decomposition. Solar energy is thus converted to a usable form by living plants instead of by man-made devices. Some people find the prospect of such an environmentally safe, solar energy economy very attractive; but, dependent as it is on renewable organic resources, it is completely incompatible with an economy of mass personal transport.

3.50 In Britain solar energy could be of great importance for certain purposes such as domestic water or possibly space heating, but it could not be used as the sole or major source of power for the present form of high energy economy. To generate from the amount of solar energy falling on Britain in one year the amount of energy consumed in 1972 (57,000 million therms) would require us to cover between 5 and 10% of the surface area of the country with solar generating equipment. A large additional area would have to be used for storage to meet the demand over long cloudy periods in winter.

Some other methods of propulsion

3.51 Nuclear fission, nuclear fusion and solar power would all be used to produce electricity. This energy could power vehicles like cars either by equipping the cars with batteries, or by the production of secondary fuels such as hydrogen and methanol, which could in turn be used directly or via fuel cells (devices which convert a chemical fuel to electricity as and when it is needed).

3.52 The only types of batteries sufficiently developed to be used in large-scale production of vehicles during the next ten years are awkwardly heavy and use large quantities of lead and zinc, supplies of which may not be sufficient. Other types of batteries appear to offer better prospects, but are still at an early stage of development.

3.53 Hydrogen and methanol can be produced by electricity from water and limestone respectively. Many technological optimists see these fuels, together with oil from coal, as the ultimate sources of power for road vehicles and aircraft when conventional oil is nearing exhaustion and is reserved for manufacturing plastics and other petrochemical products. However, it must be stressed that they are likely to be much more expensive than our present transport fuels. A recent estimate suggests that in the year 2000 petroleum fuels from coal will be 2·5 times as expensive in real terms, and liquid hydrogen and methanol 6 times as expensive, as petrol at the 1971 price (excluding tax) [10], but not much more expensive than taxed petrol in December 1973. Furthermore, the estimate for hydrogen and methanol assumes that electricity will be both widely available and cheap, and, in the case of methanol, that there will be no environmental objections to mining millions of tons of limestone and disposing of millions of tons of quicklime each year.

3.54 Hydrogen and methanol could be burned directly in engines or used to power fuel cells. A fuel cell plus a tank of chemical fuel would be equivalent to a charged battery. The dangers of hydrogen, and the complex equipment needed to produce the low temperatures to keep it liquid, seem to make methanol a much better potential fuel for transport. But fuel cells as a means of powering vehicles are still many years in the future.

3.55 Road vehicles can also be powered by the kinetic energy stored in a flywheel. The flywheel is rotated at a very high speed while the vehicle is at rest, by an electric motor on the vehicle plugged into the mains, for example, and gradually slows down as the energy "charge" is used up. The city of Berne had a flywheel-powered municipal bus service in operation over twenty years ago. Recent studies [11] have shown that at 1972 prices flywheel-powered vehicles are slightly less cost-effective than those driven by battery-stored electricity, but improving technology and rapidly rising prices for battery components could soon change that. There are many other novel technical developments in vehicular propulsion. Two examples are a West German method of storing energy in the form of latent heat and a Swedish method which uses the thermoelectric effect. The Commission is aware of these ideas but has had insufficient time to study them.

Energy crisis

3.56 The arguments set out so far may be summarised as follows. Between now and about 1985 or 1990 oil consumption may possibly be able to increase as current trends anticipate it will, but the supply will be uncertain, possibly intermittent, and very much more expensive than it was up to 1973. After 1990 at the latest, the supply of oil must decline. The only feasible substitute as a large source of energy during the next 20 years is nuclear fission, but the hazards associated with fission cast grave doubts on the wisdom of proceeding with a massive expansion of nuclear power. In any case, the conversion technology needed for using fission-generated electricity as a fuel for mass personal road transport will not be available for 20 years or more. This same conversion technology will also be needed for large-scale production of electricity from nuclear fusion or the sun, which may be possible after the year 2000.

3.57 It is clear that the supply of fuel for transport, particularly road and air transport, will be uncertain, with the possibility of crises, from now until 2000 or beyond. Continued abundance could only be assured by a policy which gave transport a firm priority in the use of oil. Striking as this conclusion is, there are still some reinforcing arguments that have been ignored.

3.58 No mention has been made of the effects of price increases on fuel consumption. These are likely to be large. The cost to the consumer of fuels derived from imported oil is made up of the following components: royalty, production cost, tanker transport cost, cost of refining, distribution, profit, etc., plus tax. In 1973 the tax was zero for international air transport, British Rail and marine propulsion, including private yachting; it was 1p per gallon for domestic air transport, 10p per gallon for bus operators and 22·5p per gallon for all other users (i.e. cars, road haulage and coaches). The variability of the tax has very important consequences, for it means that at mid-1973 prices the royalty accounted for over 16% of the price of untaxed fuel, 9% of the price of fuel for bus operators, and only 5% of fully taxed derv fuel and petrol. The royalty on 1 January 1974 was about four times the mid-1973 level. This means that, if taxes are unchanged and if there are no other price increases, the price of fully taxed fuel will rise by about 15%, whereas fuel for buses will be nearly 30% more expensive and untaxed fuel nearly 50% more expensive. The effect on the private motorist will be relatively slight, but for bus operators, railways and air transport it could be disastrous. These figures make it plain that the tax on transport fuels is a very important instrument of transport policy. We return to this point in paragraph 3.69 below, where we discuss the use of taxes to stimulate fuel economy in transport.

3.59 A brief mention should also be made of North Sea oil. It appears that the landed price of this oil in the UK will be about the same as that of oil from OPEC countries at mid 1973 prices, and less than OPEC oil at January 1974 prices. Again, this clearly gives the Government great power to influence transport policy, energy policy and the balance of payments by taxing North Sea oil and by setting the levels of production and export.

3.60 The final argument concerns global justice. There is no doubt that the pattern of world energy consumption is grossly unequal. For example, the present annual consumption of gasoline in private cars in the USA is equivalent to the annual consumption of all fuels for all purposes in the entire Third World (Asia (less Japan and China), Africa, and Latin America). Again, the fuel used to carry one passenger on an average trans-Atlantic scheduled flight is equivalent to the annual per capita consumption of energy for all purposes in the Third World. Many people find this contrast morally repugnant in itself. But, it might well be argued, the contrast is without significance unless a causal connection can be demonstrated between high consumption and wealth in the industrialised countries and poverty in the Third World.

3.61 Such a causal connection exists. Within the last year or so the oil producing nations have come to recognise the strength of the bargaining position in which they are placed by the steadily growing oil demands of Europe, Japan and the USA. They have also expressed a growing reluctance to deplete such valuable and irreplaceable assets as fast as the industrially advanced countries wish. They have therefore raised the price of oil, slowly at first, but very rapidly since October 1973.

3.62 The consequences of these price increases for the developed countries will be severe enough, but they will bear even harder on poorer countries such as India, which has been seeking, rightly or wrongly, to develop its industry by adopting techniques used in the economically advanced countries. With negligible oil reserves of its own, India has become increasingly dependent on imported oil for such vital purposes as fertiliser production. Even if, in the face of steadily rising oil prices and consequent further deterioration of its already crippling balance of payments deficit, India elected to reverse the policy of dependence on Western technology and hence on oil, it would suffer severe transitional hardships. These might be ameliorated if aid were forthcoming, either from the wealthier countries or in the form of preferential treatment by the oil-producing nations.

Energy and transport policy

3.63 Clearly there should be immediate implementation of policies to limit the consumption of energy in general and oil in particular. This must mean eliminating particularly wasteful and unnecessary consumption wherever it occurs. Domestic transport uses 14% of primary energy and $22\frac{1}{2}\%$ of oil (see Table 3.5). It is not possible to say precisely how its consumption should be restrained until all the costs and

Table 3.5: Oil consumption by transport in the UK, 1971
Units: million tons

Mode of transport	Quantity	% of transport consumption	% of all oil consumption
Rail	1·08	4·3	1·1
Private cars and motor cycles	11·94	47·5	12·4
Goods vehicles	6·51	25·8	6·8
Buses and taxis	1·02	4·1	1·1
Other road vehicles	0·37	1·5	0·4
Domestic air	0·30	1·2	0·3
International air	3·45	13·7	3·6
Domestic water	0·47	1·9	0·5
All transport	25·14	100·0	26·2*

* Less 3·6% international air to give total energy consumption of domestic transport, 27·6%.

Source: Digest of UK Energy Statistics 1972.

benefits associated with different forms of transport have been considered, as they are in later chapters. However, a number of steps suggest themselves.

3.64 (i) *Reduce the amount of travel performed.* This need not necessarily mean reducing the number of journeys made; reducing the distance travelled per journey might well be more effective. This is a matter of locational and land-use policy as well as of transport narrowly conceived. We might also question the wisdom of consuming very considerable resources, costing scores of millions of pounds each year, in actively persuading people, through advertising, to buy private vehicles, make journeys, live further from their workplace, or otherwise increase the amount of travelling they do. Withdrawing these pressures to consume resources through transport would increase individual liberty, since the smaller amount of travelling would then reflect more spontaneous needs.

3.65 (ii) *Encourage walking and cycling as means of personal transport.* It is true that the motive power for these is derived from food, and that food consumed in industrial countries like Britain is produced by methods which use very large quantites of oil and other fossil fuels (for fertiliser manufacture, mechanised farm equipment, etc.). Nevertheless walking, and particularly cycling, are very economical in energy consumption. They also fit very well with (i) above, since as journeys are made shorter it becomes easier to walk or cycle.

3.66 (iii) *Encourage the use of more energy-efficient motorised transport modes and discourage the use of less efficient modes for both people and goods*. Unfortunately, identification of the more efficient modes is not as easy as it may appear at first sight. It is fairly straightforward to calculate theoretical efficiencies for each mode on the basis of a single vehicle carrying a specified load over a specified distance. But these theoretical efficiencies differ markedly from what can be achieved in practice by a whole transport system based on the relevant mode. It is not always possible to achieve the theoretical loads while still providing the reasonably frequent standards of service required by customers. Some empty running is therefore inevitable between work journeys. These operational problems may affect some modes more than others. In Appendix 2 some theoretical and achieved efficiencies are given.

3.67 In spite of the problems, some conclusions can be drawn with confidence from these figures. With high load factors rail and bus are much more efficient than car or air transport; for freight, rail and water are much more efficient than road. With the load factors obtained in the past the distinction is not so marked, though rankings are maintained. Diversion of traffic should improve the load factors of the more efficient modes. Even with present achieved efficiencies, a 1% transfer of traffic from car to bus would reduce the oil consumed by car and bus combined by 0·5%, and reduce oil used for all purposes by 0·05%.

3.68 (iv) *Encourage more efficient use of all modes, but particularly of the one which uses most oil (i.e. cars)*. This could be done by increasing occupancy, especially for commuting journeys, in which the average number of persons per car is less than 2. Better planning and routeing of freight vehicles, including the sharing of vehicles by firms in the same locality, could also do much to increase average load factors and hence save fuel.

3.69 (v) *Encourage changes in vehicle and engine designs*. Opportunities for this are much greater in the USA, where typical vehicles are heavier, more highly powered and less highly tuned than in the UK and in Europe as a whole. It

53

has been estimated that potential fuel savings in US cars could be 5 to 15% from improvements in carburation, fuel injection, ignition and air intake; 15 to 20% from the use of leaner petrol-air mixtures; 10 to 20% from the use of infinitely variable transmission systems; and 5 to 10% from the use of radial ply tyres [12]. (The first two are not additive but are alternatives.) Similar changes in European cars would produce smaller but nevertheless very substantial savings. Vehicles could also be made lighter: a weight reduction of 10% reduces fuel consumption by about 8%. Though lighter vehicles might be less safe for their occupants, improvements in safety design and/or reductions in speed limits could easily offset this disadvantage; and if all vehicles were made lighter this disadvantage would in any case be eliminated in any vehicle–vehicle accident. In the long term very large savings could be made simply by the production and use of slower, lighter and therefore lower-powered vehicles, especially in cities (where such vehicles would bring many other benefits). These changes in vehicle and engine design should be encouraged by a suitable taxation policy. This could be an increase in the existing tax on petrol and derv fuel, a differential tax on engine size, a differential tax on vehicle weight, or some combination of these three. The Commission has been unable to determine which of these policies would be most effective, but it supports the general principle of taxation to encourage fuel economy in motor vehicles and recommends that such a policy be implemented.

3.70 (vi) *Reduce road speed limits*. It is estimated that fuel consumption can be reduced by about 30% if average speed is reduced from 70 to 50 m.p.h. For all but the longest journeys on motorways or trunk roads, such a reduction adds little to overall journey times. Lower speed limits could be phased in with the production of slower and lower-powered cars (see v) and would thus appear "fairer" and less frustrating than they might if imposed today.

3.71 (vii) *Encourage greater use of electric transport*. Any electrification of transport at present would save oil and promote the use of our most abundant energy resource: coal. Electrification sharply reduces noise and pollution from road vehicles; and battery driven vehicles would greatly ease the problems of electricity generation by helping to smooth out the day–night fluctuations of demand (most batteries would be re-charged overnight). Immediate practical measures to this end include the further electrification of rail and the reintroduction of trams and trolleybuses. In the longer term, the more rapid development of battery and other electric transport systems for road vehicles could be encouraged.

3.72 We emphasise that these options are dependent on our later consideration of transport policy.

LAND

3.73 At present British agriculture provides about 50% of the temperate foodstuffs consumed in this country. If we offer incentives for British farmers to produce more than this proportion it may be possible to move the balance of trade in our favour, and we may also become less vulnerable in the future if food-exporting countries find it expedient in times of world food shortage to restrict shipments abroad. In the absence of any such change in our agricultural policy, as population and real income are likely to rise in the foreseeable future, the consequent growth in food consumption is likely to require *both* additional imports *and* additional domestic supplies. Unless we can be sure of further development of land-saving techniques in agriculture, more domestically grown food will require more land. However, we should bear in mind that agricultural and other rural land plays an important part also in recreation and amenity, and that there is a potential conflict between the use of land for amenity and its more intensive agricultural use by such techniques as removal of hedgerows and intensive animal rearing. We must also consider whether our population should be allowed to increase indefinitely.

3.74 For these reasons land is an increasingly scarce resource, and its future value is not reflected in the current prices paid for agricultural land. Any development which permanently reduces the area of land available for agriculture in Britain must be considered with great care.

Land lost to transport uses

3.75 In 1971 the total of agricultural land in England and Wales (excluding rough grazing) amounted to some 30 million acres: the total loss to urban use during the preceding nine years was 350,000 acres or about 1·2% of the total. This may seem small, but it is equivalent to an area the size of Oxfordshire every twelve years. Moreover, the rate of loss has increased markedly over the period (see Table 3.6).

Table 3.6: *Annual loss of land from agriculture* (thousand acres)

	Net loss for all purposes	Net loss to purposes other than forestry and woodland
1961–2	29·6	17·0
1962–3	38·7	25·5
1963–4	53·9	40·1
1964–5	49·2	35·1
1965–6	65·7	48·7
1966–7	38·0	27·1
1967–8	58·7	48·2
1968–9	66·7	50·3
1969–70	70·6	57·1

Source: Hansard, 11 February 1972, cols. 449–450.

3.76 The loss of agricultural land to transport uses narrowly defined is not very great. To complete the rest of the outstanding inter-urban road programme would require about 30,000 acres, though this figure does not allow for loss of productivity of other land as a result of severance of farms, etc. Nevertheless, other transport modes, especially railways, are far more economical of space; for instance, a four-track railway (width about 60 feet) has a higher passenger and freight carrying capacity than a six-lane motorway (width about 130 feet). In terms of land lost, railways which have been allowed to become derelict are no better than railways which continue to function.

3.77 The effects of transport policy on the pattern of urban development are undoubtedly much more serious in causing loss of agricultural land. A transport system based on private motorised travel directly uses large areas of land for local roads on housing estates and for car parks at shopping and entertainment centres. For example, over one-fifth of the land used in building new estates is required for roads and parking, and this amounts to more than the area covered by the houses themselves. This policy contributes indirectly to land loss in an even more striking way by actively encouraging urban developments of low residential density. For example, the New Town of Milton Keynes has a target population of 250,000 and is being built to an overall population density of 8 people per acre [13]. The major reason for this choice was to facilitate car use. It can be compared with the residential density of 23 people per acre in Edinburgh New Town in 1971, 23 and 32 in two wards in Bath in 1964, and 59 and 66 in two parts of central Brighton in 1971 [14]. All these towns were built long before the motor age.

Land loss in production of aggregates

3.78 Road building and maintenance make demands on aggregates such as gravel, sand and crushed rock. The quantities used are large: in 1967 it was estimated that new road construction and major improvements in Great Britain used 26 million tons and maintenance a further 23 million tons [15]. This was about 25% of the total production of aggregates. In 1970 total production of aggregates was estimated to be 220 million tonnes, of which 112 million were sand and gravel and the remainder crushed rock of various kinds [16]. Nevertheless, there is no shortage of aggregates as such; they are not a limiting resource. The limitation is confined to the loss of land which their extraction involves.

3.79 This land loss is particularly severe in southern and eastern England, where sand and gravel beds are the only local source of aggregates. These beds often occur under land of high agricultural and environmental quality—along river valleys for example. Approximately 2 to 3 acres of typical gravel pit are needed to supply the aggregates for one mile of motorway: if all the aggregates needed to complete the inter-urban motorway programme were to come from gravel pits (which they will not), this would mean the loss of 2–3,000 acres. The production of marine-dredged sand and gravel has been increasing steadily in recent years, but it is still only about 10% of total production. It is not expected that marine dredging will replace land extraction as the main source of sand and gravel [15]. In the north, crushed limestone and other rock is the most common source of aggregates for road building. The quarries which produce this rock generally use up much less land than gravel pits, and the most powerful objections to them relate to their

57

destructive effect on the rural environment. This is one of the effects of transport policy on the countryside which is discussed in Chapter 4 below. Attempts are often made to minimise the loss of land through extraction of aggregates by the insertion of appropriate clauses in the planning approval for opening a pit or quarry. These nominally make approval conditional on an agreement to backfill the exhausted pit and finish off with topsoil, or to ensure by other means that the area is at least as attractive and productive as before; but often the agreement lacks teeth and cannot be enforced. New procedures are required to ensure plenty of funds for the task, either by restitution levies, or by a requirement of a bond from the developer, or by more detailed conditions in the planning consent. We understand at the time of writing that a governmental committee will shortly be making recommendations.

Conclusion

3.80 The loss of land taken directly and indirectly by transport is clearly a cause for concern. No account at all is taken, when the cost of transport is calculated, of the indirect effects of transport policy in promoting patterns of urbanisation which cause higher losses of agricultural land than would otherwise be necessary. The direct costs do, of course, appear in the road programme, but it is doubtful whether the market price of agricultural land fully reflects the long-term requirements of food production or the environmental and recreational costs involved.

OTHER MATERIAL RESOURCES

3.81 Motor vehicle production uses large quantities of material resources such as iron and steel, non-ferrous metals and rubber. It is also a most important user of many manufactured products; for example, motor vehicle production is the largest single user of carpeting. No scarcity problems arise here comparable to those connected with energy. In the first place, many of the materials used are not scarce, and probably will not be so for several centuries at present rates of consumption. Those which are scarce, particularly certain non-ferrous metals, are being replaced by substitutes —copper by aluminium and zinc by plastic, for example.

Secondly, a large proportion of the metals used in motor vehicles are effectively recycled. For other transport vehicles, such as ships and trains, the recycling is even more complete.

3.82 This is not to say that no waste occurs. Inbuilt obsolescence and rapid corrosion cause a very considerable waste of energy and resources. There is also scope for increasing the efficiency of metal reclamation from scrapped cars.

Inbuilt obsolescence and corrosion

3.83 Rapid obsolescence is a characteristic of many road vehicles; they also lack adequate body protection and consequently suffer from rapid corrosion. This is directly wasteful of the resources employed, and even if the materials are efficiently recycled there is still some loss of materials and input of energy. Vehicles do not have to become obsolescent and corrode; design standards, materials technology and assembly techniques are common to the manufacture of most cars, but some cars are built to last much longer than others and all could be built to last longer still.

3.84 A recent Government Commission on the subject estimated that the cost of corrosion in the transport industry is about £350 million per annum [17]. In its response to this report, the Department of Trade and Industry took the view that corrosion in cars could be "greatly reduced at almost negligible cost" by improved design and manufacture. But the manufacturers have concentrated on cheap spare parts rather than on initial protection, and many warranties have been reduced from twelve to six months. A new growth industry has arisen, carrying out rust-proofing treatment which should have been done on the production line.

3.85 Pressed steel construction is used for most cars and is cheap for the manufacturer, but it is seriously liable to corrosion. Box sections, in particular, often corrode within two years of manufacture (usually from the inside). If detected, this type of corrosion results in failure to obtain a DoE test certificate for the vehicle; if undetected, it may cause an accident. The external corrosion of hydraulic lines is an even graver safety risk, while corrosion of exhaust systems leads to excessive noise and air pollution. Because corrosion of such major components can decisively affect the safety and performance of a vehicle, cheap replacements

59

are in no way a satisfactory substitute for durability of the original parts.

3.86 Another source of corrosion is the use of brightwork body trim on cars. Dissimilar metals in contact, as when trim is placed on a steel body, constitute an ideal electrolytic cell under wet conditions, and corrosion is consequently very rapid. Manufacturers claim that they would lose sales if trim were abandoned, but this argument would lose its force if the unnecessary use of trim were simultaneously eliminated by all manufacturers.

3.87 It is sometimes argued that making vehicles to last longer would tend to slow down technical innovation. The Commission recognises the force of this argument, but on the other hand it notes that the application of existing technology to promote longevity and durability is being restricted in favour of increasing turnover of new vehicles and parts. We believe that the advantages of more durable cars in reducing danger and waste outweigh the disadvantages of slower introduction of technical innovations, and that, in any case, ways can be devised to incorporate some worthwhile innovations into existing vehicles.

3.88 The Commission therefore recommends that the D.T.I. should impose on all vehicle manufacturers new standards of design and finish to achieve, *inter alia*:

(i) a reasonable minimum lifetime for each vehicle under normal usage;

(ii) a significant element of protection from and inhibition of corrosion of the body shell; and

(iii) the elimination of all unnecessary bright work.

Metal reclamation and recycling

3.89 Although the recycling of metals used in motor vehicles is already relatively efficient, much could be done to improve it. Copper wiring and chromium-plated fittings, for example, cannot usually be easily separated from the body; thus these metals cannot be recycled themselves, and they cause problems of contamination when the steel body is recycled. These difficulties could be overcome by fairly simple design changes, such as grouping all copper wiring together in a self-contained package and replacing chromium-plated with sealant-treated steel or plastic. Despite the best efforts of local authorities, a significant proportion of derelict cars are abandoned by their owners and do not get reclaimed. Some financial incentive would seem to be necessary to achieve a complete recovery of old cars.

3.90 The Commission therefore makes the following recommendations:

(i) The design of motor vehicles should be subject to a universally applied code of practice to facilitate recovery of metals.

(ii) A refundable charge of the order of £50, payable to the Exchequer, should be included in the purchase price of all new private vehicles, or should be paid when the vehicle is first licensed. This should be refunded to the eventual owner upon relinquishment of the vehicle for recycling. (Any cost involved in transport to the car-shredding plant should be deducted from the sum repaid.) In the absence of an identifiable final owner the appropriate local authority should be deemed to own the vehicle.

REFERENCES

[1] Grimmer, D. P., and Luszczynsky, K.: "Lost power." *Environment*, April 1972.
[2] Herendeen, R.: *An energy input-output matrix for the U.S.* Doc. CAC no. 69. University of Illinois, Urbana. Undated.
[3] Warman, H. R.: *The future availability of oil.* Paper delivered at World Energies Supplies Conference organised by the *Financial Times*, September 1973.
[4] Institute of Fuel: *Energy for the Future.* 1973.
[5] *The Times*, 24 November 1973.
[6] *Atom*, February 1973.
[7] Patterson, Walter C.: *Nuclear reactors.* London, Earth Island, 1973.
[8] *The Guardian*, 8 November 1973.
[9] Hancox, R.: "Fusion reactor studies in the United Kingdom." Transactions of the American Nuclear Society, 1972, p. 626.
[10] Day, G. V.: *The Prospects for synthetic fuels in the UK.* Futures, December 1972, pp. 331–343.
[11] Hoffman, G. A.: Paper, *Second International Electrical Vehicle Symposium*, Atlantic City, U.S.A., November 1971.
Cf. also Post and Post: *Flywheels*, Scientific American, 229, 6 December 1973.
[12] Mallioris, A. B., and Strumbotue, R. L.: U.S. Department of Transportation, reported in *The Times*, 16 November 1973.
[13] Information supplied by the Milton Keynes Development Corporation.
[14] Figures supplied by the Corporations of Edinburgh, Bath and Brighton.

61

[15] Please, A., and Pike, D. C.: *The Demand for road aggregates*. Transport and Road Research Laboratory, Crowthorne. LR 185, 1968.
[16] *Sand and gravel production 1970 and 1971*. HMSO, 1972.
[17] *Report of the Commission on Corrosion and Protection*. HMSO, 1971.

CHAPTER 4

Other Costs of Transport

4.1 The prudent use of resources for transport is important because of the very large quantities involved. Resource costs, however, are by no means the whole cost imposed by transport upon society. In this Chapter we deal with the less tangible losses and sacrifices—matters affecting the quality of life and, indeed life itself, rather than the standard of living.

ACCIDENTS

The gravity of the problem

4.2 Most travel accidents occur on the roads, as Table 4.1 shows. The numbers affected are very great; almost one million people were killed or seriously injured on the roads during the past ten years. Each year the number killed or seriously injured is about equal to the population of a town the size of Cambridge. One reason why most accidents occur on the roads is that most travel is by road, but it is also true that accident rates per million passenger miles are much higher for road than for other modes (see Appendix 3). Although each mode uses a different definition of injury, and

Table 4.1: Deaths and serious injuries from travel in Great Britain, 1962–1971

Mode	Deaths	Serious injuries
Road	74,080	922,260
Rail	2,229	4,527
Air (domestic)	45	3
Total	76,354	926,790

Sources: *Annual Abstracts of Statistics*, HMSO.
Railway Accidents, HMSO.
Accidents to Aircraft on the British Register, HMSO.

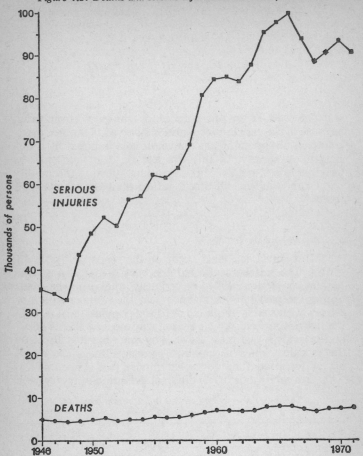

Figure 4.1: Deaths and serious injuries on the roads, 1946–71

Units: thousands of persons.

Source: Annual Abstracts of Statistics, HMSO.

one may question the adequacy of comparing simple rates per million passenger miles, nevertheless the differences between modes, certainly between road and rail, seem conclusive.[1]

4.3 If the present toll continues, nearly half the children being born today will eventually die or suffer injury on the roads. Figure 4.1 shows the trend of road deaths and *serious* injuries since 1946. Road accidents are the principal cause of death for people between the ages of five and twenty-four. Between 1966 and 1971 the annual average number of deaths and serious injuries among children under five was 3,544, among children aged five to nine 7,105, and among children aged ten to fourteen 5,592.

Official attitudes to road accidents

4.4 There is a marked inconsistency in society's attitude towards these terrible facts. On the one hand, successive Ministers of Transport, and other prominent spokesmen, declare the toll unacceptable in a civilised society. Mr. A. C. Durie, Director-General of the AA and Vice-Chairman of the British Road Federation said in 1968:

"I am convinced that death and injury on the road will[1] become one of the greatest burdens of our society as we motor into the 1980s. Hardly a single household in the land will escape the long hand of human destruction, either by removing loved ones from the home or condemning them to live only half a life permanently shattered." [1].

Mr. Peyton, then Minister for Transport Industries, said on the BBC on 4 September 1973:

"The casualties which happen daily, and as a matter of routine, on our roads are brutal and uncivilised. And anybody in my position has got to do his best to *bring these dismal figures down*" (our italics).

4.5 The figures, however, do not come down. Indeed, they would be much higher than they are if millions of potential cyclists, motorcyclists and pedestrians had not been dissuaded by the "brutal" facts from venturing upon the roads. 4.6 On the other hand it is argued that the nature of our

[1] We are aware of, but do not accept, the arguments of Brigadier T. I. Lloyd, who claims that railways are more dangerous than roads.

transport system, upon which our way of life depends, makes a large number of accidents inevitable. As long as we continue to bring down the accident *rate*, i.e. the number of casualties per hundred million *vehicle* miles, and to compare well with other countries, there is felt to be cause for satisfaction, though not for complacency. This point of view was put by Mr. Peyton at the Transport and Road Research Laboratory in March 1972:

"Road-safety is no field for complacency, yet I believe that in this country we have no cause for shame. We have made many steps forward and our record bears comparison with anywhere else in the world" [2].

4.7 One's attitude towards road accidents may be influenced by one's opinion on whether our transport arrangements are in other ways desirable, necessary or even inevitable. In later chapters we conclude that the transport system does not serve the nation's transport needs very well, quite apart from accidents and other side effects. We therefore find ourselves unimpressed by the prospect of a reduction only in casualty *rates*, if this does not also produce a reduction in the absolute number of casualties.

Road accidents and current transport policy

4.8 Another indication of the attitude of policy makers to road casualties is the monetary values they place on accidents, over and above the resource costs of deaths and injuries and the purely economic costs discussed in the last chapter. These values are intended to represent what society is prepared to pay to prevent the suffering and grief involved, and they are recommended by the Transport and Road Research Laboratory for use by the Department of the Environment in assessing alternative road schemes. The values (in 1970 terms) are £5,000 for a fatality, £500 for a serious injury and £10 for a slight injury [3].

4.9 Despite a certain repugnance for putting monetary values on death, disablement and suffering, a majority of the Commission accepts that the design and operation of transport facilities must often involve a judgement of this kind, and it is better and more honest to make the judgement explicit than to pretend it does not exist. But the Commission does not accept the values in use or the way in which they were derived. A judgement of this kind is a political, not a technical, matter and should be taken by the responsible Minister after public and Parliamentary debate. The Commission does not believe that the values now used are high enough to reflect society's assessment of all the personal consequences of death and injury on the roads. We believe that society should and does accept an obligation to provide safe conditions for its members. The obligation varies according to the circumstances. Mountaineers and others who engage in dangerous sports generally know the risks involved and undertake them deliberately; society's obligation to them is less than to those who are involuntarily exposed to risks during their normal daily lives. Above all there is an obligation to provide for the safety of pedestrians, because pedestrians are especially vulnerable. Everyone must frequently be a pedestrian; and many pedestrians, especially the very young and very old, cannot exercise the unceasing control and judgement that present traffic conditions demand.

4.10 Accidents are not the only distressing consequence of an unsafe transport system; danger generates the fear of accident, both in travellers themselves and in other people on their behalf, for example in parents for their children. Many journeys are not made which would be made in safer conditions; this restricts the activities of the would-be travellers. Once again it is walking and cycling that are most affected, and it is children, old people and the less affluent who suffer most. The perils of walking and cycling cause people to go by car instead; for example, many a mother drives her children to school, thus accepting an additional daily chore as well as adding to traffic volumes, because she is not prepared to let them cycle. We return later to these problems of personal mobility; here it is sufficient to note that they are related to road safety.

Future trends in road accidents

4.11 What future trend in road casualties can be expected if the travel projections of Chapter 2 are realised? This question is not easily answered, particularly since one does not know what new efforts will be put into road safety. But no appraisal of transport policy would be complete without some answer, however rough.

4.12 The number of casualties can be considered as the product of the number of vehicle miles and the casualty rate per vehicle mile. In Great Britain over the last twenty years the casualty rate has been falling, so that the increase in casualties has been much less than the increase in vehicle miles. Why has the casualty rate been decreasing, and how far can it be expected to decrese in future?

4.13 One important reason why the casualty rate has been falling is, as already noted, that vehicle miles by motorcycles and pedal cycles, two classes of vehicles highly prone to accidents, have declined sharply. The rate of decline cannot continue much longer, since the volume of such traffic is now only a fraction of what it was twenty years ago (see Chapter 2). If cyclists and motorcyclists are excluded from the analysis a better picture is revealed of what has been achieved by road safety measures alone. In Table 4.2

Table 4.2: Trend in road casualty rates

Year	Deaths A		B		Serious injuries A		B	
	Rate	Index 1953=100	Rate	Index 1953=100	Rate	Index 1953=100	Rate	Index 1953=100
1953	9·57	100	8·58	100	106·3	100	82·6	100
1954	9·11	95	8·12	95	104·0	98	79·3	96
1955	9·35	98	8·02	93	105·1	99	78·0	94
1956	8·39	93	7·59	88	101·7	96	75·4	92
1957	9·27	97	7·74	90	106·4	100	75·4	92
1958	8·96	94	7·38	86	103·4	98	72·4	88
1959	8·92	93	7·00	82	110·4	104	73·6	89
1960	9·02	94	7·15	83	104·3	98	74·5	90
1961	8·34	87	6·74	79	102·5	96	70·9	86
1962	7·84	82	6·46	75	98·1	92	68·8	83
1963	7·71	81	6·32	74	97·7	92	68·9	83
1964	7·85	82	6·44	75	95·8	90	68·4	83
1965	7·54	79	6·36	74	92·8	87	69·1	84
1966	7·17	75	6·11	71	89·7	84	69·0	84
1967	6·28	66	5·40	63	80·5	76	62·6	76
1968	5·61	59	4·80	56	72·9	69	56·8	69
1969	5·42	62	5·19	60	72·9	69	58·5	71
1970	5·72	60	5·05	59	71·4	67	57·8	70
1971	5·52	58	4·82	56	65·1	61	52·6	64

A. Casualties to all road users divided by the number (in hundred millions) of vehicle miles performed.

B. Casualties to road-users other than cyclists and motorcyclists divided by the number (in hundred millions) of miles performed by vehicles other than pedal cycles and motorcycles.

the casualty rates per hundred million vehicle miles are traced; cyclists and motorcyclists are included in section A, and excluded in section B. (In fact, the B figures do not represent the full adjustment necessary because they do not allow for the other road users hurt in accidents with motor-cycles and cycles. Hence the B figures give a slightly flatter-ing account of the effect that road safety measures, and all other influences except the decline in motorcycling and cycling, have had in reducing casualty rates.) The A figures do not begin to fall faster than the B figures until after 1960, because till then the annual motor-cycle mileage had been increasing every year, and with it the number of dead and injured motorcyclists.

4.14 What future change in the B rates can be expected? There are, of course, many more road safety measures that could be implemented. In particular there is still unexplored potential in small-scale traffic measures and road works designed to improve road safety and in secondary safety measures, such as wearing seat-belts, which reduce the severity of accidents. But it is also true that many of the more obvious and productive safety measures have by now been implemented, and their effect is reflected in the decline in the casualty rates shown in Table 4.2. The drinking-and-driving clauses of the 1967 Road Safety Act brought about an immediate and marked reduction in casualties. Casualty rates are substantially lower on motorways and high quality trunk roads than on other roads, and almost half the prospective inter-urban motorway was completed by 1971. (There must be some question, however, about the efficacy of building motorways *as a road safety measure*, despite their lower casualty rates, because they also bring about an increase in traffic, especially in urban areas.) The safety aspect of vehicle design has improved in a number of ways. There may be much more scope for reducing accidents by making the wearing of seat belts compulsory, and by recognising that the holding of a driving licence is not an inalienable right. The existing driving test sets arbitrary levels of competence; this could be reviewed as part of wider measures to curtail poor and anti-social driving, which should certainly include stricter and more uniform penalties for those who infringe the present laws. Nevertheless, we must sooner or later expect diminishing returns from these efforts.

4.15 Although we have not attempted to project casualty statistics into the future, we think it unlikely that if vehicle mileage does indeed double by the end of the century the number of casualties can be reduced. It is vital, of course, to persevere with research into road safety measures, and with their implementation; but if society really intends to reduce the toll of casualties it will have to find ways of limiting the growth of traffic volumes, and particularly the types of traffic and the types of situations that give rise to most accidents.

STRESS

4.16 Physiologists and psychologists agree that increased heart rate, blood pressure and perspiration are significant measures of stress, whether this be defined as fear, anger, frustration or anxiety. Experiments have shown that car drivers and passengers have an increased heart rate in congested traffic (anger) and fast-moving traffic, especially on motorways (fear). Increased heart rate has been found among airline passengers during take-off and in other tense situations, but is almost non-existent during travel by train or bus, both for the passengers and for experienced drivers. (It is however, a matter of common experience that anger and frustration may be experienced while waiting at bus stops as much as while waiting at stations or airports during a period of delay.) For some people travel by Underground is a special cause for anxiety, for it may induce claustrophobia, leading to physiologically expressed anxiety. Since fear, anger, frustration and anxiety are normal reactions to stress situations, driving becomes a particularly stressful activity to those who begin a journey in an anxious, frustrated or tense state, and for those who have a low tolerance for such feelings or are prone to them owing to personal circumstances [4], [5], [6].

4.17 A further way of measuring stress is to test a person's ability to do simple intellectual exercises after a particular experience. (This method is used for testing the reactions of astronauts and underwater explorers.) In some experiments, a car driver's ability to perform these tasks deteriorated after a three hours' drive, while three hours' journey as a passenger on a bus or in a train had no such effect [7], [8], [9].

4.18 Driving in frustrating situations produces feelings of anxiety which produce two specific reactions in drivers. First, motor skills are impaired by fatigue and by the need to concentrate. "The high numbers of road accidents and prosecutions for dangerous driving indicate that constant vigilance and the need to take split-second action are well beyond many drivers' competence" ([10], p. 34). Secondly, police studies of accidents have shown that frustration increases aggressiveness. Studies at Cornell University have demonstrated that drivers have accelerated when common sense and a normal instinct for survival would have resulted in braking or turning aside; anger and frustration have been given as the cause. Furthermore, stress caused by driving conditions has been known to aggravate existing stress disorders such as ulcers and coronary thrombosis [10].

4.19 It has also been shown that driving performance in simulated driving tasks can be affected by mood, and is lowered by any disequilibrium in a person's state of mind [11]. A group of lorry drivers decided to ban its members from driving after a serious illness, bereavement or other emotional upset; accident rates in this group of drivers were lowered significantly.

4.20 A further aspect of stress is the fear of road accidents, particularly significant for elderly pedestrians and the parents of young children. The slow walking speed and reactions of the elderly may accentuate the risks they take when crossing a road, while the natural impetuousness of children playing in the open may be a cause of parental anxiety lest they be injured by a passing vehicle. Stress is also caused for those who witness accidents or are involved in them, but are not themselves injured. It has been calculated that in 1972 some 19,000 people suffered bereavement through road accidents and nearly 250,000 suffered anxiety because a member of their family was seriously injured [10]. The distress caused to other relatives must multiply these numbers many times.

4.21 Although many people would agree that some degree of stress is necessary for a person to realise to the full his personal potential, evidence suggests that stress caused through driving cars in modern conditions can impair efficiency, cause great personal distress, exacerbate personal tensions and anxieties and lead to accidents.

NOISE

4.22 Noise is produced by most forms of mechanical transport, by road, rail or air. There is considerable evidence from social surveys that noise, from motor vehicles and aircraft in particular, is a major concern of people in urbanised industrial countries throughout the world—North America, Europe and Japan [12]. In Britain, public objections to the noise from airports and urban motorways have had sufficient political impact to ensure that noise is now regarded as a very important factor in transport planning.

The measurement of noise

4.23 It is not easy to develop a quantitative measure to express the effects of a particular noise on people. Many composite indices have been devised, taking account of both the loudness and duration of the noise, but none is entirely satisfactory. The unit most commonly used for measuring the noise climate produced by road traffic is known as L_{10}. This measures the level of noise exceeded for just 10% of the 18-hour or 24-hour daily period. The L_{10} has been criticised, in our opinion justly, because it can take no account of the fact that many people find traffic noise most annoying at night, when the actual noise level is relatively low.

4.24 For aircraft noise, which is more intermittent than road traffic noise, the preferred index is the Noise and Number Index (NNI), based on a formula which combines the loudness of individual aircraft with the number of aircraft heard during a given period. The NNI was based on a survey of noise annoyance round Heathrow in 1961, and has become very widely used in the UK for the measurement and evaluation of aircraft noise annoyance, "for lack of an obviously more suitable tool" [13]. It was based on very limited empirical work, and doubts about it were not removed by a further survey in 1968. Other formulae for the measurement of noise annoyance have been developed since 1961 in several countries. We therefore recommend that the Noise Advisory Council review the use of the NNI.

4.25 The following examples, taken from a publication of the Noise Advisory Council [14] illustrate the meaning of these indices:

an L_{10} of 70 dB(A) corresponds to the noise 60 feet from the edge of a busy main road through a residential area, average traffic speed 30 m.p.h.;

an NNI of 45 occurs near busy routes from airports, where many aircraft are heard at noise levels that interfere with conversations in ordinary houses.

The relationship between the two units can be calculated from the work of Robinson [15]. This indicates that an L_{10} of 70 is approximately equivalent to an NNI of 48 and that the loudest possible road noise, an L_{10} of 80, which occurs 20 feet from the edge of a motorway, is equivalent to an NNI of 52.

4.26 Appendix 3 also contains tables showing the numbers of residents affected by aircraft and road traffic noise. In 1970–71 approximately 2·3 million people were subjected to an NNI above 35 in the vicinity of Heathrow, and a further 300,000 were similarly affected around three other major airports (Manchester, Gatwick, Luton). In 1970 it was estimated that 9·7 million people were subjected to road traffic noise of L_{10} above 70 dB(A), and a further 14·2 million experienced an L_{10} between 65 and 70 dB(A).

4.27 According to the Department of the Environment, the situation with respect to road traffic noise has worsened since 1970. Furthermore, these figures do not include people affected by aircraft or traffic noise at work, in schools, in hospitals, while shopping, etc. Nor do they take account of the fact that many people are affected by both aircraft and traffic noise.

The importance of noise

4.28 The importance of noise as a source of annoyance is shown both by the public objections to noise and by public opinion surveys of environmental nuisances. Market and Opinion Research International, which conducts an annual survey, found in 1972 that 12% of respondents considered noise to be one of the three or four most serious problems in Britain today [16]. Although in their own local areas it was regarded as less important than such problems as unemployment and "too much traffic", it was on a par with other local pollution problems such as air and river pollution. Furthermore, in a special survey conducted in 1972 on noise alone, 79% of respondents said that noise had got worse in recent years and 43% were disturbed or very disturbed by noise.

4.29 Both this survey and the London Noise Survey of 1961, as recorded in the Wilson Committee Report [13], show that road traffic affects more people than any other source of noise. The London Noise Survey, which was restricted to people in inner London, found that 36% were disturbed at home by road traffic noise, 9% by aircraft noise and 5% by railway noise. The last two figures should be interpreted with caution, as this Survey was carried out in 1961, when piston-engined aircraft and steam engines were still common.

4.30 There is no evidence that transport noise causes physical injury and loss of hearing, as industrial noise can do. There are suggestions, however, that traffic noise may speed up the process of age-induced deafness [12]. It has been shown that traffic and aircraft noise often disturb sleep, both by making it difficult to fall asleep and by reducing the depth, and hence quality, of sleep, even though the sleeper does not actually wake [12], [17]. Variations of noise level seem to be more important in disturbing sleep than the level of a continuous noise.

4.31 Noise also interferes with the performance of both physical and mental tasks. It disrupts conversation and spoils the enjoyment of music, radio or television. Evidence is emerging to suggest that about one fifth of the population may fall into a distinct group which is very much more sensitive to noise than the rest [18]. Aircraft and traffic noise is clearly an important problem of public health and social welfare.

Future trends

4.32 In the absence of any specific measures to reduce the noisiness of road vehicles, the increase in traffic expected on present trends will greatly increase the number of people affected by traffic noise. It has been estimated that the urban population exposed to traffic noise of L_{10} greater than 70 dB(A) in urban areas will be 65% greater in 1980 than in 1970, while the number exposed to levels over 65 dB(A) will increase by 40% [17]. The numbers affected are already so high that these increases would result in almost two-thirds of the population being exposed to objectionable traffic noise. Regulations currently in force will prevent individual vehicles becoming noisier, but will do very little to reduce noise. Furthermore, regulations are effective only if they are universally observed and enforced; enforcement is acknowledged to be difficult and, at present, generally inadequate.

4.33 Railway noise is not likely to rise above its present level. New, faster trains such as the APT incorporate design elements intended to limit the noise to about the same level as that of the present electric intercity trains.

4.34 At the present time, the situation with respect to aircraft noise is in a state of great change and uncertainty. Although it has been generally agreed that the numbers of aircraft using British airports would, with existing policies, grow during the next decade, they may not increase very rapidly because of the increased size of new aircraft such as the Boeing 747, the DC-10, the Lockheed TriStar, and the European A-300B. These aircraft are also quieter than older types such as 707s, VC-10s, Tridents and BAC-111s; the older types can also be quietened by various technical modifications. These and other approaches to reducing aircraft noise are discussed below. Various authorities on aircraft noise have taken these factors into account in estimating that the number of people seriously annoyed in 1985 may be only one-third or less of the present figures (see Appendix 3). If governments, airlines and aircraft manufacturers act with a sense of urgency, that reduction can be achieved even more quickly.

Possibilities of noise reduction

4.35 In principle, specific measures to reduce the impact of noise fall into two groups: measures to prevent the noise from reaching people and measures to reduce noise at source.

4.36 The first group of measures includes sound-proofing houses and arranging rooms so that quieter rooms are shielded from the noise. This approach is of some use against road traffic noise, but is almost useless against aircraft noise, which is far more intrusive. It provides no protection in the summer to people sitting in gardens or with the windows open, nor does it protect people walking in the streets or shopping, for example. Furthermore, it is unjust in principle that people should be forced to protect themselves in their own homes against noise. Despite these criticisms of sound-proofing, the Commission would strongly oppose any move to stop the present scheme of sound-proofing grants to households near noisy airports. Other measures in this category which are of some value against road, but not against aircraft noise include placing roads in tunnels or cuttings, erecting barriers along the edges of roads and laying out towns so that heavy traffic is kept well away from people. These methods are not generally possible in existing towns and cities; they are only relevant to new towns and large-scale redevelopment areas.

Reduction of vehicular noise

4.37 Reduction of noise at source is a much more rewarding approach. This means changes in the design of vehicles. For cars, there would be no difficulty in reducing noise levels by 4 dB(A) to 80 dB(A) [19]; indeed, many cars would already meet this standard and a further reduction to 75 dB(A) would be quite possible by 1980 [20]. Goods vehicles and buses present a more intractable problem. Many of them when new still do not meet the present 89 dB(A) standard. However, it has been estimated that a noise reduction of some 5 dB(A) could be achieved by simple measures costing £50 to £200 per vehicle [17]. A five-year project for the development of a quiet heavy goods vehicle is currently sponsored by the Government and the motor industry; this is intended to reduce engine noise to the point where a vehicle with a maximum noise level of 80 dB(A) could be mass produced by 1980 [19], A similar development pro-gramme on diesel buses is clearly needed. At an engine noise level of 80 dB(A), other sources of noise on the vehicle would become important, particularly tyres, which are already a major noise source at high speeds. Nevertheless, low-speed vehicles could be further silenced by replacing the internal combustion engine as the power unit. The most important example is electrically powered buses, i.e. trolley buses.

4.38 Developments in noise reduction should be stimulated by legislation which sets lower noise emission levels and makes more effective provision for enforcement than the Motor Vehicles (Construction and Use) Regulations 1969. These regulations actually increased the permissible noise levels and made the legally acceptable method of measuring noise so impractical and expensive that 63 out of 64 Chief Constables refused to operate the system. The Commission believes that current noise measurement technology could be used to make enforcement simpler and more effective. We therefore recommend that:

(i) regulations be introduced to reduce the permitted noise levels of cars sold in the UK to 80 dB(A), and of goods vehicles to 85 dB(A), by 1978.

(ii) grants for the purchase of new buses be paid only if the vehicles reach the required standards of quietness.

(iii) police officers and traffic wardens be equipped with pocket noise measuring devices for checking the noise made by vehicles in the street. The owner of any vehicle which seems to exceed the maximum permissible noise level should be required to furnish proof, in the form of a certificate from a garage equipped with standard noise measuring equipment, within 20 days that the vehicle conforms to the regulations. This procedure could be co-ordinated through the Central Registry. It would be an offence to drive the vehicle without the certificate after 21 days.

(iv) Noise testing should be part of the annual DoE vehicle test.

4.39 The relationship between noise produced by individual vehicles or classes of vehicles and the noise emanating from a traffic stream is complicated and depends on the composition of the traffic and gradients, etc.; but, given that heavy goods vehicles account for about 10% of total road vehicle miles (Chapter 2), a reduction of, say, 10 dB(A) in the noise they produce would reduce L_{10} by considerably less. Other problems will remain, even on the most optimistic assumptions. Much annoyance is associated not with the average level of noise, but with variability, and this may well continue even if the general level is reduced. Other measures will be needed to control the noise made by people parking and collecting vehicles late at night, which a survey by Social and Community Planning Research suggests can be as annoying as the noise of moving traffic.

Reduction of railway noise

4.40 In the opinion of the Commission, railway noise could be greatly reduced. There is scope for silencing diesel-powered locomotives; even diesel multiple units, of the type used on local services, make an excessive noise when accelerating. It is hard to believe that any attempt has been made since Stephenson's day to silence railway wagons.

Reducation of aircraft noise

4.41 The new generation of wide-bodied aircraft, powered by high bypass ratio jet engines, are 10-12 PNdB quieter than those they are replacing [21]. The older types of aircraft can be quietened by fitting "hush-kits" to their engines. These can reduce noise levels on take-off by 3–5 PNdB and on landing by 8–10 PNdB [21]. It has been estimated that fitting hush-kits to all aircraft currently operated by British airlines would cost £100 million, which is 4% of their total revenue [22]. Fitting new fans to engines is more expensive, but does not reduce the range and/or payload and increase fuel consumption as hush kits do. Some experts see it as a more promising approach [22], [23]. An example of the costs of different approaches to engine noise reduction is given in Appendix 3.

4.42 These comparisons have become rather theoretical since the announcement by the Minister for Aerospace on 12 December 1973 on strengthened noise control regulations. All British airlines are required to fit hush-kits to their existing fleets before 1979. Most of the aircraft concerned are Tridents and BAC-111s, powered by Rolls-Royce Spey engines. New aircraft of these older types are required to meet the noise certification standard (which new aircraft types, such as the Lockheed TriStar, must already meet) by 1976, and Rolls-Royce is said to be working on a quieter Spey engine for this purpose. The cost of developing and fitting the hush-kits and quieter engines is put at £24 million. It is estimated that operating costs will increase by 5%, which will amount to £60 million over 8 years. When the regulations are in force, foreign aircraft using British airports will have to meet the same standards. (Concorde is excepted from all these regulations.) [24]. The Commission welcomes this move by the Government, which should do much to alleviate noise nuisance, not only around London airports, but also at such airports as Birmingham, Glasgow and Edinburgh, for which Maplin would provide no relief. Nevertheless, we believe that a number of additional measures, some of which would bring immediate relief from aircraft noise, should be implemented. We discuss these in the following paragraphs.

Conclusion

4.43 It is certainly possible to reduce road traffic noise by specific measures. But, even taking the most optimistic view of their effectiveness, there would remain a sizeable problem. Nor is it yet certain how soon the noise reductions can be achieved, how much they will cost, or how effectively they will be enforced. On the other hand (although we have not seen this discussed), personal experience suggests that the safety of pedestrians and cyclists might be further jeopardised by measures to make conventional motor vehicles quieter without any other changes, such as reducing their speed.

4.44 Hence the Commission believes that rapid and substantial reductions in traffic noise are not likely to be achieved without measures designed to limit the growth of traffic volumes and, in some places, the speed of traffic. It is necessary to consider changes in general transport policy as a means of tackling the noise problem, in addition to specific measures directed at noise alone.

4.45 Although the question of international air transport lies rather outside the scope of this report, the Commission felt that aircraft noise was too important a subject to be ignored. As with motor vehicles, advances in engine and airframe design offer considerable possibilities for noise reduction. Although the cost and the imminence of these improvements remain uncertain, the air transport industry is now directed, by legislation and regulation, to hasten the introduction of quieter aircraft. The Commission believe that there is scope for still more legislative and administrative measures.

4.46 Noise abatement in civil aviation is the responsibility of the DTI, which is also responsible for the promotion of trade and industry, including civil aviation. Noise abatement is likely to suffer as a result; the Progress Report for

1973, *Action against Aircraft Noise*, issued by the DTI, shows a certain preoccupation with economic aspects. Perhaps for the same reason, there has been an apparent dilatoriness in the establishment of adequate monitoring centres at Heathrow. As recently as August 1972 the Secretary of State for Trade and Industry rejected a Select Committee proposal that he should share responsibility for noise abatement in civil aviation with the Secretary of State for the Environment (who is also Chairman of the Noise Advisory Council, without executive power.) We recommend that the responsibility for civil aircraft noise be transferred to the Secretary of State for the Environment.

4.47 New motorways are subject to Public Inquiry procedures. New airways are not: they may be announced to the public only a few days before use of the new routes begins. We therefore recommend that the introduction of new aircraft routes be subject to Public Inquiry and that existing routes be regularly reviewed by the appropriate authorities. Somewhat similar considerations apply to the introduction of minimum noise routes, which are approved by the Noise Advisory Council. A minimum noise route is defined as a path which overflies the minimum number of people; but strict adherence to this principle should not be allowed to impose severe noise on small minorities. We therefore recommend that minimum noise routes be not applied automatically to existing urban areas.

4.48 We have noted the introduction of a noise tax in France by a Government decree of 13 February 1973. The tax is paid by passengers departing from Orly and Roissy-en-France at a rate of 1 franc for a passenger departing to a destination in French territory and 3 francs for a passenger to any other destination. The tax is collected by the Aéroport de Paris and is used to pay grants for soundproofing both private dwellings and public buildings. Recommendations on how the money is to be spent are made by an Advisory Committee, which includes representatives from the affected areas. We recommend that a noise tax be levied on all passengers (of two years old and over) departing from UK airports, and that legislative provision for this tax be made forthwith. We further recommend that passengers on aircraft which have been certified to have engines emitting noise below a level to be decided should be exempted from the tax.

4.49 There are curbs on night take-offs of aircraft at Heath-row, Gatwick, Luton and Manchester airports during the summer. However, there are no such restrictions on night landings, and the total number of night movements was still high during summer 1973, despite the small number of take-offs. As a matter of social justice, everyone has a right to freedom from constant disturbance at night by aircraft noise. Some airports outside the UK, c.g. Orly, Zurich and Washington National, place a total ban on aircraft movements at night. We therefore recommend that night movements at airports in the UK be subject to a substantial tax (to be used for noise abatement), graduated on a basis of stringent criteria as to noise levels.

4.50 In 1920 the right of an individual to sue for noise nuisance from aircraft was removed. As a result, the aircraft industry is now in a uniquely privileged position. In 1920 it was thought that, unless common law was altered in this way, aircraft research would be inhibited; but today more research on quieter aircraft is needed. The right of the individual to sue has been retained by the USA and France, and their aircraft industries have not noticeably suffered. Under the Protection of the Environment Bill, local authorities will be given new powers to control noise from construction sites and similar works, and to designate noise abatement zones in which they will be able to control noise from premises. Nothing is said about the control of aircraft noise. We recommend that the right of an individual to take legal action against nuisance from aircraft noise be restored and that local authorities be empowered to take proceedings in public nuisance against aircraft noise.

4.51 Aircraft noise is largely confined to the areas near airports and is now treated as an important factor in all airport planning decisions. Maplin is undoubtedly the most important airport proposal currently under discussion, and the question whether it will contribute substantially to the alleviation of noise is the subject of intense debate. We believe it is right that noise should be given high priority in planning decisions. However, we have not been able to study in depth the necessity for, or the proper location of, a third airport for London, and we do not therefore express any opinion on Maplin.

4.52 By far the most important type of pollution associated with transport is the air pollution produced by petrol and diesel-engined motor vehicles. This will be the main subject of this section. Other transport sources of air and water pollution not considered further include:

—pollution of the sea by spillage of oil during transport by tanker or production in off-shore wells. It has been estimated that in 1969 this amounted to over 600,000 tons world-wide ([25], p. 267); the contribution of transport is in proportion to its consumption of oil (about one quarter of the world total);
—pollution of rivers and eventually of the sea by oil spillage from refineries (300,000 tons in 1969) and waste lubricating oil from industry and motor vehicles (450,000 tons in 1969) [25]; one quarter of the former and a much larger proportion of the latter can be attributed to transport;
—emissions of exhaust gases and unused fuel by aircraft— a serious problem in the near vicinity of airports, particularly Heathrow;
—exhaust fumes from diesel railway locomotives;
—air pollution caused by dust in underground tube railways, which is currently of some concern to London Transport [26];
—water pollution as a result of accidental spillage of materials being transported by road, rail or water. Three people died when the Mersey Ship Canal caught fire in 1971;
—dereliction and spoliation of land used for dumping old motor vehicles, tyres, etc.

Composition and sources of pollution from motor vehicles

4.53 The main pollutants by quantity emitted by petrol engines are carbon monoxide (CO), unburnt hydrocarbons and nitrogen oxides (NOx). The first two are the result of incomplete combustion of the fuel, while the latter results from the chemical combination of atmospheric nitrogen and oxygen at the high temperatures which occur in the engine. Other pollutants are carbon particles (smoke), also resulting from incomplete combustion; lead from the lead anti-knock compounds added to petrol; aldehydes, which generally have an unpleasant smell; and polynuclear aromatic compounds, which are produced in relatively small amounts but have caused concern because of their carcinogenic (cancer-inducing) properties.

4.54 Diesel engines, when properly adjusted, are significantly less polluting than petrol engines. They produce very much less carbon monoxide, less hydrocarbons and aldehydes and about the same amount of nitrogen oxides. Since they do not use fuel with lead additives, they emit no lead at all. However, they are likely to emit smoke and noxious-smelling compounds if they are incorrectly operated or maintained [27], [28].

4.55 The amounts of the various pollutants emitted by petrol and diesel engines vary greatly according to whether the engine is idling, accelerating, cruising or decelerating. They also depend very much on how worn the engine is and how well-adjusted. Figures for total amounts emitted are relatively uninformative, since the factor which determines the effects of pollution is the concentration in the most severely affected place, i.e. busy city streets. However, the following estimates have been made for 1968 in Great Britain [29]:

carbon monoxide	7,000,000 tons
hydrocarbons	1,100,000 tons
nitrogen oxides	400,000 tons
particulates	125,000 tons
aldehydes	20,000 tons
lead	10,000 tons

The effects of motor vehicle pollution

4.56 In assessing the health and nuisance effects of air pollution from motor vehicles, it is difficult to distinguish the effects of air pollution from other sources, such as industry and domestic heating [28]. It is also difficult to distinguish the effects of different individual pollutants, since they commonly interact with each other, sometimes in a synergistic way (producing enhanced effects). The most is table case of this synergism is photochemical smog, which nosuch a great problem in Los Angeles and other North American cities. This smog is caused by reactions between nitrogen oxides and hydrocarbons (both from motor vehicles) when subjected to bright sunlight. Since conditions favouring the formation of photochemical smog seldom occur in Britain, the problem is not considered to be significant, although its constituent compounds have been detected in London [30].

4.57 Carbon monoxide is the largest pollution component of motor vehicle exhaust, and it is an extremely poisonous gas. Motor car exhaust is the largest source of CO emitted to the atmosphere; but, even in the busiest city streets in Britain, the concentrations of CO are never high enough for long enough to produce widespread ill effects [31]. Nevertheless, there are some suggestions that it may harm, for example, drivers in heavy commuter traffic if they are older, smoke heavily or otherwise have a low blood oxygen level, e.g. because of heart trouble [32]. Nitrogen oxides may be more of a hazard [28]. It is known that in higher concentrations they have a more permanent effect on the body than CO, but little is known of long-term effects resulting from continuous exposure to low concentrations, such as are found in busy roads. Unburnt hydrocarbons are not generally considered to be a danger to health. But some attention has been paid, particularly in West Germany, to the hazards of polynuclear hydrocarbons, such as benzyprene, which are well known as carcinogens. Little seems to be known of the dangers of the present atmospheric concentration of these compounds, or of the relative importance of motor vehicles as a source.

4.58 The situation with respect to motor vehicle lead emissions is rather similar. Lead is a dangerous cumulative poison; but, because the symptoms of lead poisoning are so vague (tiredness, etc.), it is difficult to establish what level of lead in the blood is associated with definite symptoms. It is also difficult to relate the concentration of lead in the air to the amount in the blood, partly because food is also a major source of lead taken into the body. There is the further complication that some of the lead in food may originate as atmospheric lead. All these uncertainties have left considerable scope for argument about the health danger of lead from petrol engine exhaust. The Commission, recognising both the uncertainties and the dangers surrounding the subject of atmospheric lead pollution, recommends that there be no further increase in the amount of lead dispersed in the atmosphere.

4.59 In addition to the health dangers, there are other obvious effects of exhaust pollution from motor vehicles. Smoke in exhaust fumes produces deposits of greasy dirt on clothes, houses and roadside plants. It also produces widespread and sometimes acute feelings of nausea.

4.60 We conclude that, in this country at least, atmospheric pollution by motor vehicle exhausts is not an acute threat to human health, but it cannot be concluded that it is not a long-term threat. Chronic exposure to some of the pollutants may have long-term harmful effects, especially if the amounts emitted continue to increase. Motor vehicle pollution is, moreover, a most objectionable contaminant of the environment. Considerations of social justice also arise from the fact that pedestrians and cyclists, i.e. non-motor car users, are particularly affected.

The control of motor vehicle pollution

4.61 If no steps are taken to control the situation, the quantities of pollutants emitted by motor vehicles would increase approximately in accordance with the trends in vehicle mileage given in Chapter 2. This means that pollution would increase by about 50% up to 1980 and would almost double by 1990.

4.62 Measures are now being introduced to prevent the rise in exhaust emissions and, indeed, to reduce them. All approaches to the problem involve reducing the emission of pollutants at source. Some reduction in the quantities of CO and hydrocarbons produced can be achieved by relatively small modifications to the engine. Further reductions, such as are now required in the U.S.A., are being achieved by fitting devices to the exhaust system. The disadvantage of this approach is that it increases fuel consumption by 10 to 20%. Since the catalysts are made ineffective by impurities, particularly lead, in the exhaust, these must be removed from fuel. The capital cost may be £50 to £150 per car [33]. Measures, modest compared with those in some other countries, were to have been introduced here to control lead pollution directly by reducing the maximum permitted lead content of petrol. These have now been postponed.

4.63 More fundamental approaches could be more effective and economical than the methods already described, but none has received large-scale support from Government or industry. One measure, already in limited use, is burning liquid petroleum gas instead of petrol; the necessary conversion costs about £150 per car. A restriction on the maximum size of engines would contribute greatly to reducing pollution. So would the more fundamental step of replacing the internal combustion engine by an entirely different type.

4.64 Estimates of the cost of various measures are given in a Transport and Road Research Laboratory publication [20]. The capital cost of meeting present U.S. standards is estimated at £40 per car, equivalent to £50 million per annum for the U.K. as a whole. The cost of any increased fuel consumption would be additional. Removing lead from petrol would mean blending a different mix of fuels so as to obtain the high octane number petrol needed by modern high compression-ratio engines; this is estimated to cost 1p per gallon, or £40 million per annum.

Conclusion

4.65 The consensus of expert opinion on motor vehicle exhaust pollution is that, while not an acute short-term danger, it may well be a long-term danger to health, and it is undoubtedly an offensive annoyance to millions of people. The Commission recommends that the lead content of petrol be progressively reduced, although we recognise that this will involve some increase in fuel consumption. Significant reductions in the emission of other exhaust pollutants can be achieved by quite small modifications to the engine, and the Commission would like to see these modifications incorporated in all new vehicles as soon as possible.

4.66 Further reductions in exhaust emissions can be achieved only by fitting devices to the exhaust system. We do not believe that step to be justified, especially as it would result in considerably increased fuel consumption. A more promising approach would be to seek reductions in pollution simultaneously with other improvements. For example, two of the most effective ways of dealing with the problem would be to reduce vehicle mileage and to reduce the engine size of vehicles used in towns and cities. Although pollution control could not by itself justify major changes in transport policy, it might be a welcome additional benefit of changes undertaken for other reasons.

THE QUALITY OF THE URBAN ENVIRONMENT

4.67 The decline in the quality of the urban environment is one of the sad themes of our time. It has many causes, and their effects cannot easily be distinguished, but there is no doubt that transport—and not only road transport—is one of the more serious. Railways did great damage in the 19th century. The self-contained nature of the railways and the long time since they were built have enabled towns to grow back round them to some extent, in ways which tend to reduce the harm done; yet there are many places where railways still constitute a severe scar on the urban environment. But the ubiquity and volume of road traffic are such, even without the future growth envisaged in Chapter 2, that it is already by far the most intrusive form of urban transport.

4.68 Our cities and, in particular, our middle-sized towns are the products of many centuries of growth and change, for the most part harmoniously blending old and new. Most of the most precious artefacts of the British heritage are in our towns, and many of them are now in danger of destruction by the growing traffic flows. The visual pollution caused by modern traffic in historic towns, and the damage being done to buildings, require urgent action (see Appendix 7).

4.69 Some of the most serious effects of traffic have already been described: road accidents, danger, noise and fumes. Traffic also intrudes unpleasantly on the visual scene, especially large vehicles which are often completely out of scale with the surrounding urban fabric and destructive of its visual harmony. Parked vehicles often impair the look of streets, and "temporary" car parks on unused ground are an eyesore. Vehicles are often parked in places off the street where their presence is quite incongruous, for example in churchyards or in the forecourts of public buildings. As well as the vehicles themselves, the traffic signs and street furniture necessary to control and direct the flow of traffic are prominent and uncompromising objects not easily fitted into the urban scheme. Street lighting is often brighter and

87

the columns higher than would be necessary in the absence of traffic.

4.70 As traffic volumes grow and drivers seek routes away from congested main streets, these effects become more widespread, even in the absence of one-way streets and traffic management schemes designed to get more use—by vehicular traffic—from the existing road network. Roads are widened or completely remodelled to increase their capacity for vehicular traffic. In the process, the spaces between buildings in towns and cities are encroached upon or brutally transformed. The visual harmony of the neighbourhood is thereby destroyed, for this harmony depends even more on the spaces between buildings than on the buildings themselves.

4.71 New roads have numerous effects on the environment. Before they can be built, it is usually necessary to demolish houses and other buildings, creating social problems and causing personal distress in addition to the environmental impact. Some of the buildings destroyed have been of great historic or architectural value: typical examples from a few of our larger cities are Queens Square and Horsefair in Bristol, Eldon Square in Newcastle, Charing Cross in Glasgow, and Barings Bank and the Coal Exchange in London. Partly to avoid such problems, routes for new roads are often sought through or alongside open space. Open space is scarce in most towns; but just as serious are the division of the open space, or its further separation from the buildings it serves, the visual disruption and the loss of peace and quiet. Examples of this encroachment and division are on the east side of Hyde Park, London, and on Newcastle Town Moor. New roads, even without the traffic they carry, usually create further barriers to movement for short journeys, especially for those made on foot, on routes crossed by them. They are often visually intrusive and, if elevated, can cast their shadows over houses and other buildings. Their obtrusive presence may form a psychological barrier even when it is possible to walk under them. They fragment a neighbourhood and make people feel cut off.

4.72 The process of construction creates noise, dust, visual intrusion and traffic congestion, both on the site itself and on the streets through which contractors' vehicles pass. For example, it was reported to us that in Neasden "pile drivers used on site brought noise levels up to 110 dB; vibrations from compressors used almost round the clock shook houses, endangering structure and causing crockery to slip off tables. People suffered from sleeplessness, deafness and pain in the ears and were distracted by worry" [34]. Hydraulic equipment could have been substituted for pile drivers, and compressors and pneumatic drills could have been muffled, as they were later. Under Clause 52 of the Protection of the Environment Bill, the local authority may serve a notice regulating the way in which works are to be carried out; and this applies to the erection, construction, repair or maintenance of roads. We do not regard this permissive section as sufficient. We therefore recommend that, for all (major) road works in built-up areas, control of noise levels and vibration from heavy machinery be written into the contract; and that during the course of the work the Public Health Inspector should regularly inspect the site.

4.73 New roads in urban areas may also create environmental advantages if they divert traffic from streets less suited to carry it. Of course all new roads attract some traffic from older roads, and thus tend to produce immediate environmental benefits on the latter. If this merely serves to attract or permit new traffic to start making use of the relieved roads, or of other roads to reach the new road, these benefits will soon be lost. If, on the other hand, the potential for additional traffic growth is not there, as may be the case in low-density suburban areas, or is forestalled by traffic restrictions in the relieved roads, the benefits may be of lasting value. One of the critical needs in urban areas, we believe, is to understand this phenomenon and to learn to distinguish between the situations where new roads will, or can be made to, give lasting environmental benefits and those where they will not.[1]

[1] One of the few attempts to study in detail what the environmental improvement might amount to in an area relieved of its through traffic by the construction of a new road was made in London in connection with the (since abandoned) inner motorways plan. The conclusion drawn from this study was as follows: "The base-year results showed that the environmental quality of the zone is already so affected by the traffic volumes as to be unsatisfactory in almost all respects. In 1981 (i.e. the year by which it was intended that the motorway would be in operation), it is predicted that the over-all situation will be little changed, the increase in locally generated traffic largely counterbalancing the beneficial effect of the removal of almost all through traffic from the area" (*London Transportation Study*, volume 3, paras. 23.2.68 and 69).

4.74 New roads are not the only physical alterations required if much larger traffic volumes are to be accommodated in towns. In central areas at least, car parks are usually necessary; these may be multi-storey car parks, or may be provided in the basements of buildings, or underground beneath squares or other open spaces. This adds to the pressure to demolish buildings. Multi-storey car parks are at best uninteresting and unsympathetic buildings; they break up the continuity of the streets in which they are built and are out of scale and obtrusive within the small central area of an English city. The design of other buildings is unfavourably affected by the need to incorporate car parks, and even underground car parks cannot be made completely unobtrusive. Outside central areas and suburban centres it is rarely necessary at present to make such severe physical changes in order to accommodate cars, although it is difficult to see how car ownership can rise to the predicted levels unless provision is made for off-street storage. In particular, the tendency to provide garages or car parks adjacent to houses, where they can only be reached by driving cars across the pavement, creates further hazards for pedestrians.

4.75 The impact of transport policy on new towns, or new areas in existing towns, has already been noted in connection with land. Motorisation tends to encourage dispersal and low densities, thus using more land than would otherwise be required. Aesthetically the resulting town form is at best dull and often depressingly monotonous. The need to provide access for and to store large numbers of vehicles also creates problems at a more detailed level of architectural design. It is a requirement difficult to reconcile with the formation of squares, terraces and streets, which most people find so pleasing in the towns that we have inherited from our ancestors.

THE IMPACT OF TRANSPORT ON THE COUNTRYSIDE

4.76 It is not easy to separate the effects of transport from the many other pressures on the countryside. The effects of traffic and road-building are similar to those in towns; they affect fewer people, but are more serious in other ways. The lack of pavements and lighting means that motor traffic is often more of a threat to pedestrians in the country than in the towns. Traffic usually moves faster in the country, and this increases the effect of noise. Traffic noise is more prominent because of the relatively low level of other background noises, and it carries much farther where there are few buildings to act as barriers.

4.77 New roads, especially motorways with their vast intersections, are not easily fitted into the gentler sort of English rural landscape. They may not be out of place in wild and rugged country, and may even enhance the landscape in some areas, but their traffic is bound to disrupt the peace and remoteness that such places offer. In the Lake District, for example, the proposed development of the A66 will create a road which, in the opinion of the Lake District Planning Board and the Countryside Commission, will be totally out of scale with the delicate landscape, and will provide a lorry route with all its inherent problems of urban intrusion and noise in an area noted for its solitude and unspoiled beauty. Similar suggestions have been made about the proposed improvements to the A591 between Kendal and Keswick, including the proposed Ambleside by-pass between Ambleside and Loughrigg. These effects are inherent in major roads; good design and landscaping are important, and standards have greatly improved since the M1 was built, but they can only soften the impact: they do not remove it.

4.78 Motorways are built to absolute standards of grades and horizontal and vertical curvature to allow safe speeds of 70 m.p.h. In difficult country these standards result in exorbitant costs and unjustifiable scars on the countryside. The Commission therefore recommends that, in areas of scenic beauty which present engineering difficulties, standards of design should conform to lower speeds and speed limits of 45 or 50 m.p.h. should be imposed. The Commission is aware of the danger of having short sections of motorway with restricted speeds and has in mind rather longer sections, suitably signposted, where the physical characteristics of the motorway are more closely related to the nature of the countryside.

4.79 The growth of road freight transport has meant that heavy lorries use often totally unsuitable roads at the beginning or end of their journeys, and create not only danger for residents, but also noise, pollution and damage to walls and buildings. Road improvements to relieve this problem may destroy the traditional character of the narrow, winding country lanes, thus depriving the countryside of what for many people is a special feature. This has happened in the Peak District and Yorkshire Dales National Parks, where quarry traffic is now a major environmental nuisance.

Commuting

4.80 An important effect of current transport policies is that they encourage the commuting habit, and in particular the trend towards long-distance commuting. This has been, and still is, primarily associated with railways. But cars have made a difference to the pattern of residential development associated with commuting. When long-distance commuting was entirely by rail, it was mainly to large cities, especially London, from other urban areas. The car commuter, however, no longer finds it necessary to live near a station; he can drive all the way to the city, or he can drive to an intermediate station. Higher speeds on railways and high-speed, high-capacity roads have extended possible commuting distances. Villages in the more distant parts of the Home Counties, e.g. those north of Bedford, Bletchley and Aylesbury, regarded in 1960 as well outside the London commuting range, are now within it. And the influx of commuters into rural villages is no longer a phenomenon restricted to the Home Counties. Although London has always been the main focus of long-distance commuting, rail commuting to other main cities such as Liverpool, Manchester, Birmingham, Leeds and Bradford has existed for a long time, and long-distance commuting to these cities also is increasing. Middle-class and professional people, who once lived in city centres and later in suburbs, are now moving to dormitory towns or villages many miles away from their work. By commuting 20 or 30 miles to work by road they impose a heavy financial and aesthetic burden on both town and countryside.

4.81 These developments contribute to the road and traffic problems already described. It is less easy to assess their more general environmental and social impact on the countryside. Good effects include the rehabilitation of old buildings which might otherwise have perished, and the introduction of more money and opportunities for service employment into areas which might otherwise be relatively restricted and impoverished. On the other side is an inevitable loss of physical and social character. It seems inevitable that if the commuting habit grows the harmful effects on the countryside will increase more rapidly than the good. The growth of commuting also has important effects for cities: it is a cause for concern that the richer and more influential people who earn their living in a big city can dissassociate themselves from its problems by living elsewhere. If they do not contribute financially to the costs of the cities there is a danger that the cities will become increasingly hard-pressed in the same way as American cities, where large areas have degenerated into working class ghettoes, torn apart by roads on which the more affluent drive from country to city.

Second homes

4.82 The growth of second homes, also, must be related to transport policy. The growth in the number of second homes owned has been extremely rapid in recent years, from some 120,000 in 1968 to some 315,000 in 1972.[1] An important difference from commuting is that the great majority of journeys, probably over 90%, to and from second homes are made by car. The journeys can also be very long: a large survey on second homes indicates that only 8% of them are within two hours' travelling time of their owners' main home and 48% are five or more hours away.[36]. Although the journeys are of course made less often than commuting journeys, the traffic effects when they are made must be more pronounced.

4.83 The effects on the countryside of second home ownership are otherwise similar to those of homes owned by commuters, at least when second homes take the form of houses and cottages (at present roughly half are houses and

---

[1] These estimates are derived from surveys, based on very large random samples, conducted by AGB Ltd. Second homes include both permanent structures (houses and cottages) and static caravans which are permanently rented. The immediate source of this information is Downing and Dower [35]. Other surveys quoted by them suggest that the number of second homes in permanent form was some 20,000 in 1951 and that the rate of growth has generally increased since then.

cottages and half are static caravans). There is already some evidence that second homes have taken away from the housing stock houses that might otherwise have been used to provide first homes for the local population, though very often their most likely fate would have been to become entirely derelict and ultimately to disappear. The supply of unused houses must be exhausted soon, if it is not so already. The growth that took place in the five years 1968–1972 could be sustained at a comparable rate in future only by building new houses or by providing more static caravans or similar dwellings. Apart from its effect on the stock of houses, the demand for second homes has caused house prices to rise in many areas.

4.84 But the percentage of people with second homes is still extremely low, both absolutely and in comparison with some other European countries. There is every reason, both from the steepness of the present rate of growth and from experience abroad, to expect that (as long as economic growth continues) there will be a further rapid growth in second home ownership; and this cannot but have a serious effect on the countryside. The impact on traffic may increase even more rapidly, as the supply becomes exhausted near the major centres of population and people go further afield.

Over-visiting of beauty spots

4.85 Second home ownership is one aspect of increasing recreation. There are two trends: the number of holidays and day trips is increasing [37], and so is the use of the car for these purposes. The danger is that the places that are the goals of these journeys will be spoilt by over-visiting. In some places this is a threat to their physical characteristics. For example, at Stanage Edge in the Pennines, where there can be as many as 600 climbers at one time, the handholds on the recognized climb are being eroded [38]. At Frensham Great Pond in Surrey the pressure of visitors and their cars has been largely responsible for the erosion in some places of almost two feet of soil and the associated loss of heathland vegetation [39]. Similar erosion is taking place at Malham in the Yorkshire Dales [40], in the New Forest [41] and in many other places.

4.86 More commonly, however, the threat is to the enjoyment of the visitors themselves; the attractions they seek they unwittingly destroy by their overpowering numbers. It is not just the numbers of people but the numbers of cars. To provide access by car puts pressure not only on the main roads but also on the local country roads near the destination, roads which are themselves part of the local landscape. The parking of cars produces a major problem. Perhaps most important of all, access by car results in a scattered pattern of arrivals over a wide area, rather than concentration of arrivals at a few points as with public transport. The fact that both cars and visitors are scattered over a wide area frustrates those who value remoteness and quiet and are prepared to walk to find it; and it increases litter and damage. One way of tackling this problem is by parking controls, supplemented where necessary by the provision of shuttle buses and similar forms of transport. Experiments along these lines have been conducted in the Goyt Valley in the Peak District and elsewhere, and have met with the approval of most visitors. Traffic management schemes, not necessarily the same as the Goyt Valley project, are needed in many of the National Parks, and in other popular areas subject to heavy pressure by visitors.

4.87 The problem of over-visiting is most acute at well known beauty spots. The National Trust has recognised it as a serious problem and has adopted a policy of restricted advertising to reduce visitors: "a fairly equable way of stabilising visitors is to restrict publicity . . . It is not, however, necessary to advertise all our houses to the general public, nor need there be sign-posting from main roads to remote beaches" [42]. A survey of visitors to the Watendlath Valley in Cumberland showed that 15% of car drivers (or 37% of those who made any suggestions for improving the valley other than that it should be left alone) wished to see bans or restrictions on car use. Among walkers interviewed (most of whom had originally arrived in the area by car) 43%, or 70% of those who made any positive suggestions, wanted such bans or restrictions [43]. A survey of visitors by car to nine popular beauty spots in the Yorkshire Dales National Park in 1967 found that 55% of respondents agreed with the statement that "spots like this are getting too crowded [40]."

Recreational travel

4.88 The problems, however, are not confined to well-known beauty spots. All parts of the coastline of England and Wales are under pressure. Seventy per cent of built second homes are at the seaside [36]; camping and caravan sites account for 3·5% of the whole coastline of England and Wales and their number is increasing ([38], pp. 202–3). Most day trips are to the coast ([38], p. 94). The most acute problems are felt in the South West. The number of visitors to Cornwall rose from 2,090,000 in 1964 with 187,000 at the peak, to 2,840,000 in 1972 with 242,000 at the peak [44]. Most visitors come by car; congestion is caused not so much by the arrival and departure of visitors as by their attempts to use their cars during their holidays. The effects are particularly severe in the towns in wet weather [44], and can result in complete traffic paralysis. Similar congestion can be observed in many other parts of the country. In the Scottish Highlands, tourist traffic causes acute congestion every summer in such towns as Dunkeld, Pitlochry and Kingussie.

4.89 The social implications of the whole trend of recreational travel are again disquieting. Household surveys show that people in households with cars each make approximately twice as many recreational trips as people in households without cars, and for certain purposes, for example summer excursions to the coast or country, the difference is wider [45], [46]. In addition, the range of choice of those without cars is much narrower. Surveys of visitors to popular tourist spots show that the great majority come by car. Unfortunately, it is not possible from survey data to trace how the position of those without cars has changed over the years, but the decline in rail and bus services has made access harder. For example, services giving access to many scenic parts of the Dartmoor, Peak District and Yorkshire Dales National Parks have ceased, and others serving, for example, the Snowdonia National Park are threatened. In all parts of the country, not only in the most remote areas but also, for instance, in Sussex and Kent, bus services have been reduced, and on Sundays many have been completely eliminated [47]. The growth of coach excursions may have partly compensated for the decline in public transport, but coach travel is not well suited to the needs of individuals and small groups.

4.90 It is beyond the scope of this report to suggest planning measures to control recreational demands on the countryside and to mitigate their effects. What is clear, however, is that such measures have not yet been worked out; and, until they are, one must beware of the consequences of stimulating or unleashing these powerful forces. This is just what the road programme has done,[1] and will continue to do, although, as will be seen in Chapter 8, the encouragement of recreational travel is nowhere mentioned among its aims or likely effects.

4.91 Social justice and conservation alike also suggest the encouragement of public transport to supply access to the countryside for town dwellers. This consideration too must be seen in the context of the other transport arguments which are presented in later chapters.

CONCLUSION

4.92 Much of this chapter has been concerned with qualities which could broadly be called aesthetic, including both the harmony and beauty of our everyday surroundings, which are largely man-made, and also the wildness, remoteness and tranquillity that only the natural environment provides. This is therefore an appropriate place to say what importance the Commission believes should be attached to such things. There is sometimes a tendency to treat them as frills or luxuries, agreeable enough but not ranking high among the many claims on society's attention and resources. Equally it is sometimes suggested that we need not be too much concerned on behalf of posterity about the destruction of such qualities: people who have never experienced them will not miss them. We do not accept these views. We believe that aesthetic qualities and the harmony of his physical surroundings meet a spiritual need in man which cannot otherwise be satisfied. If these qualities are destroyed, our descendants will indeed miss them, even if they do not know exactly what it is that they are missing, and their lives will be diminished.

[1] For example, there is a clear connection between the motorways built in the last fifteen years and the growth in the number of second homes. The problems of Cornwall mentioned in the text are likely to be exacerbated by the building of the M5: it is expected that the traffic volumes observed in peak months in 1971 will be more than doubled.

4.93 This judgement is not merely a projection of our own tastes, unsupported by any other evidence. The beauty of the natural and man-made environment has always been one of the main inspirations of art and literature, especially perhaps of English literature and poetry. The artists and writers cannot be dismissed as few and untypical; unless their work had appealed to millions of less gifted people in successive generations it would not have survived.

4.94 Another spiritual need is to feel a sense of continuity with the past. The language, literature, customs and institutions that we inherit supply this to some extent, but we need continuity in visible and tangible things as well. If we destroy what our ancestors built and can no longer recognise the scenes they knew, we cut ourselves off from the past, impoverishing ourselves and disinheriting our children.

4.95 We have considered various problems caused in whole or in part by our present transport arrangements. These problems are serious, and the expected growth in vehicle mileage will tend to increase their severity. Their effects can be mitigated to some degree by specific remedial measures; but, however successful such measures are, major problems will remain which we believe can only be solved by changes in general transport policy.

REFERENCES

[1] Durie, A. C.: *Motoring into the 1980s*. Lecture presented to the Insurance Institute of London, 22 January 1968.
[2] Speech reported in *Care*, the RoSPA newspaper.
[3] Transport and Road Research Laboratory: *Current costs of road accidents in Great Britain*. TRRL report LR 396. Crowthorne, 1971, page 4.
[4] Morgan, C. T.: *Physiological psychology*. McGraw Hill, 1965.
[5] Perry, M. H.: *Aggression on the road*. Tavistock, 1968.
[6] Lynn, Richard: *National differences in anxiety*. Paper no. 59, Economic and Social Research Institute, 1971.
[7] Buckout, R.: *A working bibliography on the effects of motion on human performance*. USAF Technical Document no. 62–77, IV, 1962.
[8] Dieckmann, D.: "A study of the influence of vibration on man." *Ergonomics* I, 347, 1970.
[9] Dudek, R. A., Ayoub, M. M., and El-Nausi: "Performance and recovery under prolonged low level vibration." *Proceedings of the 4th International Ergonomics Association Conference*, July 1970.

[10] Hillman, Henderson and Morley: *Personal mobility and transport policy*. PEP Broadsheet 542, 1973.

[11] Heimsted, Ellingsted and Dakock: "Effects of operator mood on performance in simulated driving tasks." *Perceptual and motor skills, 25, 729, 1967.*

[12] Organisation for Economic Co-operation and Development: *Motor vehicle noise*. OECD working document. Paris, 1971.

[13] Committee on the Problem of Noise: *Noise: final report*. Cmnd. 2056. HMSO, 1963.

[14] Noise Advisory Council: *A guide to noise units*. HMSO, 1973.

[15] Robinson, D. W.: *The concept of noise pollution level*. NPL Aero Report Ac38. National Physical Laboratory, 1969.

[16] Crawley, R.: Market & Opinion Research International, London —personal communication.

[17] Transport and Road Research Laboratory: *A review of road traffic noise*. TRRL report LR 357. Crowthorne, 1970.

[18] Bryan, M.: "Noise laws don't protect the sensitive.' *New Scientist*, 27 September 1973.

[19] Noise Advisory Council: *Traffic noise: the vehicle regulations and their enforcement*. HMSO, 1972.

[20] Burt, M. E.: *Roads and the environment*. Transport and Road Research Laboratory report LR 44. Crowthorne, 1972.

[21] *Flight*, 25 October 1973.

[22] Masefield, Peter G.: "The road to Maplin." *Flight*, 10 August 1973.

[23] Smigh, M. J.: "Hush-kits or new fans." *Flight*, 10 August 1973.

[24] Department of Trade and Industry announcement, as reported in *The Times*, 13 December 1973.

[25] *Man's impact on the global environment*. Report of the Study of critical environmental problems. MIT Press, Boston, Mass., 1970.

[26] *The Guardian*, 23 October 1973.

[27] National Society for Clean Air: *Air pollution from road vehicles*. Brighton, (no date).

[28] Sherwood, P. T., and Bowers, P. H.: *Air Pollution from road traffic—a review of the present situation*. Transport and Road Research Laboratory report LR 352. Crowthorne, 1970.

[29] Wood, C. M., and others: *Pollution in Greater Manchester*. Manchester University Press, 1973.

[30] Derwent, R. G., and Stewart, H. N. M.: "Elevated ozone levels in the air of central London." *Nature*, 241, pp. 342–3.

[31] Lord Ashby: "Pollution across frontiers: three cases." *The Public Health Engineer*, March 1973.

[32] NATO Committee on the Challenge of Modern Society: *Air quality criteria for carbon monoxide*. Brussels, 1972.

[33] Hopper, W. C.: *The problem of gasoline engine exhaust control*. Stichting Concawe report no. 12/72. The Hague, 1972.

[34] Bargmann, E. E.: *The disruption of an environment and its effect upon people, including a report on Neasden, p. 3*. Appendix to the Hampstead Motorway Action Group's Stage 3 submission 11 to the Greater London Development Plan Enquiry entitled *The medical and social effects of the motorway upon Hampstead*.

[35] Downing, Peter, and Dower, Michael (for the Countryside Commission): *Second homes in England and Wales*. HMSO, 1973.

[36] Bielckus, C. L., Rogers, A. W., and Wibberley, G. P.: *Second homes in England and Wales*. Wye College, University of London, 1972.

[37] *Leisure in the countryside*. Cmnd. 2928. HMSO, 1968.

[38] Patmore, J. A.: *Land and leisure*. David and Charles, 1970, p. 121.

[39] Dr. David Streeter, Department of Biology, University of Sussex: personal communication.

[40] West Riding and North Riding County Councils: *Recreation traffic in the Yorkshire Dales*. 1969.

[41] Forestry Commission and others: "Conservation in the New Forest." Reported in *Rural transport in crisis*. The Ramblers' Association, 1973.

[42] *National Trust Newsletter*, Autumn 1973.

[43] Cumberland County Council: *Traffic in the Watendlath Valley*. 1972.

[44] Information supplied by Cornwall County Council Planning Department.

[45] Sillitoe, K. E.: *Planning for Leisure*. HMSO, 1969.

[46] North West Sports Council: *Leisure in the North West*. 1973.

[47] Ramblers' Association: *Rural transport in crisis*. 1973.

CHAPTER 5

Mobility

5.1 Chapters 3 and 4 dealt with the costs and adverse side-effects of transport. Now it is time to consider the other side. What are the blessings and enrichment of life that flow from movement and mobility, and are they always worth the attendant costs? Can it be said that society, through the trends which reflect the choices of millions of individual people, has decided that the costs are worth while? How in fact has the mobility of different classes of people been affected by the changes that have taken place over the last few decades, and would a continuation of the trends provide a satisfactory way of providing for the mobility needs of the future? These are the central issues with which we deal in this chapter.

Benefits from modern transport

5.2 It is impossible to assess, except in a very broad way, the beneficial effects of modern means of transport. Without trains, lorries, cars, buses and planes, Britain would be an utterly different place. Her population would probably be smaller, still largely agrarian, and very poor in material things. There would be no large cities and no big factories. One can speculate endlessly on the implications, and some people might doubt whether, on balance, life was really any better as a result of these potent inventions. But the majority would certainly not wish, even if it were possible, to give all these things up, in spite of all the trouble they cause.

5.3 The train and the bus were vital to the economic development of the country and the growth of cities. London, in particular, was and is rooted in its railway system. Lorries have added much to efficiency but have not radically altered the structure of the economy. Similarly cars and planes have been superimposed on the earlier system, for those able to use them, and have made many activities much easier to undertake than previously. Numerous suburban and rural communities have been developed on the basis of the motor car as an essential form of transport, although this process has not gone anywhere near so far as in some other countries. But, as we have seen, about half the households in Britain do not possess a car; and to most of those that do own a car, although it represents an exceedingly useful and greatly valued possession, it is not something on which their lives depend. Nevertheless for a sizeable minority it has become essential in the sense that without it they could not continue to live and work where they do. Nor must one underestimate the great attachment that many people have for their cars, and the expense that they are prepared, perhaps irrationally, to lavish upon them.

5.4 The popularity of the private car, and the wish of so many people to possess and keep their own cars, is entirely understandable, especially in present circumstances. A car may be a person's most valuable possession, and he naturally takes a pride in it. It may also seem to him the most beautiful of his possessions, and he will value its appearance. It adds to his personal convenience and even enriches his life. It transports him and his family on holiday. It is useful for many kinds of day trips, to relatives, to the country or to recreation centres. It is available for unpremeditated expeditions. It can aid family shopping and can act as a kind of hold-all into which the family's impedimenta can be put higgledy piggledy. It is specially valuable in any emergency. Thus it is not surprising that many people buy a car as soon as they can afford one.

5.5 In addition to these pleasures and satisfactions that the convenience of a car bestows on its owner, driver and passengers, there are also emotional satisfactions which a person may experience but of which he may not be conscious. For a young person the right to drive a car confers initiation into adult status. A car insulates its occupants, and especially its driver, from the outside world. He crawls back into his private cocoon for temporary retreat. The driver feels king of his own little universe; the people outside seem things, not persons; for one part of his day he is not required to acknowledge others around him. And he can live in a fantasy world of his own making, rehearsing for his next brush with reality. He feels that he has the destiny of others in his own power, and he may exult in the mastery of man over machine. Driving can be a challenge to his manipulative and judgmental abilities, and, as the car becomes an extension of his own ego, so even the smallest scratch on its bodywork can seem a personal injury. The car may appear to him as a symbol of freedom, so that he may feel resentful, like an invalid, if the car is out of action. The car constitutes a symbol of both power and status, enabling a driver to confer benefits on others (such as offering a lift) and (according to the type of car that he drives) feel a member of a desirable social class. At the same time the car may enable a person to feel an equal member of a modern democratic society which has conquered space and is on the way to conquering time. It can be an outlet for aggression, giving rein to feelings of pugnacity and to the desire to prove oneself superior to others. It can also be a psycho-sexual outlet.

5.6 It might seem that these unconscious motivations are merely a *chimera*, and have no counterpart in reality. Advertisers, however, are well aware of them, and they and car manufacturers are prepared to spend large sums of money using these motivations to help to sell their products. Hence it must be presumed that these psychological satisfactions are as real as those consciously conferred by the appearance and ownership of a car and the conveniences attached to car travel.

5.7 The Commission, in advocating that less use be made of the private motor car, is well aware of these satisfactions, and indeed members have experienced them themselves.

5.8 Air travel, for the majority, occupies a very different place. It permits them occasionally to take holidays in more distant places, or with greater ease, than they would otherwise do. For the small minority who fly on business trips, however, the speed of air travel saves enormous amounts of valuable time and makes many trips worth while that would not otherwise be made.

Society's choice?

5.9 The introduction of cars and aircraft has brought profound changes, and for many people great benefits. But have these benefits outweighed the costs described in earlier chapters, and if so would a continuation of the trends, on the scale officially projected, still be advantageous? Many people would claim that the benefits are worth the costs and would argue that, whatever a minority may say, it is obvious that society as a whole agrees: if it were not so, these developments would never have come about. The trends are themselves sufficient evidence of society's choice. In this spirit the Buchanan Report, *Traffic in Towns*, after discussing the growth in vehicles and traffic officially forecast, went on to ask whether that growth would really come about. The view was expressed that a total of 25 million vehicles, including enough cars to give an average of one car per family, "must be regarded as virtually certain" and that "nothing would be more dangerous, at this critical stage in planning for the new mobility offered by the motor vehicle, than to underestimate its potential". The Report went on to say: "It is sometimes maintained that these increases will not come about, that would-be owners of cars will be deterred by congestion and frustration, but we think this attitude would amount to a miscalculation of the mood of the country. The population appears as intent upon owning cars as the manufacturers are upon meeting the demand" ([1], paras. 49 and 51). The Steering Group of *Traffic in Towns* also concluded: "There is no doubt that the desire to own a car is both widespread and intense. The number of people who genuinely do not desire to possess their own private means of transport must be very small." The final paragraph of the Steering Group's report started as follows:

"It is impossible to spend any time on the study of the future of traffic in towns, even so short a time as we have been able to give, without being at once appalled by the magnitude of the emergency that is coming upon us and inspired by the challenge it presents. There is another source of fascination. We are nourishing at immense cost a monster of great potential destructiveness. And yet we love him dearly. Regarded in its collective aspect as 'the traffic problem' the motor car is clearly a menace which can spoil our civilisation. But translated into terms of the particular vehicle that stands in our garage (or more often nowadays is parked outside our door, or someone else's door), we regard it as one of our most treasured possessions or dearest

104

ambitions, an immense convenience, an expander of the dimensions of life, an instrument of emancipation, a symbol of the modern age. To refuse to accept the challenge it presents would be an act of defeatism" ([2], paras 7 and 55).

5.10 *Hansard* provides more recent examples. The opening speaker in a debate on motorways in the House of Commons on 14 May 1973 said [3]:

"It is apparent that the public are determined to own their own cars if they can afford to do so. United Kingdom expenditure on purchasing cars and running them, in the most recent year for which figures are available, was £3,600 million. In addition, more than £500 million was spent on buses and coaches, making a total of more than £4,000 million on road transport. That compares with expenditure on rail travel by the public of £264 million. It is clear, therefore, that the public are anxious to spend their money on road travel rather than on other forms of transport ... It is clear that the public choose road transport rather than other forms. That is true in passenger mileage, as 91 per cent went by road and only 8 per cent by rail."

5.11 The Under-Secretary of State for the Environment said in reply: "Of course this (the forecast growth in the vehicle population) may not happen. It is suggested that man's enchantment with the car is over. The figures for vehicle registration scarcely bear this out ... We are concerned that everyone should enjoy the mobility which the motor car can bring."

5.12 Such quotations could be multiplied almost indefinitely. The attitudes expressed, and the belief that the trend illustrates what society wants, are the fundamental inspiration of policy. Governments of quite different political complexions have therefore supported an ambitious and expensive road programme (which is discussed in detail in Chapter 8) on the basis only of some very general arguments. Similarly, in London, it was the belief in some kind of political imperative to provide for mobility that led the Layfield Panel to accept a road plan with an admittedly very low rate of return, and to propose modifications and additions to it without even calculating the cost [4].

The concept of "mobility"

5.13 Influential though these arguments are, we think they are oversimplified. "Mobility" is not an easy concept to define. In ordinary parlance, it usually refers to the ease with which a person can move about or the amount of movement he performs. But what is important is not movement as such; it is *access to people and facilities*. Access, not movement, is the true aim of transport. One may have access to facilities without moving much at all. An immobile person may have water and gas at the turn of a tap and electricity at the flick of a switch, have his refuse collected, receive calls from his doctor and deliveries from the shops, be informed and entertained by wireless and television, talk to his friends on the telephone, all without stirring from his house. In a well endowed town a person may have access to a vast range of facilities with very little travelling. While possibly less mobile in the ordinary sense of the word than someone who travels greater distances to work, school, and recreation or to visit friends, he may nevertheless be better placed, since the act of travel, with the time, cost and personal effort involved, is something which he usually would prefer to avoid.

5.14 The true goal of planning, the real meaning of mobility, is therefore access, and this is not automatically to be identified with any one means of travel. It can only be provided by the careful location of facilities and a combination of different modes, including motorised modes and—very often—walking and cycling. Shops and places of entertainment, for example, must not be located where they can be reached only by car, or, for that matter, only on foot or by any other single mode, because not every mode is available to every traveller. Different modes conflict with each other, so that an increase in the use of one mode may reduce the ease of using another. A narrow interpretation of mobility is liable to neglect, and possibly to harm, the interests of some people.

Private costs and social costs

5.15 Whatever planners may decide, individuals will try to optimise their own positions within the circumstances in which they find themselves. Millions of transport decisions are made by individuals who are not required to account for all the consequences; many of the disadvantageous effects fall not on the decision-maker himself but on third parties. When the individual decides how to travel to work, whether and how to make a trip into the country, he considers the costs to himself, in time, expense, comfort and perhaps risks. He seldom considers the delays, expense, discomfort and risks that he imposes on other travellers, though these may far exceed his own; nor does he take into account the noise, fumes and environmental nuisance he will cause. The same is true of freight travel. The business man choosing a supplier, the supplier choosing how to send the goods, the lorry driver choosing his route, all weigh up the consequences to themselves, not to the community. Indeed, if they did otherwise, they would soon be out of business. If they were forced to bear all the consequences of their decisions themselves, either directly or indirectly by paying compensation to others adversely affected, there could be better grounds for saying that their decisions represented society's choice; but there is little reason to suppose that their decisions would then be the same as they are today.

Constrained choices

5.16 It is not only because of these externalities—the costs borne by people other than the decision-makers—that one cannot say that the decisions now taken represent society's choice. They may not even represent the decision-maker's own preferences, since he can only choose from the options open to him, which he may find unsatisfactory.

5.17 For example, take someone who lives in a busy city street and uses his car a great deal, thus adding to the traffic on the street. He might be willing to accept some restriction on the use of his car in order to obtain more agreeable living conditions. But no self-restraint on his part alone could bring about such an improvement. Even if he gave up his car altogether, the street would not become noticeably less noisy, dirty and unsafe; it would merely be harder for him to get away from it.

5.18 Social research has shown that this example represents the actual position of many people. The research took the form of a game in which people were asked to choose between options which in real life rarely present themselves

107

as alternatives. In particular, they were able to improve their residential or shopping environment at the expense of a longer journey to work, or alternatively to shorten their work journey times at the expense of a deterioration in their environment. Forty-four per cent of those interviewed chose to improve their environment; only 3% chose to reduce their journey times [5].

5.19 Similarly, if the pleasure of visiting a place in the country is diminished by the presence of too many people and cars, a person might be prepared to go less often or to travel by a less convenient means in return for finding the place less crowded and more pleasant when he does go there. But again individual self-restraint could have no such effect. One is not offered the choice one really wants. Surveys again suggest that this in fact is true of many people; many visitors to beautiful places in the country, including people who arrive by car, would actually welcome restrictions on car use (see para. 4.86). Similarly, those who oppose the building of a new road will undoubtedly use it if it is built, but that does not mean that they have changed their minds in favour of it; they can only respond to the choices they are given.

5.20 There are many similar examples of travel which people make only because they are not able to choose between all the alternatives that are in fact possible. A person living in a dispersed city may have to use motorised transport because there are no adequate shops or other facilities within walking distance. People who would like to walk or cycle may decide not to do so because conditions are disagreeable or unsafe. People who would rather use public transport than go to the trouble and expense of running a car may find public transport so deficient that they feel obliged to run a car. Similar deficiencies compel housewives to give up their own time, energy and freedom in order to act as chauffeurs to their families (see para. 4.10). These are all examples of unwanted or forced travel. Of course the travel is wanted in the sense that it represents the best of the available alternatives, but it is wanted only because other possible alternatives, which would be preferred, are denied.

5.21 In these examples the idea that society either in whole or in part has somehow chosen to accept the full costs of mobility is seen to be simplistic, because the choice is not presented in that way. To the individuals whose choices have collectively the effect that we have described, one option is open and the other is not. If they choose A when they are not offered B it cannot be inferred that they prefer A to B. But, as we have shown, inferences of this kind lie at the bottom of transport policy in this country.

The dynamics of travel growth

5.22 It is important to understand the dynamic nature of transport decisions. At any particular moment the situation and options confronting a decision-maker are themselves the consequence of millions of decisions taken by others in the past, and his decision will affect the options of others in the future. The effects of each individual decision may be negligible, but cumulatively they constitute the trends described in Chapter 2. Although the trends are the collective result of what many individuals have chosen, it does not follow that anyone has chosen or approves of the collective result. If everyone acts rationally but separately in his own interest, a communal situation may arise which is in no one's interest.

5.23 As an example, imagine a city that has grown up before the motor age, in a typical compact form, with some of the finest residential neighbourhoods in the central area. With the development of fast transport (by rail or road) some people build houses in the outskirts, thinking they would rather live where they can have immediate access to the countryside and still be able to find their work and pleasure in the city. But then others come and do the same, and those who made the original move may find that they are as far from the country as ever, that their transport link to the centre is becoming congested, and that their city is very different from the one they used to know. Those who live in the inner city are more distant from the country than ever before. These results were not intended by anyone at the outset, and there can be no presumption that they represent a better, let alone the best, alternative. Even if the more far-sighted citizens anticipated the result, they were not in a position, as ordinary citizens, to alter it. Their choice was only to move or to stay; to shape the growth of the city in some other way would have demanded powers which no individual possesses. Only collective action, in the form of a planning policy implemented by the appropriate authorities, could have brought about any different result.

5.24 The origins of the trends in transport that we have described are, of course, much more complex than this simple example. Nevertheless, one can recognise similar mechanisms which result in trends that are in the long-term interest of practically no one.

5.25 The process starts with rising incomes and proceeds through a vicious circle. As incomes rise, car-owning families tend to make more and longer journeys; in particular they make more car journeys, especially if they become two-car families. Then their use of public transport falls, except for very long journeys. Meanwhile non-car-owning families acquire cars and change their travel habits in a similar way.

5.26 The reduction in travel by public transport means less fare revenue for the operators, who may thereby be forced to reduce services or increase fares, or both. This reaction leads to the loss of yet more customers. Some will make fewer or shorter journeys; others will resort to walking or cycling; others will switch to the use of a car, for some journeys at least, and may indeed by obliged to acquire one for the purpose.

5.27 More car travel means more congestion, which makes the buses slower and less reliable, thus deterring their customers still further and encouraging more car use. Delays also add to bus operating costs, once again obliging operators to economise on service and increase fares, with the same consequences as before. On the other hand, road congestion bolsters the use of rail services, where they exist. As has happened in London, discouraged bus passengers will transfer to trains, along with car owners who in less congested conditions might have used their cars.

5.28 Congestion also adds to the difficulties of pedestrians and cyclists. This may suppress altogether some journeys by people who are dependent on those modes and who find adverse conditions particularly difficult to cope with. Since some pedestrian journeys are made to bus stops and railway stations, *some public transport journeys may never be made*. On the other hand worsening conditions for pedestrians and cyclists may induce some people to go by public transport on journeys which they would otherwise have made, not neces-

110

sarily to the same destinations, on foot or by cycle. Car journeys are substituted for some journeys which would otherwise have been made either entirely on foot or by cycle, or partly thus and partly by public transport. Very often someone who otherwise would not have travelled at all has to act as driver.

5.29 As traffic grows, so does its environmental impact on the recognised main roads, on other roads which become pressed into service in an attempt to avoid congestion on the main roads, and on the local roads on which almost all journeys start and finish. Traffic management schemes designed to increase street capacity worsen the impact on the environment and also make life more difficult for cyclists and pedestrians, thus encouraging yet more use of motor vehicles. This is serious in itself; it also helps to strengthen the motive of travel "to get away from it all" and requires ever longer journeys to be made for that to be possible.

5.30 These various tendencies create and are reinforced by locational changes. As car ownership grows, it becomes possible for people to live further away from their work, sometimes in places not served by public transport. They may not necessarily move house; they may, for example, stay in the same house if their firm moves or if they change jobs, whereas previously they might have moved closer to their work or taken another job instead. The desire to avoid congestion may influence firms in their own locational decisions. Increasing car ownership makes it more possible for them to choose locations which their employees, customers and other visitors can reach by car rather than by public transport. As a partial counterbalance to these tendencies, congestion induces some people to live where their regular journeys are short and easy. Figure 5.1 shows the main interactions that have been described and how they increase car travel and congestion. For the sake of simplicity, the diagram does not show corrective tendencies, in particular the possibility that road congestion may encourage the use of rail transport.

5.31 The effects described can take place without any road building or other action on the part of central or local government. But the resulting increase in vehicle miles is likely to give rise to pressure to provide more road capacity

111

Figure 5.1: The dynamics of personal travel

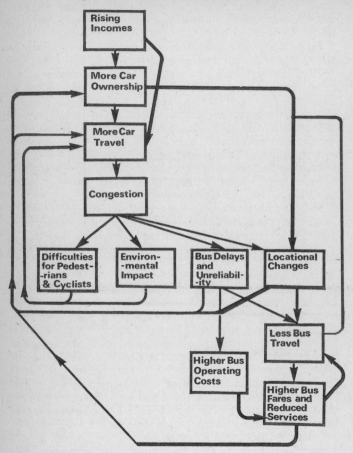

112

by road widening, road building or traffic management. The provision of more road capacity intensifies the various processes shown; in the short term, by encouraging more travel by car and less by public transport, with all the consequences that flow from that, and in the longer term by encouraging car ownership and locational changes. In addition to the changes that can take place within a given stock of buildings, road building gives rise to the tendency mentioned in Chapter 3.77 for new development to take place at low densities and in a form difficult to serve by means other than car.

5.32 Road provision is likely to have a similar effect in encouraging the growth of road freight traffic. Initially it makes road freight transport cheaper, and hence encourages people to use road in preference to other modes and to patronise more distant rather than closer suppliers. Business men are encouraged to locate factories or other buildings requiring goods movements near new roads, on sites that are poorly served by rail. The dispersal of the population encourages more freight traffic, for some purposes at least, such as deliveries to shops and houses.

5.33 The process is considerably more complex, subtle and protracted than we have been able to describe in the last few pages. Little work has been done on some important aspects of travel, so that our knowledge is more sketchy than it need be. But there is ample evidence of the existence of the vicious circles described.

Effect of traffic growth on public transport

5.34 The problems of public transport are the best documented. The decline in both passengers and services was noted in Chapter 2, although of course the statistics do not discriminate between cause and effect. Table 5.1 shows that fares have risen faster than the cost of living generally, and much faster than the costs of acquiring and running cars. Surveys and behavioural studies of the reasons why people do or do not use public transport suggest that frequency and reliability are regarded as even more important than price, except to the very low income groups. The decline in public transport services has meant a decline in frequency, except on BR's Intercity services (on which custom has increased), and on certain suburban services. Trends in reliability are more difficult to measure, but there seems to be widespread agreement that, in cities at least, reliability has deteriorated. A survey of London car-users conducted in 1970 showed that 29% of them thought that London Transport's services had deteriorated in the previous year; the most common cause of complaint, particularly among those who used the services most often, was bad time-keeping.[1] Traffic congestion is certainly not the only reason for the unreliability of buses, either in London or elsewhere; staff shortages are also important. But staff shortages are not unrelated to the vicious spiral of declining public transport that has been described. The financial difficulties of operators lead to low wages and job insecurity and make it hard for them to compete in the labour market, while traffic congestion makes

Table 5.1: *Personal transport: indices of cost to the consumer*
Current prices (1953 = 100)

Year	Railway fares	Bus and coach stage service fares	Prices of new and second-hand cars and motor-cycles	Running cost of motor vehicles	Total consumer expenditure on all goods and services
1953	100	100	100	100	100
1954	101	102	100	99	102
1955	107	107	101	100	106
1956	112	NA	109	102	111
1957	115	NA	113	108	115
1958	119	128	115	106	118
1959	122	131	111	107	119
1960	139	137	109	108	120
1961	151	144	109	111	123
1962	163	152	106	115	126
1963	170	158	95	116	129
1964	173	169	94	117	133
1965	185	180	94	126	139
1966	197	193	94	131	144
1967	201	201	96	136	148
1968	207	213	101	145	159
1969	223	223	103	154	163
1970	240	253	111	159	172
1971	281	297	121	168	184

Source: Annual editions of *Passenger Transport in Great Britain*, HMSO.

[1] *Source:* Opinion Research Centre, a survey on car users carried out for London Transport in 1970.

the job disagreeable and embitters relations between staff and passengers.

Effect of traffic growth on cycling

5.35 The decline of cycling was also recorded in Chapter 2. The mileage performed in 1971 was only one-fifth of that performed in 1952. Clearly increasing affluence, which allows people to use more comfortable means of travel, must explain some of this. But it takes a certain amount of determination to attribute a decline of this order to "demand" factors alone; increasing traffic with its attendant risks, noise, fumes and general unpleasantness must also have deterred many would-be cyclists. That cycling is becoming riskier is well established statistically: there are fewer accidents to cyclists as cycling itself has declined, but the casualty rate in terms of bicycle miles travelled continues to rise.

Table 5.2: Casualties to cyclists per hundred million miles travelled

Year	Type of casualty Fatal	Serious	Slight	Any
1956	6·4	96	385	487
1961	9·6	137	519	666
1966	13·2	173	590	776
1971	16·0	204	673	893

Source: Annual editions of Road Accidents in Great Britain, HMSO.

5.36 The common-sense view that cycling has been discouraged by deteriorating conditions also finds some statistical support from the fact that, whereas cycling on all rural roads declined by 48% in the six years 1960 to 1966, it declined by only 16% on unclassified rural roads, which presumably remain comparatively agreeable for cycling in spite of traffic increases [6]. It is also not surprising to learn that parents are unwilling to let their children cycle, and that even in places where most children have bicycles only a very small proportion of journeys to school are made by bicycle [7].

Effect of traffic growth on pedestrians

5.37 The study of pedestrian travel has been neglected. Indeed most travel surveys do not even count pedestrian journeys as movements. Nothing is known of the way in which pedestrian volumes have changed over the years, or of the changing conditions. The difficulties that poor conditions cause to many less active pedestrians are nevertheless well established: these people include the young, the old, the disabled and those temporarily handicapped for some reason, for example mothers pushing prams or with young children. Common sense suggests that the increase in vehicle miles must have increased pedestrians' difficulties. The accident statistics show a slight upward trend in pedestrian casualties over the years; of course, they reveal nothing of the suppression of would-be pedestrian travel or the delays, frustration and general unpleasantness that increasing motor traffic has brought. A recent report from the Transport and Road Research Laboratory suggests, after taking all relevant conditions into account, that "current trends seem to be moving against the pedestrian" [8]. A memorandum sent to the Commission by the Pedestrians' Association for Road Safety draws particular attention to the confusion caused to pedestrians, particularly to children and old people, by traffic management measures adopted in an attempt to accommodate more traffic on the road—measures such as "split phase operation of traffic lights, one-way roads, green arrow signals, road markings, new traffic signs and symbols."

Unwanted car ownership

5.38 The dynamic process described above starts with rising incomes leading to an increase in car ownership. This initial car ownership is desired by the owners themselves, whether or not it is desirable to society, but the description then suggests how later in the process people are led to acquire cars which they would rather be without. The extent to which present car ownership is unwanted in this sense is difficult to gauge, since studies have been concerned only to establish what present levels are and to explain and predict them by relating them to objective characteristics such as income and residential density. The Commission has not found any published studies inquiring into the reasons for car ownership, especially into the relationship between levels of car ownership and town form, conditions for pedestrians and cyclists and the quality of public transport. However, women's organisations, which have kept closely in touch with the problems over the years, have always maintained that unwanted car ownership exists,[1] and a number of individual examples from particular localities have been brought to the attention of the Commission; it is plausible to suppose that a similar decline in facilities for walking, cycling and public transport will have produced a similar reaction elsewhere. It is also likely that some of the growth in two-car households is accounted for by the inadequacy of the alternatives and therefore represents unwanted consumption.

Locational effects

5.39 Some of the locational effects of the dynamic process that we have described would be difficult to observe: no statistics can be collected of people who did not move house when the location of their jobs changed but who would have done so if they had not possessed a car. The tendency for the distance between home and work to increase has been described in Chapter 4. There is also a tendency for facilities of various kinds to become larger and fewer: for example, schools, recreational centres, hospitals, doctors' practices, shops. The total number of shops has been declining for many years; between 1961 and 1971 there was a net reduction of 57,000 shops in Great Britain, more than 10% of the 1961 total. Most of this reduction was accounted for by a decrease in the number of independent shops, a category which includes the small, easily accessible neighbourhood shops. The independents' share of turnover also fell in this period from 60% to 53% [10]. Official studies predict that both the number of shops and the place held by independents will continue to fall [11].

5.40 This concentration of facilities of various kinds usually arises for reasons independent of transport. The initial

[1] The following extract is taken from [9]. It describes a visit of a deputation of representatives of four women's organisations to the Parliamentary Secretary to the Minister of Transport in October 1970. "At the outset, the deputation was seriously disturbed to hear Mr. Heseltine affirm that the British Public no longer wanted to use the railways as a means of transport. He maintained that the trend showed a constant falling off of both rail and bus traffic, and he was unmoved by the delegation's contentions that if a service was allowed to run down until it became almost unusable, it forced large numbers of people, sometimes unwillingly, to put cars on the road."

impetus comes from the desire to take advantage of economies of scale. But it does have direct consequences for transport and for personal mobility. Travel on foot or by cycle becomes harder; some pedestrian journeys are probably no longer made and others diverted to motorised transport; motorised journeys themselves become longer.

5.41 The growth of car ownership has now made it possible for entrepreneurs to plan large-scale developments catering especially for a car-borne clientele. Cash-and-carry centres, hypermarkets and regional shopping centres are often sited in places difficult or even impossible of access for those without cars. For example, the Sunday market outside Melton Mowbray, in Leicestershire, attracts 15,000 people and 4,000 cars, which are driven an average of over twenty miles to reach it [12]. It is apparent that what seems a desirable solution for the car-borne harms those members of the community without access to cars. They are obliged to pay higher prices at the local shops, if these indeed are able to survive the competition from stores of the hypermarket variety, which live off the town but not in it and which pay little to its support. The results in the decay of town centres, destruction of community life and loss of convenience through the division and isolation of essential services may be very grave.

5.42 Much the same is true of enterprises which cater for rural or semi-rural recreation. The pattern is for facilities to expand with the growth of car ownership, and for public transport users to be gradually excluded from the enjoyment of these facilities as bus and rail services have declined or ended. Country parks and similar ventures, often highly profitable concerns, are obvious examples. Likewise, those country houses which have turned themselves into great rural recreation and leisure centres are frequently beyond the reach of the car-less.

Traffic generation

5.43 The tendency for road provision to create new traffic is another phenomenon that has been noted for a long time. An official study of London's roads published in 1937 drew attention to "the remarkable manner in which new roads create new traffic", citing in particular the effect of the opening of the Great West Road on the former route: "The new route, as soon as it was opened, carried $4\frac{1}{2}$ times more vehicles than the old route was carrying; no diminution, however, occurred in the flow of traffic along the old route, and from that day to this, the number of vehicles on both routes has steadily increased" [13].[1]

5.44 In America, too, it has long been noted that there is a tendency for efforts to deal with growing traffic and congestion by road building to be self-defeating. An American author wrote in 1963:

"Post-war urban growth has brought with it traffic and transportation problems of unprecedented complexity and difficulty. Our efforts to find satisfactory answers to these problems have not been wholly successful, mainly, I think, because we have not correctly assessed them. We have assumed that where there was an obvious lack in street and highway capacity or parking, we could solve the problem simply by providing what was needed, either by making better use of what we had or by building new facilities. However, we have been learning during the past ten or fifteen years that this piecemeal approach is not adequate to cope with the increasingly difficult transportation problems which seem to arise from the very successes of traffic and highway engineering.

"As traffic engineering measures and new streets and highways have added capacity to road systems, more motor vehicles have been put into use almost immediately. New roads and more motor vehicle miles of travel have gone hand in hand in the United States" [14].

5.45 Experience in large towns and cities all over the world provides overwhelming evidence of the tendency for traffic volumes to adjust to the road capacity provided. All large cities experience severe congestion and traffic difficulties, but in none of them does the traffic "grind to a halt", except temporarily as the effect of breakdowns of different kinds. Roads outside towns produce a similar effect, though on a different scale.

[1] The report did not, however, draw the conclusion from this observation that road building was an ineffective way of dealing with congestion; in fact, it used the same illustration in support of the claim that "one can hardly conceive the degree of congestion that would now prevail . . . but for the relief afforded by the arterial roads."

Changes in personal mobility

5.46 What has been the effect on personal mobility of the trends we have described? Shortage of information makes it hard to answer this question precisely. The lavish transport studies during the last decade have usually been based on a large survey of the situation prevailing at one time, rather than on an attempt to monitor on a continuous basis how the situation has been changing over time. Also, they have not approached the problem from the point of view of personal mobility or the provision of access to facilities, but have concentrated heavily on the problems of motorised travel and traffic.

5.47 One conclusion that emerges with certainty is that the past twenty years have witnessed a drastic deterioration in the position of those without cars. As has been seen, the quality of the modes open to them has deteriorated, and prices have risen far more rapidly for them than for the purchasers and users of motor cars. Even after the rapid growth in car ownership of the past twenty years, 45% of households, containing 49% of the population, do not own a car. The conspicuous growth in the number of cars, their impact on the environment and their use by the more affluent, articulate and influential members of the community seem to have led to the false assumption that car ownership is now nearly universal. Not only is this not true, but among large classes who include the poor, the old, the young and the infirm, it is unlikely ever to be true.

5.48 In car-owning households not everyone can treat the car(s) as his own individual means of transport. Those who cannot drive only have the advantage of a car when accompanied by someone else. Table 5.3 shows the wide variations in licence holding by age and sex, and, for the economically active population, by socio-economic group.

Table 5.3: Adult Population without a Car Licence
(Great Britain) 1973

		% with no licence
Sex	male	33
	female	75
Age in years	16–20	63
	21–29	41
	30–59	47
	60–64	66
	65+	85

Socio-economic group	Employers and managers	17
	Professional	8
	Intermediate non manual	30
	Junior non-manual	50
	Personal service	76
	Skilled men (including foremen supervisors)	38
	Semi-skilled manual	64
	Unskilled manual	81
	Farmers and agricultural	34
	Others	27

Source: Provisional data from the National Travel Survey, 1973.

To relate licence holding to car availability one must turn to other survey data. Being a licence-holder in a car-owning household does not mean that one has a car readily available: a recent survey [15] of housewives with young children in the Outer Metropolitan Area found that 30% of those with licences in car-owning households did not have a car available for their everyday use, and, notwithstanding the high levels of both car ownership and female licence-holding in that sample in this most affluent region in the country, 70% of all housewives interviewed did not have a car available to them every day.

5.49 Non-licence holders may, of course, gain much from the family car. Many journeys, particularly holiday or recreational journeys, are by their nature family occasions. And of journeys where one member of the household acts as chauffeur for others, by no means all are unwanted (in the sense described earlier), because they include many which would not be made by other means even if the latter were vastly improved. But most journeys made in the ordinary course of daily life and social contact are ones which we think people ought to be able to make as individuals, independently of the rest of their family.

5.50 Another obvious reason why members of car-owning households do not always have access to a car is that the car is already being used by someone else. The extent to which cars are not available for this reason could only be ascertained by surveys of a kind which have not so far been undertaken, but it must be considerable—hence the familiar problem of the house-bound housewife.

5.51 To understand what the constant decline in their mobility has meant to those without a car, we must turn to the descriptions given by organisations concerned with the welfare of particular social groups and to those few academic studies which have considered transport problems from this point of view.

Difficulties of the handicapped

5.52 According to an official survey there are in Britain about 700,000 impaired people, of whom some 290,000 are permanently disabled and said to be unable to work. Of these about two in five, over 110,000, said that they were unable to work simply because they could not get to and from a suitable workplace. Of those who are working 16%, some 90,000, stated that they encountered difficulties in the travelling involved. For 10%, over 55,000, the disablement restricts the distance they are able to travel with present transport facilities. Other groups with similar problems are pregnant women, mothers with small children and anyone with shopping to carry.

5.53 A study in the USA in 1968 showed that there can be a considerable economic return on investment in transport for the handicapped or disabled. There were nearly one and a half million employable but "transportation handicapped" persons in the USA. Calculations showed that, if only 100,000 of these could be mobilised and returned to work, annual earnings of over \$450 million would be generated, \$40 million of which would be returned to public coffers in income tax.

5.54 Age Concern carried out a widely based study of the problems faced by old people and concluded that "the problems of public transport are little more than an irritation for many people. For the elderly, however, they can mean hardship. Even those who can afford a car may find driving increasingly tiring or dangerous. But in most cases the old have no alternatives. They rely on public transport for practical needs, to get their pension, to visit the doctor, ... and for avoiding the greatest danger in old age, isolation."

Difficulties of country dwellers

5.55 Serious hardship is suffered also by people who live in the country and do not own cars. The closure of rural branch lines and of local stations on main lines has isolated them in a very real and serious way from neighbouring towns and cities, and recent widespread reductions in bus services have made the situation even worse. Some surveys show that country people have found ways of getting to work or to school by sharing lifts in neighbours' or workmates' cars or by means of private bus services provided by employers and education authorities. These services cannot be used by the ordinary public, as they are not stage carriage services, but they do constitute a form of subsidised transport in rural areas.

5.56 However, the needs of country dwellers are much wider than travel to work and school. Shopping trips, business trips, and visits to doctors, dentists or hospitals are equally essential for all sections of the community and (as we suggest in Appendix 6), there are a great many people for whom the lack of transport and the inconvenience and expense of such services as still exist create serious personal difficulties. It is hard and sometimes impossible for country people to travel into nearby market towns to shop; they are therefore thrown back on the resources of the village shop (if it still exists) which has a more limited choice and higher prices. Visits to the doctor are very difficult for people living in a village without a doctor. Bus timetables rarely fit in with morning surgery times, and buses may have stopped running by the time of the evening surgery. The needs of patients going to hospital are generally well catered for, but not those of their friends or relations wanting to visit them. The hardship is particularly acute in rural Scotland and Wales and the remoter parts of England; it is sometimes not possible to visit someone in hospital and return the same day, and in many places Sunday visiting has become impossible because there are no services.

5.57 Just as the old and the poor suffer most acutely from lack of public transport in towns, so in the countryside their hardship is correspondingly worse, as distances are greater and facilities more scattered. The situation now is in some ways worse than before the First World War; at least in those days the local carrier would undertake commissions for those unable to visit the nearest town, or provide a cheap means of transport, albeit slow.

5.58 But there are other requirements apart from those relating to material and physical well-being. "Quality of

123

life" implies access to a reasonable level of cultural and social facilities, and it is in this area that country people perhaps suffer most dramatically. Children may have a special bus to take them to or from school, but they cannot participate in school activities which take place out of school hours because there is then no way for them to get home. The absence of evening bus and train services cuts down the social, recreational and educational activities of people of all ages. Trips to a local theatre or cinema are impossible when the last bus leaves at 8 p.m.; equally when night-school classes or the meetings of a local natural history group continue to 9 p.m. such opportunities may be denied to the country dweller, and few people like to be beholden to a neighbour for a trip which is not absolutely essential. Even a journey to visit one's family or friends in a nearby town or village may require long waits between connections, making a total travelling time of several hours.

5.59 The sheer inconvenience of travel in rural areas has now reached the point when the possession of a car is often essential, even though it may mean a considerable sacrifice for a family on a low income. Given the alternative of having to depend on totally inadequate or even non-existent transport services, there is really no "choice"; indeed, evidence has reached the Commission of families who could ill afford it having to put two cars on the road to provide for the essential needs of the wife and children. Such cases are not a reflection of a growing desire for car ownership, as is commonly assumed from the statistics, but an indictment of a public transport system that has become quite intolerable.

5.60 Another side to this problem is that of city dwellers who wish to escape into the countryside to enjoy the quietness and physical beauty the human spirit needs.[1] The physical expansion of cities itself has made it more difficult to reach the countryside, but particularly acute is the problem of reaching the remotest and loveliest areas of Britain, many of which are, in England and Wales, designated National Parks. Services to and into National Parks have declined steadily in recent years, at the very time when private cars have become an increasing environmental nuisance in these areas. But the individual wishing to visit a National Park or Area of Outstanding Natural Beauty may well find that he has to

[1] See Appendix 6.

use his car, particularly on a Sunday. We have now reached the stage when many famous and historic areas in Britain cannot be reached by public transport, except perhaps by means of coach excursions. *Even where there is public transport, its existence tends to be ignored in official brochures.* Tourism is a growing industry catering for visitors from home and overseas, the latter usually being without private transport, and regular, scheduled bus and train services to places of interest will not only provide that level of access needed by the tourist, but will encourage the dispersement necessary if over-used centres are not going to be spoilt by weight of visitors.

5.61 The problem of some people without cars will diminish as car ownership spreads and as more people learn to drive. But it should be realised that people unable to drive or without the use of a car for particular journeys are likely to constitute the majority of the population for as long as one can foresee, simply by reason of age—old and young— or physical deficiencies or lack of income to support two or three cars per household. The difficulty and unit cost of providing them with services will grow as the market shrinks; if the services are allowed to decline, however, so will their level of mobility, and the gap between them and those with access to cars will widen. One result will be an increase in unwanted car ownership and use.

Difficulties of car-drivers

5.62 How have the trends affected the position of people who do have cars? The motorway and trunk-road programme has undoubtedly made many longer-distance journeys faster and easier. Elsewhere it is generally harder and less agreeable to use a car than it was twenty years ago, although in real terms it is cheaper (as Table 5.1 showed). Moreover car owners do not always use or want to use their cars, for every journey they make, and they too suffer from the declining quality of the alternatives. The position has thus become worse for car users in some important ways. Nevertheless, a great many people have become car owners during the last twenty years and their mobility has improved in many respects, even if not to the level of the car owners of twenty years ago. Which of these opposing tendencies has been the stronger must vary greatly from place to place and from person to person. In the country those who have acquired cars have generally experienced a great increase in their personal mobility, whereas in big cities it is quite possible that, even for those who have acquired cars, there has been no net increase in mobility, at least in their ordinary daily lives as opposed to holiday and other out-of-town trips. The reason for the difference is that the self-defeating character of increasing car use applies strongly in cities and very much less in the country—hardly at all in some areas.

5.63 The extreme, and best documented, example of the self-defeating process is in London and especially central London, where the usual process of traffic growth has been assisted by traffic management measures and a limited amount of road building. The net result is that the streets are more crowded—since cars have replaced many of the two-wheeled motor vehicles—but the total number of travellers by road has in fact declined over the last 15 years or so as Table 5.4 indicates. Travellers as a whole have certainly not benefited from this; it is hard to believe that any class of travellers has benefited.

5.64 The ultimate source of this problem is physical capacity. It is not physically possible to accommodate more than a small proportion of the vast mass of journeys that have to be made each day into and within large towns on the basis of one or two people per vehicle. And if the problem of car availability will not disappear as car owner-ship increases, the problem of capacity can only grow. Conditions now found only in larger towns and cities and in some smaller towns at certain times of day will spread to other towns and other times of day, frustrating mobility as well as causing environmental problems.

SUMMARY

5.65 The argument in this chapter has of necessity been long and intricate; a summary may therefore be helpful. The premises underlying current transport policy are that mobility is itself desirable, and that the trends demonstrate that society has chosen mobility, based on the car, notwith-standing the heavy costs involved. We have suggested that this is an oversimplified view of the position. Mobility, in

Table 5.4: Daily arrivals in central London between
7 a.m. and 10 a.m.
Unit: thousand travellers

Year	BR or Underground	Bus and coach	Car	Motor cycle	Pedal cycle	Total road travellers
1961	882	209	104	23	12	348
1962	905	215	108	23	10	356
1963	884	191	111	20	9	331
1964	887	191	115	19	8	333
1965	884	180	117	16	6	319
1966	876	175	116	12	5	308
1967	884	172	115	11	4	302
1968	840	167	124	9	4	304
1969	856	157	116	7	3	283
1970	848	151	124	7	3	285
1971	843	146	128	6	2	282
1972	818	144	128	7	2	281
1973	805*	144	128	9	3	284

* This figure is not final.

Source: London Transport Board

Notes: 1. For the purpose of the road counts on which these figures are based, central London is defined as the area bounded by Grosvenor Gardens and Park Lane in the west, Marylebone Road and Euston Road in the north, Shoreditch and Aldgate in the east and the Thames in the south.

2. There are various estimations involved in arriving at these figures, which should be regarded as approximate only.

the sense of having the facility to move or perform great amounts of travel, is not in itself desirable. It is access to people and facilities that matters. Since those who travel or send goods do not have to take account of all the costs that their decisions impose on society, it cannot be said that the outcome of their decisions reflects society's choice. Since their choices are heavily constrained by the options made available to them, it cannot be said that their decisions reflect even their own true preferences. On examination of the facts we find that the mobility of the majority of the population, i.e. those without cars available, has been declining, and that the mobility of some car owners is also declining. Future increases in car ownership will not solve the problem of availability and will accentuate the problem of capacity.

5.66 This discussion suggests a gloomy judgment on the

trends and policies of the last twenty years: the sacrifices made and costs incurred have not resulted in a satisfactory transport system. But it also suggests a much more hopeful conclusion for the future. Society does not have to choose, as is sometimes suggested, between an expensive and damaging transport system on the one hand and the acceptance of poor mobility and restricted living on the other. The changes in policy required to reduce the costs of transport seem to coincide well with those required to create a system of transport which will serve the needs of all citizens and make use of all the possible means by which mobility can be provided. The changes necessary and the means of achieving them are the subjects of subsequent chapters.

REFERENCES

[1] *Traffic in Towns, Report of the Working Group.* HMSO, 1963.
[2] *Traffic in Towns, Report of the Steering Group.* HMSO, 1963.
[3] *Hansard*, 14 May 1973, columns 1204, 1205.
[4] *Greater London Development Plan, Report of the Panel of Enquiry.* HMSO, 1973, paras. 12.30, 12.59, 12.61, 12.69 and 12.79.
[5] *Traffic Disturbance and Amenity Value*, Social and Community Planning Research, December 1972, page 19.
[6] *Traffic Survey at 1300 Sites.* TRRL Report LR 206, 1968, Table 17.
[7] Hillman, Henderson and Whalley, *Personal Mobility and Transport Policy.* PEP, 1973, pp. 5, 6, 66, and 67.
[8] *Roads and the Environment.* TRRL Report LR 441, 1972, p. 26.
[9] National Council of Women: *Survey of Public Transport*, 1972.
[10] "Provisional results of the Census of Distribution 1971", *Trade and Industry*, vol. 11, No. 7, 1973.
[11] *The Future Pattern of Shopping*, NEDO, HMSO, 1971.
[12] *The Guardian*, 23 November 1973.
[13] Bressey, C. H.: *Highway Development Survey*, HMSO, 1937, p. 25.
[14] Kennedy, Norman: "Evolving concept of transportation engineering." *Traffic Engineering and Control*, July 1963.
[15] Political and Economic Planning (as yet unpublished research).

CHAPTER 6

Instruments of a Transport Policy

6.1 We have shown that the transport system contains fundamental deficiencies which can only be put right by policy changes. Not only does the transport system fail in many ways to meet the needs of large numbers of the population; the way it is organised virtually precludes it from doing so. Dynamic processes are creating long-term changes in the system that are to the ultimate advantage of only a minority, and even for them, we believe, a different approach could offer advantages.

6.2 The dawning recognition of these deficiencies has led people to demand an integrated transport policy. But what does that mean and what form should it take? It certainly does not mean that some huge central authority should control all transport decisions. What is required is a framework of institutions and procedures that will ensure that, before transport decisions are taken, the full range of options is considered and all the consequences taken into account. In later chapters we consider how government—central and local—should study its problems and what particular changes should be introduced. This chapter discusses the instruments that could be used by society to tackle transport problems and compares their potential with the use now being made of them.

The legal framework

6.3 Transport is moulded by the legal framework in which it operates. Some of the vicious circles described in Chapter 5 would not arise if the legal framework were different. For example, when the mounting volume of traffic disturbs the peace and quiet of residential streets, it matters not how highly people prize these amenities; they have no legal right to them and cannot protect them from the encroachment of traffic. Nor does the law protect pedestrians and cyclists from the violation of their traditional liberties by the force of motor traffic. Public transport passengers also have few rights. A manufactured article of poor quality can be returned to the shop, but if a bus or train is late or full the disappointed customer has no redress. This is a growing anomaly since the rights of consumers in other fields are continually being strengthened.

6.4 Some reinforcement of the rights of individuals with respect to amenity is both possible and desirable. For example, grants are paid to residents near Heathrow, Luton and Manchester Airports to help sound-proof houses. Although these do nothing to mitigate nuisance outside the home, nevertheless they are at least an acknowledgement that people have a right to compensation when their amenities are disturbed. This major point of principle is explicitly accepted in the White Paper, *Putting People First* [1].

6.5 Another significant and welcome change is the Land Compensation Act, 1973, which permits certain compensation payments for loss of amenity due to road-building schemes, although it is an extremely limited measure and could even do harm. For example, it could encourage the greater use of traffic management as an alternative to new roads, because the disamenity effects of traffic management schemes do not have to be compensated, although they can be worse than those of road building.

6.6 It is important to extend these rights, but the Commission's view is that the best way to reduce the environmental impact of transport is by general transport planning and regulation in order to prevent the conflicts from arising.

6.7 Pedestrians now have some common law rights, for example the right to be able to cross the road without unreasonable delay, and it is possible that more could be done to improve their legal position and that of cyclists. But problems of definitions and enforcement put a strict limit on what can be achieved by legal means. The best approach again is to plan in a way which prevents the problems from arising.

6.8 At first sight the prospects of improving the legal rights of public transport passengers seem brighter, since theirs is the familiar legal relationship of customer and supplier.

The problems of definition are also less formidable: it is easier to specify standards for the reliability of bus services than for the adequacy of conditions for pedestrians. But it would still be difficult and expensive to establish that failures of reliability had occurred and to compensate customers; and the attempt to do so might have unfortunate effects, such as encouraging bus and train drivers to make up for delay by driving too fast.

6.9 The difficulty in enforcing the rights of individual passengers makes it all the more important to strengthen their collective power. The need for collective consumer representation is acknowledged in principle by the existence of the Transport Users' Consultative Committees. There are nine such committees in England, one in Wales and one in Scotland, and one central body, the Central Transport Consultative Committee for Great Britain. The chairmen of these committees are appointed by the Secretary of State for the Environment, who also appoints the members, after consulting with appropriate organisations. On the passenger side the committees are restricted to considering the service offered by British Rail, including its subsidiary services; for freight they are concerned with the National Freight Corporation and the British Transport Docks Board. In London, the London Transport Passengers' Committee, which is appointed by and reports to the GLC, is concerned with both the bus and railway operations of London Transport. Elsewhere the Committees are only concerned with buses when the possibility arises of replacing a rail service by a bus service. The Committees may not consider either the fares charged by BR or any reductions in BR services short of complete withdrawal. Their activity is limited to considering withdrawal of rail services and matters to do with quality of service. These committees correspond to the bodies set up to represent consumers' interests in other nationalised industries, for example the Electricity and Gas Consultative Committees. The effectiveness of any of these committees is questionable, and the TUCCs have been shown to be the least known and probably the least effective of all [2]. They have themselves complained of the inadequacy of their powers [3].

6.10 The Commission recommends a complete overhaul of this system. From 1 April 1974 the new county councils will be responsible for transport planning within their areas; there should therefore be a transport consumer council for each county council area. These consumer councils should be concerned with all surface passenger transport services supplied to the public within their areas, whether by nationalised undertakings such as British Rail and the National Bus Company, by municipal undertakings, by private bus companies or by taxi and car-hire firms. They should have powers to investigate and follow up complaints, including powers to conduct surveys on buses and trains. They should be empowered to bring prosecutions where appropriate against operators on behalf of customers. For example, if a council received complaints that a taxi firm was failing to send taxis when promised, it should be able both to make its own investigations and to prosecute on the basis of evidence collected. Transport operators should be obliged to publish the findings of any investigations carried out by the consumer councils and to make an appropriate reply. If the consumer councils were not satisfied they should have the right to take their complaints to the county councils, which would be obliged to conduct their own investigations, publish the results and state what action they intended to take. Consumer councils should have the power to appoint non-executive directors to the boards of local transport undertakings and non-voting members to the appropriate local authority committees. Consumer councils should be elected or appointed in such a way as to guarantee their independence; the Chairman and perhaps other members should be paid[1] and they should have adequate funds to conduct the kind of investigations described. They should be financed either from the rates or by means of a tax levied on local transport undertakings.

6.11 At a regional and national level, similar councils should be set up with powers in relation to national transport undertakings and central government equivalent to those of the local councils at local level. Members of regional and national councils should be elected by local councils.

6.12 The first important task of these councils should be to represent and protect consumers' interests. The material provided to the Commission by the women's organisations and others shows how deep and widespread is their dis-

[1] See Note of Reservation on p. 279.

satisfaction with public transport services, and how often it is caused by details that escape the attention of high-level transport planners: details such as the lack of porters and seats at railway stations, or shelters at bus stops, poor co-ordination of timetables, buses that are difficult for elderly and infirm people to mount, insufficient provision for parcels and luggage, and inadequate marking of the route numbers on buses. But effective consumer councils would also have an important influence on general transport planning. The inadequacies of public transport services and the helplessness of the individual citizen to do anything about them are the main cause of unwanted car use and car ownership; hence they are a cause as well as an effect of the vicious spiral of decline.

Regulation of vehicles, drivers and traffic

6.13 Numerous regulations prescribe the kind of vehicles allowed on the roads, the condition in which they must be kept, the people allowed to drive them and the manner in which they may be driven. The object of these regulations is usually safety, but sometimes it is amenity, in particular the control of noise and fumes; and the rules of the road are designed not only to ensure safe and efficient traffic movement, but also to safeguard the rights of pedestrians.

6.14 The last decade has seen an increasing awareness of the possibilities of using regulations for purposes wider than those for which they were first devised. Their power to protect certain areas from traffic was indeed recognised much before that: a generation ago Abercrombie in his City of London Plan discussed the use of traffic lights and other controls limiting the volumes of traffic in the "precincts" which he wanted to see created all over London. The powers of local authorities to regulate the routes of heavy lorries have recently been consolidated and amplified in the Heavy Commercial Vehicles Act 1973, with the object of facilitating protection of the environment.

6.15 But attempts in recent years to develop and extend established methods of traffic control have had quite another purpose. Starting in London in the early 1960s, traffic management has been employed to increase the capacity of roads, in terms of the flow of vehicles they can accommodate. Greater safety is also claimed as an objective. Parking controls, one-way streets and the systematic use of traffic lights, sometimes controlled by computer, have been the main instruments, accompanied by minor measures of road widening or building.

6.16 Such schemes attempt to treat a rather narrowly conceived problem: how to move vehicles making a given pattern of journeys as expeditiously as possible. Similar techniques, and extensions of them, can also be used to solve the wider problem of how to accommodate the movements of people and goods. The essential difference is that controls would be used selectively, to facilitate the movements of some travellers, or the use of some kinds of vehicle, and to discourage others. In pedestrian precincts all vehicles may be banned, with possible exceptions for delivery vehicles and buses, and with special provision for disabled people. Elsewhere vehicles may be permitted subject to conditions on their behaviour and, implicitly, on their number: for example, speeds may be severely restricted by speed limits or "sleeping policemen", i.e. ramps built in the road. There is a wealth of experience of pedestrian and environmental management schemes in Germany and, indeed, in this country. There are numerous ways in which buses can be given priority: by reserving whole streets or lanes for their use, either exclusively or with other specified vehicles such as taxis or delivery vehicles, by exemption from turning restrictions, by actuating traffic signals in their favour, and so on.

6.17 Controls can impinge on parked or stationary vehicles as well as on moving vehicles. It was in London in 1958 that parking meters were first introduced. Initially, the intention was only to prevent unsafe and disorganised parking and to clear the way for moving vehicles. But it was soon realised that parking controls were also a powerful instrument of transport policy, because they could limit the possible number of journeys by car to the controlled area. Parking controls can also be used selectively: for example, permits may be issued to residents only, or spaces may be reserved for special classes of people such as doctors or the disabled. Ordinary parking meters embody a principle of self-selection: it is up to the individual car user to make up his mind whether the price is worth it or not. The successful development of parking control as an instrument of transport policy in towns depends, however, on the powers of planning authorities to obtain control over private parking space.

6.18 A full description of the measures available to control moving and parked vehicles, and the advantages and limitations of each, would require a report in itself (see for example [4], [5], [6]). The Commission's view is that these measures constitute an indispensable element of transport policy, the potential of which is still hardly explored. They are usually cheap to implement and have been shown to provide excellent value for money. In London fourteen bus-lane schemes were investigated by before-and-after studies. It was claimed that the value of savings in operating costs to London Transport and in passenger time in one year was more than double the cost of installing the schemes, and that conditions for other traffic were not seriously affected and in some places were improved. Some increase in accidents was reported; but it was hoped that this result could be eradicated by alterations in the design and enforcement of the schemes in question [7]. Good results are claimed from the implementation of bus priority measures elsewhere, but unfortunately the results are not often presented in a form which allows value for money to be assessed [8]. Management measures are the only action that can be implemented fairly quickly and they lend themselves to experiment and adaptation, as the construction of new roads or railways clearly does not.

6.19 The potentialities of management measures for purposes other than the control of traffic flows and speeds are so obvious that it may be wondered why we are so slow in developing them and why there are so few such schemes intended to help pedestrians, buses or the environment. Legal obstacles are part of the answer. Before the Town and Country Planning Act 1968 and the Transport Act 1968 it was not possible to make selective prohibitions of vehicles or to create foot streets (except on grounds of safety). Although the first example in a public street was approved by the Minister of Transport in Bedford Street, Norwich, in 1967, even now, legal obstacles limit the implementation of some potentially useful measures such as the "sleeping policemen"; and we recommend that the laws should be revised. Another, perhaps more important, obstacle is the belief that such measures constitute restrictions on individual freedom, or at least would be so regarded by the general public.

6.20 We have said enough to refute the idea that the absence of rules is to be equated with freedom. No one would call the ordinary rules of the road an infringement of liberty; clearly there would be chaos without them. We recommend the kind of regulations discussed in this chapter as a logical extension of the rules of the road, made necessary by the growing traffic volumes.

6.21 The belief that traffic regulations would be regarded as restrictive by a hostile public is not based on a serious study of public opinion. There has been little social survey work on this subject, but such questions as have been asked, as part of general questionnaires, have revealed that many members of the public understand the problem and are prepared to accept traffic regulations as part of a "package deal" to improve the environment and public transport. Tables 6.1 and 6.2 present the results of questions asked in social surveys in 1963 and 1969 respectively. They show that

Table 6.1: Gallup Poll Survey*

	Respondents with current driving licences	Respondents living in conurbations

Do you agree that some limitations on the use of cars in the larger towns will be necessary in the future?

Yes	86%	82%
No	10%	11%
Not stated	4%	7%

Would you accept some limitations in the use of cars if this meant that congestion would be eased and that you would be able to use your car to full advantage at other times?

Yes	80%	65%
No	10%	9%
Not stated	10%	26%

Do you think that the character of our ancient towns should be preserved even if it means keeping out private cars in some way?

Yes	61%	61%
No	31%	27%
Not stated	8%	12%

* This survey was carried out in October and November 1963. The sample was selected by quota methods, within areas selected randomly, so as to represent all adults (16 or over) in the United Kingdom. The total number of respondents interviewed was 2,154, but we have confined this analysis to respondents with current driving licences and respondents living in conurbations; these two categories overlap.

a large majority of people were in favour of firmer controls on the use of cars. Although the latter survey was confined to a very limited geographical area, we believe the results are of interest, since it is the only thorough study of its kind that we have come across.

*Table 6.2: Metra Survey**

	Households without cars	*Households with cars*	*All households*
All households—			
actual	212	330	544
weighted	597 = 100%	852 = 100%	1453 = 100%
The use of motor vehicles in towns must be controlled even more in order to protect the environment.			
Agree strongly	40%	30%	34%
Agree	42%	43%	42%
Disagree	10%	19%	15%
Disagree strongly	1%	4%	3%
Don't know	7%	4%	5%
Much more could be done to enable motorists to use their cars in towns.			
Agree strongly	11%	22%	17%
Agree	32%	31%	31%
Disagree	34%	31%	32%
Disagree strongly	15%	11%	13%
Don't know	8%	5%	6%
In large towns, we should concentrate on improving public transport and should discourage motorists from using cars.			
Agree strongly	41%	27%	33%
Agree	44%	38%	40%
Disagree	8%	22%	16%
Disagree strongly	1%	11%	4%

* Fieldwork on this survey took place in November and December 1969. Interviews were carried out in 544 households selected by random means in predominantly rural areas of Bedfordshire, Buckinghamshire, Cambridgeshire, Essex, Hertfordshire, Northamptonshire and Oxfordshire. Wherever appropriate, interviews were conducted jointly with husband and wife.

Regulations on vehicle performance

6.22 It is surprising that, although it has now been realised that traffic and parking regulations can be used for purposes much wider than those for which they were originally intended, little thought has been given to extending the use made of regulations on the vehicles themselves. The tacit assumption at present is that regulations should not seriously interfere with the performance characteristics of motor vehicles. If this constraint were set aside, an area of policy of great potential would be opened up. For example, if there were limits on the maximum speeds which vehicles permitted for use in an urban area were physically capable of attaining, the impact on safety, noise, fumes, fuel consumption and the choice of mode for longer journeys might be dramatic. The Commission has not been able to explore this area of policy and recognises that, since the stock of vehicles takes years to replace, quick results could not be expected. But we believe that the possibilities should be investigated for the longer term. The Institute of Fuel in the recently published report of its Working Party [9] recommended legislation governing the engine size and power-to-weight ratio of petrol-operated vehicles, (and also the use of private cars in urban areas). We recommend that further study be made of this proposal as a start to a consideration of more far-reaching possibilities.

Pricing policy

6.23 Pricing is the normal method of limiting the effective demand for costly goods and services. It allows fine gradations and lets travellers decide in the light of their own circumstances whether the price is worth paying. We pointed out in Chapter 5 that many of the adverse consequences of transport decisions fall not on the traveller or decision-maker but on others, and that if the decision-maker had to bear the consequences he might act differently. It is not possible to make each traveller bear all the consequences, but he can be made to pay a sum which corresponds to the nuisance imposed on others.

6.24 At present, pricing is used hardly at all as an instrument of transport policy. The charges made by transport operators for their services are ordinary commercial transactions and relate only to the operators' own costs, not to the total social costs. There is, of course, the vehicle excise duty which raises from vehicle owners revenues that are probably large enough to cover the overall costs of maintaining road facilities. The scale of charges made for licences is related to the classes of vehicles in a way intended to reflect the relative damage done to the roads. Thus, while a private car pays only £25, the heaviest lorries pay over

£400 annually. But since the duty is not related to mileage it is possible for any individual vehicle to do much more, or less, damage than it pays for, if it does more or less mileage per annum than the average vehicle in its class. There is certainly a case for some reform in the system of duties by adjusting the amount to be paid by vehicles of each class[1] and perhaps by changing the definition of the classes; but a tax of this form, unrelated to the amount or type of use made of individual vehicles, can never be a sensitive instrument of transport policy.

6.25 Fuel tax is at present used not as an instrument of transport policy, but purely as a means of raising revenue, although exemptions from fuel tax have been granted to buses as a way of assisting them (see para. 6.43 below). Since the tax paid is related to the amount of fuel used, and hence to the amount of use made of a vehicle and to its weight and load, it is potentially a more sensitive instrument of transport policy than vehicle licensing. Even so, the amount of tax paid cannot be related at all closely to the damage and nuisance caused by particular vehicles on particular journeys; and attempts to discriminate between classes of vehicles would invite cheating. For these practical reasons the Commission believes that, whatever adaptation is made of fuel tax, a combination of regulation and subsidy is likely to be also necessary to cope with the problems caused by lorries.

6.26 We are fully aware both of the attempts made, and of the difficulties encountered, in devising practical pricing schemes for bringing the consequences of their actions home to road users. The possibilities of road pricing have been studied mostly as a means of controlling congestion in urban areas. One suggestion is that vehicles should be fitted with electronic meters which would respond at "pricing points" to circuits placed in the road surface. The incidence of the pricing points could be readily varied between different areas and different times of day and week. The meters issued to large vehicles could carry a higher charging rate than those issued to small vehicles. Pricing points could be located with the object not only of easing congestion but also of achieving environmental aims. A cruder, but much simpler, method of

[1] See Chapter 10.104–105, and also the suggestions put forward in [10].

road pricing in towns is to create a daily licensing zone in the centre of the town. Admission of a motor vehicle would require a supplementary licence valid for one day only.

6.27 Objections have been raised to these and similar ideas on grounds of equity; although the intention is that those who most need to travel by car would pay and the rest be squeezed out or travel by other means, in practice it is likely that the rich would pay and the not-so-rich would be squeezed out. Exactly the same objection can be raised to parking meters, which are now widely accepted. The question of equity is not a simple one and must be judged in relation to the total transport policy, including the way in which the revenues from road pricing are disposed of. If road pricing were used as a means of protecting and improving the bus system, which is available to all, and if the charges were not so high as to be prohibitive for the poorer car owner on special occasions, it need not be objectionable.

6.28 We believe that the simplicity and low operating cost of daily licence schemes are important advantages over the vastly more sophisticated meter systems. There are many places in addition to town centres where simple methods like this, and even ordinary tollgates and ticket systems, may be both effective and desirable. They should be regarded as weapons in the armoury of local transport planners, along with other traffic and parking controls. The right combination of measures for any given town or place will depend on its particular circumstances. But changes in the law are required to enable charging schemes to be added to the controls available to local transport planners.[1]

Grants and subsidies

6.29 Grants and subsidies are the obverse of pricing measures. Their purpose is or should be to reduce the price of certain transport services below that which would result from commercial considerations alone. There are several reasons why this might sometimes be desirable.

6.30 First, in transport the direct costs (economic and social) associated with providing additional services are commonly low relative to the average costs including overheads; for instance, if a bus is running half empty, the cost of taking on

[1] See Note of Reservation on p. 279.

140

additional passengers is very low, provided they are not so many as to necessitate an additional bus or to cause uncomfortable crowding for the original passengers. Similarly, when a motorway is carrying far less than its traffic capacity the cost of using it is very low. Provided, therefore, that the facility is going to be open to traffic anyway (e.g. if there is no question of withdrawing the bus or closing the motorway) and provided that low prices do not generate so much traffic as to create congestion costs, there is a case for letting people use the facility at prices below average cost, and for subsidising the capital cost, and perhaps the running costs too. This is a general argument for charging lower prices during off-peak periods and on very much under-utilised facilities, provided—let it be repeated—that the facilities are to be offered to the public anyway.

6.31 Secondly there could in theory be external benefits from certain types of transport. In that case a subsidy serves to encourage use, just as a tax serves to discourage the use of types of transport that give rise to external costs. In practice, in British conditions today, we know of no important instances where this argument for subsidy can be put. There is, however, the possibility of countervailing subsidies where the use of one form of transport, by reducing the demand for more objectionable forms, leads to a reduction in either the external costs (e.g. noise, accidents, social injustice, etc.) or the internal costs (e.g. congestion, new investment) of the latter. Ideally, in such situations, we believe the correct policy is to tax or otherwise restrain the transport users who are imposing these costs on society. But if for practical, political or other reasons it is difficult to do this, a "second-best" policy may be to attract users away from the more objectionable to the less objectionable form of transport by means of subsidy.

6.32 Thirdly, there may be grounds of social justice for retaining low prices. The principal example occurs when people have been attracted to live or work in certain areas by the availability of transport services which, for one reason or another, become increasingly costly (per passenger) to run. Sharp increases in price, like withdrawals or drastic reductions of services, can come as a major blow to people who are dependent on, and have been lured into a state of dependency by the existence of, the transport services in question. Society may have an obligation in such situations to soften the blow by means of subsidy, at least for a period of years.

6.33 Finally, there are arguments for subsidy on grounds of income redistribution or social need. One of the difficulties with transport is that the same service can be a trifling luxury for one passenger while it is an essential requirement for another. We certainly would not class transport in general as an essential service deserving of subsidy for that reason alone, any more than we would say the same of food and clothing. But there are classes of society, consisting of underprivileged households or underprivileged members of other households, who depend vitally on certain transport services being available at reasonable prices, and we would support the subsidisation of such services where there is no other acceptable way of meeting the needs of the people in question. Low fares on country services and reduced fares for children are important examples. For old age pensioners or other classes whose real problem is poverty affecting their ability to obtain all their requirements, not transport in particular, we would look to higher pensions as the proper answer rather than concessionary fares. Nevertheless, if cheap off-peak fares or free travel can be justified on grounds of existing spare capacity (see our first argument for subsidies, para. 6.31), we would see them as an excellent way of helping old people, who seldom need or wish to travel in the peak hours, and who can be encouraged in this way to make journeys which they otherwise would not attempt.

6.34 A common objection to subsidies is that they reduce the spur to managements to be efficient. But this depends on the way in which the subsidies are given. We are strongly opposed to "open-ended" subsidies, i.e. simply paying off the deficit at the end of the year. This view sometimes leads to a preference for subsidies for capital expenditure rather than operating expenditure. We believe there is little merit in this distinction, which may cause considerable waste (see for example [11]). The money should be spent where it will do most good. If one aim is to interrupt the vicious spiral described in Chapter 5, by not allowing prices to rise and services to decline when customers are lost to cars, operating subsidies are more likely to be appropriate than capital subsidies. The way to stimulate management is to relate the

142

size of the grant to the results achieved, not to specify ways in which it can be spent.

6.35 If monopoly is the prime cause of management inefficiency, can anything be done to reduce the degree of monopoly that prevails? Nothing can be done about the railways, but it would be possible to reduce the monopoly position of bus operators. Some people have suggested a much freer system of local competition and a reduction in the powers of Traffic Commissioners to grant licences. Others, accepting the case for having all the services in an area under unified control, have argued that local authorities should make contracts with suppliers to provide the local scheduled services for a given term of years. The desire to renew their contracts would then be the spur to efficiency. If the local authority required the bus operator to provide a fuller service than could be paid for from fares alone, or wanted fares to be kept down in the interests of some wider transport policy, the contract could be drawn up accordingly. The Commission has not investigated these ideas and is not making any recommendations about the organisation of the bus industry. We mention them only to show that ways of reducing monopoly powers, or mitigating their unfortunate effects, can be suggested which are compatible with the payment of grants and subsidies.

The use now made of subsidies

6.36 There have been considerable changes in the last few years in the way that subsidies and grants can be paid to public transport operators. There is no need to describe the present situation in all its complexity, especially since it is about to change again when the new local authorities take up their powers in 1974. But a brief historical sketch and an appraisal of the present and proposed arrangements will be illuminating. (The financial relationship between central and local government, and the grants that central government can pay to local government, raise rather different issues which will be considered in the next chapter.)

6.37 Before the 1968 Transport Act, the accepted philosophy was that public transport should be a commercial undertaking and should not be subsidised or helped by the state. In practice, since the railways had made losses for many years, central government had been obliged to step in to

143

make up their deficits because it was unthinkable that they should be allowed to collapse. There was no general policy for subsidy and no recognition that subsidies might be used as an instrument of wider transport policy.

6.38 In addition, some municipal bus undertakings in effect received a subsidy from the ratepayers. The amounts were never large, indeed it is likely that municipal bus undertakings as a whole made some small contribution to the rates.

6.39 The 1968 Transport Act was intended to provide a new financial basis for the operation of British Rail. The Board was freed of past debts and was intended to act basically as a commercial organisation in future. It was recognised, however, that some passenger services were valuable to the community even though they might not pay their way. This was thought to apply particularly to some rural services and also to some commuter services in conurbations. It was therefore provided that either the central government or the new Passenger Transport Executives which the Act set up in the major conurbations or the GLC (under a separate Act passed at the same time) could pay British Railways for operating services that were socially important but not commercially viable.

6.40 The 1968 Transport Act also recognised that there would be occasions when rural bus services should be provided which were not commercially viable; it empowered county councils and local authorities to make grants to bus undertakings for the provision of a service "for the benefit of persons residing in rural areas." The central government would repay to the local authority half the grant made. No similar provision was made for purely urban bus services, but it still remains possible for municipalities to subsidise their own undertakings through the rates. The GLC now has similar powers in London, as, when specifying London Transport's financial target, it can, if it wishes, authorise the services to run at a loss.

6.41 These operating subsidies, both to British Rail and to bus undertakings, were regarded as exceptional provisions, only to be contemplated when special "social" considerations over-rode the "economic" considerations that should normally apply. This is a limited view of subsidies; we believe that (at least when a comprehensive charging policy cannot be applied) subsidies are a perfectly respectable way of achieving general economic aims. It is quite possible that greater benefits could be achieved, when the total transport system is considered, by subsidising profitable services rather than unprofitable ones.

6.42 The 1968 Act also provided for grants to be paid by central government to local authorities or by central government or local authorities to any other person for expenditure of a capital nature incurred "for the provision, improvement or development of facilities for public passenger transport in Great Britain". It was realised that, if grants were paid by central government to local government for expenditure on roads (as was and is the practice) and nothing equivalent were payable for capital improvements on public transport, this would have a disturbing effect on local authorities' investment decisions. It would encourage them to spend money on roads, rather than on public transport improvements, simply because most of the money spent on roads could be recovered from central government.

6.43 Another section of the 1968 Transport Act (section 32) empowered central government, but not local authorities, to make grants to bus undertakings for the purchase of new buses. The main purpose was to encourage operators to equip themselves with one-man buses, which were seen as part of the solution to the economics of bus operation ([11] questions 2179, 2186c). Section 33 of the Act allowed bus undertakings to claim back half the tax paid on fuel. This was intended as a simple way of giving general financial support to bus undertakings.

6.44 The Local Government Act 1972, which comes into force in 1974, removes the distinctions between capital and operating grants and profitable and non-profitable services, at least as far as payments by local authorities are concerned. It enables county and district councils to make grants towards "any costs incurred by persons carrying on public passenger transport undertakings wholly or partly in the county or district".[1] Metropolitan County Councils are similarly empowered to assume responsibility for the operations of the Passenger Transport Authority, in their area, from 1 April 1974.

6.45 What is still lacking, however, is any recognition that

[1] Local Government Act, 1972, Section 203.

subsidies may be an appropriate instrument of freight transport policy. There is no denying that it may be in the community's interest to influence the pattern of freight transport that results from purely commercial processes, or that subsidies may be one way of doing this. The Commission believes that because of the practical limitations of pricing policy, subsidies are one of the instruments that ought to be used.

6.46 A topical example from inland waterways may illustrate this. (As will be seen in Chapter 10.15ff. the Commission does not believe that inland waterways can make a substantial overall contribution to the solution of freight problems. But they may help in certain areas, and the rules should therefore be set in a way which enables them to play a useful part where they can.) The Department of the Environment has so far refused to sanction improvements to the Sheffield and South Yorkshire Navigation on the grounds that there are doubts whether the improved canal would attract enough of the traffic predicted by the British Waterways Board and its consultants to achieve either the commercial rate of return forecast or the environmental and road traffic benefits that it is agreed would arise if the scheme were successful. The Department's attitude has been criticised by pro-waterway bodies on the grounds that the guarantees of use from potential customers for which the Department is now asking go beyond what the firms concerned could reasonably give. Whether or not this is so, the incident does illustrate why subsidies should be regarded as legitimate instruments of freight policy. If substantial benefits would flow to people other than the users of the canal from its use, and if potential customers are likely to be wavering, then to reduce the charges by means of subsidies would be a way of ensuring that the other benefits would be obtained. Exactly similar arguments apply to subsidising the operation of town distribution schemes or rail freight services, ideas which are considered in Chapters 8 and 10. If subsidies are a way of guaranteeing their use and so bringing about all the community benefits that would flow from the reduction of road goods traffic, then it is in order to subsidise.

Company cars

6.47 Business executives are frequently given a company car.[1] If the sums involved were not so substantial one could call it a "fringe benefit". This is sometimes a necessity (e.g. for some representatives and salesmen), sometimes a straightforward supplement "in kind" to income, costing the company much less (at the executives' marginal rate of taxation) than a direct payment would cost. Nineteen per cent of new cars are company cars available for domestic use. We understand that the Inland Revenue levies a charge of £45 per annum on this benefit. The Commission recommends that the distortions implicit in these arrangements should be corrected and that the related tax laws, statutes, or interpretations should be overhauled. The inspector should add to the executive's taxable income what it would cost him to procure in the open market the benefit which he receives from having the use of a car outside working hours.

Locational and land-use planning

6.48 It has been stressed throughout this report that the aim of transport policy should be to provide access to facilities, rather than simply to encourage mobility in the sense of making travel easier, and that there are advantages both to the traveller and to society in reducing travel by keeping journeys short. Clearly, the length and pattern of journeys and the choice of mode are largely determined by the land-use pattern and the number and location of the facilities that attract journeys. Control over these things is therefore an instrument of transport policy no less than control of the transport facilities themselves.

6.49 The degree of control which planning authorities can exercise over locational decisions varies considerably. It was seen in Chapter 5 that changes of location, causing important changes in travel, can take place within a given stock of buildings. For example, a man can move house and make longer journeys to work in consequence; or a firm can move its offices from one building to another, with all sorts of effects on the journeys to work of its employees. Nothing can

[1] According to figures supplied by the Department of the Environment.

147

be done within present planning powers to control such locational changes; nor does the Commission believe that it would be appropriate, or perhaps even possible, to extend planning powers so as to bring them under control. But changes in the rules governing transport itself would have some indirect effect on them. For example, the man contemplating moving out to the country might think twice about it if he found that he could not drive straight from his new home to his office but would have to change somewhere on the outskirts.

6.50 Planning authorities do, of course, have considerable powers over the location and size of new developments. Powers over private developers take the form of withholding permission to build or granting permission subject to conditions. The implications for transport should be one of the most important factors taken into account when planning permission is being considered. These implications are not now always spelled out, and the standard conditions that have been attached, especially about parking, have often been exactly the reverse of what was required. The common form has been to lay down the minimum number of parking spaces that should be provided within a new building of a given type as a ratio of its floor space. The idea was that if these buildings were to attract a certain number of car journeys, it should be the responsibility of the developers to make sure that the cars were provided for off the street. But the effect of forcing developers to provide more car parking spaces was simply to encourage more car journeys. It is now realised that in the interests of wider transport planning, it is important to set maximum rather than minimum limits on the number of spaces to be provided; but there is still a tendency to set these limits by reference to a standard formula of so many places per square foot. There is no reason why the number produced by such a formula should bear any relation to the transport needs of an area.

6.51 Planning permission should take account of the implications for freight as well as personal transport. It would very rarely be appropriate for planning authorities to specify the modes of goods transport to be used. But they should ensure that the locations chosen do not rule out modes which might otherwise have been appropriate. In particular, factories or industrial estates should not normally

148

be sited in places which can only be served by road transport.
6.52 It may be questioned whether present planning powers
over private developers are adequate. It can be argued that
the negative powers of withholding planning permission are
in practice so circumscribed, especially where redevelopment rather than completely new development is in question,
as to be virtually nullified. It can also be argued that even if
these impediments were removed, purely negative powers
are not enough and that planning authorities should have
much more power to initiate development. The Commission
has not attempted to investigate these complex issues,
which have vast implications beyond the field of transport
planning. We accept that changes in the law may be required if the full potential of locational planning within
transport planning is to be realised. But we also believe that
present powers are not being fully used. We recommend that
it should be standard procedure for the transport implications of any application for planning permission of more
than a specified size to be set out before the application is
considered by the appropriate committee of the planning
authority.
6.53 Planning authorities can already have a more positive
influence over the locational decisions of public authorities.
Some decisions, for example about the provision of schools,
libraries and recreational facilities, are taken by the same
local authorities acting in another capacity. Even where, as
in the provision of hospitals for example, this is not true,
good liaison should permit planning authorities to make their
views known at an early stage. It seems that decisions on the
size and location of the facilities provided by public authorities can still be taken with very little reference to convenient
access to them for their customers, still less to the wider
transport and traffic implications; this is especially likely to
happen when more than one council is affected. Chapter 5
drew attention to the tendency for some facilities of various
kinds to become larger and fewer. There may be good reasons
of internal efficiency for this, and the Commission does not
suggest that considerations of convenient access and wider
traffic implications should dominate the decision. But
neither should they be neglected, and it is at least possible
that in some cases—recreational facilities such as libraries
and swimming pools are among the most likely examples—

a good case could be made out for the provision of more numerous and smaller facilities.

6.54 The interaction between transport and land use must also be taken into account at a more strategic level of planning when planning authorities are concerned with general questions of the shape of their towns rather than with particular decisions on individual planning applications. An appropriate long-term strategic aim would be to remove these problems at their source, rather than solving them, by encouraging the development of a more suitable pattern of land use. Access to people and facilities should usually be the dominant influence governing the form of new towns or new areas of expanding towns. At present, the planning of new and expanding towns is largely governed by the wish to achieve "full motorisation" or to come as near to it as possible. Consequently, new towns have been built to a dispersed, low-density pattern, which is exactly the reverse of the pattern required to keep journeys short or to encourage walking, cycling and the use of public transport. All the arguments in the preceding chapters suggest that the latter is the right approach to new town design.

Conclusion

6.55 This chapter has attempted to show how wide and various are the means that are available to planning authorities, or could be made available to them by suitable changes in the law, to control transport. The wider the range of possibilities, the harder it becomes how to decide what should be done in any particular situation. This is the problem considered in the next chapter.

REFERENCES

[1] *Putting People First*. HMSO, October 1972.
[2] Consumer Council: *Consumer Consultative Machinery in the Nationalised Industries*. HMSO, 1968, p. 50.
[3] *Central Transport Consultative Committee Annual Report for 1972*, HMSO, 1973.
[4] Thomson, J. M.: *Methods of Traffic Limitation in Urban Areas*. OECD, Paris, 1972.
[5] *Techniques of improving urban conditions by restraint of road traffic*. OECD, Paris, 1973.
[6] Haycock, G.: *Implementation of Traffic Restraint*. TRRL Report LR 422, 1972.
[7] GLC Press Release No. 480, October 1973.

[8] *Bus Priority*, TRRL Report No. LR 570, 1973.
[9] Institute of Fuel: *Energy for the Future*, 1973, p. 24.
[10] Sharp, Clifford: *Living with the Lorry*. University of Leicester, 1973.
[11] *Urban Transport Planning*, Second Report from the Expenditure Committee, House of Commons Paper 57, Session 1972–73, vol. II, pp. 124, 140, 141.

CHAPTER 7

Decision Making in Transport

The issues

7.1 In our democratic system, major decisions of social policy are determined ultimately by the political process. In large-scale economic projects facts must be collected and interpreted in the light of broadly acceptable criteria. If these are formalised and quantitative, they are likely to exclude important social factors that do not readily fit into a numerical framework of analysis. Such social factors, however, are open to public debate and, through the political process, their influence can be made to prevail notwithstanding the results of more formal methods of analysis. For example, it was decided to build the third London airport not at Cublington, the site recommended in the Roskill Report, but instead at Maplin.

7.2 Transport policy in this country, however, has not been guided consistently by broadly accepted goals. Until recently, major decisions were guided for the most part simply by predictions of future demand for road capacity. The attempts to build roads to accommodate the predicted increase in vehicles have perpetuated and reinforced existing trends in transport activity. This policy would be satisfactory only if it were generally agreed that a continuation of current trends would be the best way of fulfilling the social functions of a transport system. As indicated in Chapter 5, however, the inadequacies of the policy have caused a change in the climate of public opinion which has had some influence at least on local transport planning. Prediction of trends, in this new thinking on transport objectives, is relegated to a minor role. Emphasis is coming to be placed on the prior setting of social goals and the subsequent search for economic ways of realising them. Clearly this emphasis entails a radical change in our way of looking at economic activity in general and particularly at those large segments, such as transport, that are more directly under public control.

7.3 In this chapter we shall examine the traditional approach as well as the prediction-guided techniques that still constitute so large a part of what passes for transport policy, and we shall review some of the changes that are now taking place. Finally we shall briefly assess a method that is growing in popularity, namely cost-benefit analysis, in order to draw attention to some of its limitations, especially in matters of transport.

The traditional approach to transport problems

7.4 Whatever social goals are adopted, and whatever body is responsible for their implementation, it needs to be recognised in any rational approach that the various means of transport are closely inter-related and that variations in the volume or quality of any one or several means of transport has effects on the usefulness or attractiveness of the others. Do the authorities act in such recognition?

7.5 A few years ago this question could have been answered with a clear "no". Road building and maintenance, transport operation (whether making use of the roads or not) and land-use planning were carried out in almost total isolation from each other. Not only were road provision and transport operations separate, in the sense of being the responsibilities of quite different people, they were also inspired by quite different principles.

7.6 The job of the road planner has, traditionally, been to provide for the existing or anticipated volume of traffic, and also for the travel of other road users in reasonable conditions of speed and safety. It was no part of his task to query people's reasons for travel, or to inquire into alternative ways of meeting the needs for access or the supply of goods that their journeys served. His job was simply to provide the facilities that would allow road users to conduct their own affairs.

7.7 That view presupposes a very simple answer to the question how much money should be spent on the roads: the money should be sufficient to provide for the anticipated growth of traffic at the standards of service laid down. There might be different ways of making the necessary provision, such as different schemes for road widening and building, and in choosing between them it was important to get the best value for money. But the question of cost arose only in the comparison of means, not in the justification of ends. Road building was not necessarily allotted all the money that this principle required: schemes might have to be postponed or even, in rare cases, cancelled because of a shortage of funds. But such events were seen as unfortunate setbacks due to adverse circumstances, not as reasons for querying the basic approach.

7.8 Road planners also had responsibilities for environmental protection and for safety, but it was generally accepted that these considerations could be taken into account at the design stage. For example, in choosing the best route for a road it would be important to by-pass towns or town centres and to avoid doing unnecessary damage. In the same spirit, the design standards of different classes of roads were formulated with safety as a major consideration. But it was rare for a concern with safety or environmental improvement to be the inspiration of a road building proposal; nor was the possibility considered that the environmental harm done by even the least damaging of the alternative road schemes should preclude the adoption of any one of them. Thus safety and the environment, although regarded as important, were nevertheless treated as secondary considerations, traffic flow being the primary consideration.

7.9 The road planner had no special responsibilities for public transport or road freight operation. Buses and lorries were, indeed, a part of the traffic flow which had to be provided for like the rest, and some unusual design might be needed in order to allow them to stop or unload. But there was no suggestion that they deserved priority and, of course, no possibility of diverting to their use any funds allocated to road building and maintenance. Again, railways and water transport were quite separate, and their operations were guided by completely different criteria. They were run simply as commercial enterprises which had to show a profit.

7.10 These general attitudes were to a large extent embodied or reflected in the law. It was seen in Chapter 6 that before 1968 virtually no provision was made for central or local government to give grants to transport operators, even if such grants could have been used to reduce road expenditure. (In these circumstances, it is not surprising that until now only one town, Stevenage, has made a serious trial of this scheme. The results suggest that public transport provision may, indeed, be a good substitute for road building) [1]. Before 1968 there was also a marked bias in the purposes for which central government gave money to local authorities for road building schemes. Grants could be given for schemes designed to increase general road capacity, especially on trunk roads. But grants could not be given for traffic management schemes or schemes designed to bring about environmental improvements or to create pedestrian precincts.

7.11 The relatively low place traditionally given in road planning to safety is indicated by the fact that before the Local Government Act 1972 (which comes into force in April 1974) county councils and equivalent authorities had only permissive and not mandatory powers to deal with road safety. This is probably the main reason why little attention has been paid until relatively recently, in spite of pioneering efforts in the 1930s, to ways of reducing accidents by small and cheap road improvements or traffic measures designed specifically for that purpose. Recent work suggests that such measures can pay very handsomely, at least on the basis of the values currently allocated to road casualties (see [2], for example).

7.12 The traditional approach, briefly outlined above, was not always inappropriate; changing circumstances and, above all, the rapid growth in traffic have made it so. The principle of predicting the volume of future traffic and then attempting to provide for it is clearly unsophisticated, but so long as traffic volumes were low it was not likely to result in any significant misallocation of resources. Nor was there any reason to give priority to public transport or to any other class of users of the streets so long as it was possible to provide roads on a scale that would permit all users to travel without impeding each other. While the amount of road building required was small it was correct, by and large, to think that environmental and safety considerations could be taken care of by good design. Finally, so long as public transport operations could be financed from fare revenue and still offer a good standard of service at a price that most people could afford, the use of different criteria for public transport operations and for road building were defects of theoretical interest only. But aims which could be reconciled while traffic volumes were low have come increasingly into conflict as traffic has increased. Inconsistencies of approach can no longer be regarded as trivial, and we are now impelled to treat as an interrelated whole many problems which formerly could be dealt with quite adequately one by one.

7.13 The complaint that society and government have been slow to react to these changing circumstances is scarcely fair. Great changes in law, institutions, attitudes and skills have been required, all of which take time to bring about. In view of the difficulties involved, the rate of progress in the last six or seven years could be called astonishingly fast. The Commission agrees with all that has been done so far by way of changing the institutions and the approach. We want to go much further in the same direction.

Local transport planning

7.14 If the Government's present plans go ahead, most of the institutional obstacles to comprehensive local transport planning will have disappeared by the financial year 1975/76. Broadly speaking, county councils will then be empowered to spend the money they can raise from the rates, and money supplied by central government for transport purposes, in whatever way seems to them most helpful, and they will have most of the powers of control that they need. There will still be gaps in their powers, to which we have drawn attention in Chapter 6. But the legal and financial arrangements will make a comprehensive approach at least possible.

7.15 It does not follow, of course, that a correct approach will necessarily be adopted. The Department of the Environment is urging on local authorities the need to adopt comprehensive policies "based on an adequate level of evaluation and study" and to consider "an appropriate range of options" ([3]; similar language is used in [4]). But in the Commission's view more specific guidance should be given about the form that a comprehensive analysis of the problems should take and the measures that should be considered and implemented first.

7.16 More thought should also be given to the quality of

156

decision-taking at local levels. The powers and responsibilities of local authorities in matters of transport should be more widely known. There is clearly a lack of sophistication among the councillors and officers who have to grapple with the growing complexities of transport problems. The smallest local authorities are the worst off in this respect; the larger towns and cities attract better people. The new grouping into larger authorities is bound to be a help here, but there is still great need for education and training, and on this the current transport literature is wholly silent.

7.17 The Commission's recommendations are set out in the next four chapters; but there are two related points in the Department of the Environment's recent circular *Local Transport Grants* [4] which we find disquieting and which should be mentioned here. First there is the suggestion, especially in paragraph 5 of the circular, that transport expenditure within local authority areas should continue at about the same level in total as in the past. In the Commission's view, the amount of money spent on transport at present is itself a cause for concern. Management rather than investment is required to solve the problems of personal mobility, safety and environmental protection which should have first claim on the attention of the new county councils; and the Commission believes that there are more urgent claims on public expenditure in other fields, housing for example, than in transport. Although it may be helpful to indicate to county councils the *maximum* amount of money that can be made available to them for transport purposes, the Commission believes that it would not often be possible to justify spending the amounts currently envisaged, and suggests therefore that the burden of proof be placed on those who continue to argue for increasing transport expenditures. Secondly, paragraph 10 of the circular states that "in the early years of the new system it is likely that some TPPs (Transport Policies and Programmes) will consist of little more than projects already in the pipeline". The implications of this are not acceptable. Projects already in the pipeline are likely to be old-fashioned road schemes, many of which were thought of the best part of a generation ago, and none of which are the fruit of the more comprehensive thinking now officially recommended. If the approach to transport problems has now been changed, it is illogical not to re-examine all schemes based on an approach that has since been abandoned.

National transport planning

7.18 At first sight, less progress has been made in putting national transport planning on a comprehensive basis. No one apparently is concerned to consider long-distance transport problems as a whole: road building, railways, long-distance buses, water transport and air transport are all the responsibilities of different people who pursue their own plans with little or no regard to the impact of their activities on one another. This is defended officially on the ground that there is relatively little interaction between the different modes; it is said that these serve different purposes, and that even where they do compete the impact is small enough to be disregarded for the purposes of long-term planning. We consider these arguments in Chapter 10 and conclude that the interaction between road, rail and air should not be ignored.

7.19 National road planning is still inspired by the idea that future traffic growth should be anticipated and provided for. The starting point of any estimate of future needs for inter-urban roads is, as yet, a comparison of expected traffic growth on particular routes and the existing capacity of the routes. At a later stage, when a formal appraisal is being made of particular investment proposals, predictions of how specific roads would be used are made on the assumption that general traffic growth will be of the order described in Chapter 2. It is no longer true, however, that roads are accepted into the "firm programme" without any formal attempt to assess whether the expense in resources is economically justified. An evaluation of each road section is now undertaken in which the benefits to users in time savings, savings in running costs and a reduction in accidents are set against construction and maintenance costs. Environmental factors are not included in this analysis, but it is claimed that account is taken of them before a decision is reached.

7.20 As will be seen in Paras. 10.39–10.65, other reasons besides traffic growth are given for the national road programme, but most of them derive their rationale from the expected growth of traffic, which is regarded as the chief source of social benefits. In Chapter 5 we gave reasons for

158

doubting whether traffic growth in itself is desirable either for society as a whole or even, in the longer term, for the road users themselves, especially where, as in present methods of calculation, the problems arising from the continuous growth of traffic are left out of account.

7.21 It may be argued that, whether traffic growth is regarded as desirable or not, it is in any event going to take place, and that therefore it is only realistic to base future planning on it. But the Commission believes that traffic growth can be controlled, even outside towns, by direct methods; by the provision of alternative facilities; and by the indirect effects of those measures that are going to be necessary anyway to control traffic in town and country. In addition, there are reasons for thinking (see paras. 7.29–7.34 below) that the predictions of future growth of vehicles and traffic, even without deliberate measures of control, have been exaggerated. It is possible that the number of vehicles and the amount of travel may even decline in the future.

7.22 For all these reasons the Commission does not believe that the present approach to long-distance travel problems is soundly based. The introduction of more formal economic appraisals of particular road schemes is, of course, a considerable advance. Yet, as we indicate later, these methods of appraisal are not by any means to be regarded as conclusive.

7.23 The subjection of road schemes to an economic appraisal implies that the traditional gap between the criteria used to assess road proposals and those used to assess railway proposals, or the proposals of other transport operators, has narrowed. But it has not completely disappeared, since the economic criteria used for roads are less stringent than the commercial criteria used for the railways. Economic (cost-benefit) criteria attempt to take all the benefits into account, whereas on commercial criteria account is taken only of the revenues collected, and these are but a fraction of the benefits to users. Thus, if it were possible for the railways to devise a charging system under which each traveller paid for any improvement exactly what it was worth to him, there would be no difference between the two sets of criteria. This of course is not possible, and users of a railway service generally pay less than the maximum they would be prepared to pay. For example, in May 1973 extensive works were completed on the East Coast main line through Peterborough; one of the effects will be to save five minutes for each passenger journey. The British Railways Board estimates that the total yearly number of passenger hours saved will be 229,500, and that after the high-speed diesel train is introduced in 1978 this total will rise to 550,000. If all these time savings were evaluated at the rates generally used to assess road schemes, the Board calculates that they would give one-year social rates of return of about 24% for 1974 and 57% in 1978 over and above the favourable commercial rate of return on the project.

Road maintenance

7.24 Traditionally decisions on road maintenance, a major item of public expenditure, have been made, like decisions on road building, by reference to what is required to achieve certain standards and without any formal attempt to assess the benefits to users of adopting one level of maintenance rather than another. According to the Marshall Report of 1970 ([5], Chapter 5, paras. 28–29), research is now proceeding on ways of measuring the outputs of road maintenance, including the benefits of improved safety, less wear and tear on vehicles and time savings.

7.25 In the meantime, the Marshall Committee recommended that the different standards which now obtain in different parts of the country should be replaced by a uniform and higher set of standards ([5], Chapter 4, paras. 12–13). The Committee's recommendation was based on an analysis which showed very great variation between different parts of the country in expenditure per mile on roads of the same class. This finding suggested to the Committee that resources were being misapplied, and further analysis showed that only half the variation was explicable by objective differences such as weather and terrain ([5], Chapter 2, para. 7). It was argued that the adoption of a uniform set of standards must improve the situation ([5], Chapter 1, para. 5, Chapter 4, paras. 4, 12, 21) and that the standards should be higher than these generally obtaining at the time because existing treatment was not always adequate to prevent road failure ([5], Chapter 4, para. 14, Chapter 11, Appendix 1, para. 5). It was recognized that the achievement of the higher standards would take a number of years. Estimates of the extra cost of adopting them were not given in the report and have not been published since, but the *Public Expenditure* White Paper suggests that it is sizeable [6].

7.26 There is some ambiguity in the Marshall Committee's discussion of the need for uniform standards. The Committee found that there was no uniformity in the way that the same tasks were categorised and described, for accounting and control purposes, in different parts of the country ([5], Chapter 2, para 5; Chapter 11, para. 3). Clearly any scientific comparisons or progress in the measurements of benefits depend upon the adoption of a standard terminology. It is also true that, if expenditure on maintenance varies between different authorities in a way which is not accounted for by objective differences in their situation, there must be indeed, as alleged by the Committee, a misallocation of resources somewhere. But to set a uniform standard with respect to performance or expenditure does not necessarily remove the misallocation and could well increase it; all it removes is the evidence of misallocation. The fact that some roads have failed, even if their failure invariably brings serious disbenefits to road users, is not a sufficient reason for recommending a general and uncosted improvement in standards. There may be more specific ways of dealing with the problem, and the cost of any recommendations should be ascertained even if, for the time being, the benefits can only be judged rather than calculated.

7.27 In 1971/72, road maintenance and cleansing in Great Britain cost £206 million; by 1976/77 it is estimated that it will cost £299 million (at 1972 prices) [7]. It is clearly desirable that the benefits arising from these large sums should be calculated in a way which permits comparisons to be made with expenditure for other transport purposes. The Commission recommends that the necessary research should continue. In the meantime it does not believe that the necessity for generally higher standards of maintenance has been shown, and it recommends that the decision to adopt the initial standards recommended by the Marshall Committee should be re-examined.

PREDICTION OF FUTURE TRAFFIC

7.28 Inter-urban road planning is, as suggested earlier, still largely inspired by the idea that the future growth of traffic should be provided for. Although the Commission does not approve of this approach, it is clearly of some importance to be able to predict future traffic correctly. A variety of estimates have been made, but those of the Transport and Road Research Laboratory (TRRL) are the most influential. They were incorporated in the projections set out in Chapter 2, and are the basis of the assessment of inter-urban road requirements. Other methods, particularly those that have been used in local rather than national transport planning, differ in form and have some claims to be theoretically preferable, but rest on similar assumptions and have produced broadly similar results. It is sufficient therefore to consider the Transport and Road Research Laboratory's methods.

The TRRL's predictions of car population and travel

7.29 The amount of car travel (expressed in vehicle-miles) is the product of three factors: the size of the population, the number of cars per head, and the number of miles travelled per car. In order to predict future car travel the TRRL adopts the Government Actuary's population forecasts and, on the basis of past observation, assumes that the annual mileage per car will remain at its present level. The crux of the problem is then to forecast cars per head. The method assumes that this quantity will grow according to a logistic curve, which in effect means that the present rapid increase in the number of cars per head will gradually slacken off until a saturation level is reached. The shape of this curve depends on the present number of cars per head and its rate of increase, both of which are known, and the saturation level; hence the forecasting problem is reduced to predicting the saturation level. This level was forecast by the TRRL in 1965 from a statistical analysis of data from British counties and American states which suggested that in counties and states where the number of cars per head was relatively high the annual percentage increase in that number was relatively low. It was concluded that in Britain the number of cars per head would ultimately reach the level of 0·45, on the condition that restrictions in the use of cars would not become any greater. Given a "moderately restrictive" attitude to the use of cars the saturation level was put at 0·40 cars per head. 7.30 It was calculated that the saturation level would be reached by 2010, and that most of the increase would occur by 1985. In fact the number of cars per head has not increased as fast as predicted in 1965, but the TRRL still expect the same saturation level to be reached effectively by 2010. Table 7.1 compares the 1965 forecast with the most recent forecast.

Table 7.1: Forecasts of cars per head in Great Britain, made by the Transport and Road Research Laboratory in 1965 and in 1972

Years to which forecasts refer	Forecasts made in	
	1965	1972
1970	0·2473	0·21*
1975	0·3188	0·27
1980	0·3730	0·32
1985	0·4078	0·36
1990	0·4277	0·39
1995	0·4386	0·41
2000	0·4441	0·43
2005	0·4469	0·43
2010	0·4487	0·44

* Actual.

Sources: J. C. Tanner: "Forecasts of Vehicle Ownership in Great Britain", *Roads and Road Construction*, November 1965.

A. H. Tulpule: *Forecasts of vehicles and traffic in Great Britain, 1972 revision*, TRRL Report LR 543, 1973.

Criticisms of the TRRL methods

7.31 The statistical inferences on which these forecasts are based are weak in two ways. Although the data indicate a tendency for a high level of cars per head in any area to be associated with a low percentage increase in cars per head, this is a weak general tendency only, with many exceptions. For this reason, only a very rough estimate of the saturation level of cars per head can be obtained: indeed, the most recent (1972) TRRL estimate suggests that the value could lie between 0·38 and 0·70 ([8], p. 3). But this broad estimate itself involves an extrapolation well beyond the range of the observed data. The latest year for which figures were included in the 1972 figures was 1970. In that year, the national figure of cars per person stood at 0·21 and the highest figure for any county, Surrey, was 0·29. To extrapolate to 0·45 from these data is quite unwarranted as a statistical step.

7.32 An even more important criticism is that a statistical exercise of this kind throws no light on the causal or behavioural connections between car ownership and other things. There is an implicit assumption that many other things necessary for the forecast to be fulfilled will in fact happen, among which the more important are the following:

(i) that the past trends in the cost of owning and running cars, and in the costs of public transport, will continue. It was seen in Chapter 5, Table 1, that the costs of owning and running cars have risen less than the prices of consumer goods in general. This must have had an effect on levels of car ownership, and some assumption that a similar state of affairs will continue is implicit in any extrapolation of past trends;

(ii) that there is little connection between the demand for car ownership and the quality of other means of providing access; or, that there *is* a connection and the quality of the other means will continue to decline. Common sense suggests that if it is easy to satisfy mobility needs without a car, people will not buy so many cars. Studies in many countries show that car ownership is inversely correlated with density: an obvious explanation is that in high density areas it is generally possible to satisfy more needs by short journeys on foot or by public transport. It was also suggested in Chapter 5 that some people buy cars only because of the decline of alternative services. The quality of other services can be controlled and should be improved; this would have some effect on future car ownership levels.

(iii) that road building will proceed at a pace which allows cars to be used with the same facility as at present. This condition is probably more important in justifying the assumption that the average annual vehicle mileage will remain constant, but there is probably some connection also between the quality of service offered by the roads and the level of car ownership.

(iv) that the growth of car ownership and use will not

164

bring other restraints into operation. In towns especially it is easy to see how, as ownership grows, difficulties arise not only in using them but in parking them and storing them. This problem can be resolved by building car parks and garages, but this adds to the expense of car ownership and impairs one of its main advantages, namely its instant availability.

7.33 These points are particularly relevant to the ownership of a *second* car in a household, which is often a reflection of thoroughly inadequate public transport. The TRRL forecasts imply that nearly half the cars owned would be second or third cars in the household.

7.34 The future levels of car ownership should therefore not be thought of as an unalterable datum. The last three conditions mentioned in para. 32 above show that the level of car ownership depends in part on the general development of transport policy. It is true not merely that current trends could be altered if governments intervened for that purpose, but that any policy designed to maintain existing trends is sure to run into increasing difficulties. For example, the most recent TRRL report on car ownership raises the question whether the forecasts are plausible in the light of problems of road capacity (among other things) and comments:

> "On the question of road capacity, considerable extensions to the present motorway network are already programmed or are in the preparation pool, together with large programmes of improvement to principal and other roads. If built, these roads would be able to carry a substantial part of the expected increase in traffic, and more intensive and more efficient use of existing roads will also help. Except in the more heavily built-up areas there is little reason to believe that lack of road space need act as a major deterrent to traffic growth" ([8], page 5).

But, if the fulfilment of this forecast requires such massive action by society, the forecast itself changes its character: *it ceases to be a prediction and becomes a statement of intent.* And the justification of the intent is presumably the presupposition that further growth of motorised traffic is a desirable goal of society. This forecast then is reasonable only so long as it can be shown that people really do aspire to this aim, in the full knowledge of all its consequences. But the argument as presented appears to rest only on an inference from the trends, and in Chapter 5 we showed why such an inference is not valid.

7.35 The other determinant of the traffic level in any given year is the size of the population. Here, at least, is a variable independent of transport policy, but it is a variable which is notoriously hard to predict. This is borne out by the TRRL's forecasts of future traffic growth, which have been distinctly affected by the downward revision of the Government Actuary's population estimates, as shown in Table 7.2. Projections made in mid-1973 show a further slight downward provision.

Table 7.2: *The estimates of future population in Great Britain used in the TRRL's 1965 and 1972 car forecasts*
Unit: millions of people

Year to which population forecasts refer	Forecasts made in 1965	1972
1970	55·1	54·2*
1975	57·1	54·9
1980	59·0	55·9
1985	61·1	57·0
1990	63·6	58·3
1995	66·5	59·6
2000	69·6	60·9
2005	72·5	62·4
2010	75·5	63·9

* Actual.

Sources: As for Table 7.1.

Conclusion on forecasts of car travel

7.36 Since, for a number of reasons, future car ownership and travel appear to have been over-estimated, there is obviously a need for more sophisticated research on the determinants of car ownership. At present the choice of forecasting method is governed at least as much by the availability of certain data as by the sort of data that are really required. The Commission concludes that all transport plans based on existing trends should be re-examined

166

on assumptions of lower future levels of car ownership and travel. It also recommends the following research programme:

(i) Large surveys, on a continuous or repeated basis, to monitor the growth of car ownership in such a way that it can be related to external factors which can be influenced by transport policy, in particular by the levels of service offered by alternative means of transport, including walking and cycling.

(ii) Detailed studies of the motivation of car ownership and use. These studies should be particularly addressed to the question:

"What changes would be required in alternative transport systems, land-use patterns, and the environment for people to forgo willingly certain ways of using cars or the ownership of the first or subsequent cars in a household?"

(iii) Experiments in particular places to see how car ownership and consumer satisfaction are affected by different combinations of restraint on the use of cars, improvements in walking and cycling facilities, and improvements in public transport and the environment. These experiments are referred to again in Chapters 8 and 9.

Forecasts of goods vehicle traffic

7.37 The TRRL's forecasts of future goods vehicle traffic involve the following steps [9]:

(i) Future ton-mileage is forecast by reference to the expected growth in Gross Domestic Product (GDP).

(ii) It is then predicted how this total will be divided between the different modes of transport.

(iii) The number of road *vehicle* miles required to accommodate the ton-miles attributed to road transport is forecast by reference to the changing size of lorries.

7.38 In the first step, only ton-miles on lorries and rail are taken into account. It is considered that water transport, pipelines and vans can be ignored, since the quantities involved are small and the traffic is specialised. The most recent forecasts assume that GDP will increase at 3% per annum and that ton-miles by road and rail will increase at the same rate.

7.39 In the second step, it is assumed on the basis of recent trends that rail ton-mileage will remain constant; in other words, that all the increase will accrue to road transport.

7.40 In the third step, it is assumed, again on the basis of recent trends, that the average carrying capacity of lorries will increase at a rate of $2\frac{1}{2}\%$ per annum until 1980, that from 1980 to 1990 it will increase at a rate of 2% per annum, and thereafter, as far as the forecasts go, at a rate of $1\frac{1}{2}\%$ per annum. Thus the increase in lorry miles over the future is expected to be less than the increase in road ton-miles.

7.41 The forecast that GDP in Britain will increase at a rate of 3% is not too optimistic if judged in the light of the economic growth achieved since the last war, though it may seem so in the light of the energy crisis. As people grow richer, the volume of goods they consume is unlikely to keep pace; instead, they are likely to substitute higher quality and more expensive goods for cheaper ones. In particular, the service sector of the economy can be expected to grow faster than the manufacturing sector. Service industries, of course, also generate goods traffic, but presumably much less than manufacturing industries. Thus, although a constant ratio of ton-miles to GDP has been observed both in Britain and in other countries for many years, there are some *a priori* reasons to suppose that the ratio will not remain constant as GDP continues to grow.

7.42 In particular, American experience, in which the ratio of ton-miles to GDP has remained roughly constant for a decade or more, is far from conclusive. But it does raise the question of the causal relationship between ton-miles and transport policy. The Commission has not been able to investigate this relationship in any depth, but the connections are of two kinds:

(i) Transport arrangements based primarily on the motor vehicle require great tonnages of material to be used and hence transported—materials for road construction and maintenance, and materials for vehicle production and use. The vast American road-building programme must have generated an enormous amount of movement of materials. It is also of interest that if pipeline traffic (which is presumably largely oil) is excluded the ratio of ton miles to GDP in America has declined steadily in recent years ([9], Table 3).

(ii) A transport policy based on motor vehicles goes hand in hand with a land-use policy of dispersal and low density; this has been particularly evident in the USA. The greater this dispersal the greater the mileage that has to be covered to supply people with a given volume and variety of goods.

We may tentatively conclude therefore that American experience is not at variance with our conjecture that the constant relationship between GDP and ton mileage will cease to hold at some point. A changed emphasis in transport policy can itself significantly affect the relationship.

7.43 Finally the relationship between ton-miles accounted for by lorries and lorry-miles is determined not only by the carrying *capacity* of lorries but also by their utilisation—the amount actually carried per lorry. Increasing fuel and labour costs and the likely implementation of traffic management schemes will put pressure on operators to increase the utilisation of their vehicles. The TRRL make some allowance for greater utilisation, but probably not enough. In addition, the Commission believes that there is scope for planning authorities, especially in towns, to intervene more directly to bring about better vehicle utilisation; this topic is discussed in Chapter 8.

Conclusion on goods traffic forecasts

7.44 This Commission does not accept the view that rail traffic should continue only at its present level. In Chapter 10 it is suggested that the first target for British Rail should be to capture 50% more ton-miles than at present. This increase, which we suggest should be achieved within five years, is equivalent to two-thirds of the increase predicted in road ton-miles between 1975 and 1980. We would expect the railways to continue to increase their share in future, especially in the longer term when the effects will be increasingly felt of land-use and locational policies designed to encourage rail movement.

7.45 Both for reasons of forecasting method and because of the scope for intervention to alter current trends, we conclude that current forecasts of road goods traffic are likely to be high. We therefore recommend, as for car traffic, that road plans should be re-examined in the light of lower goods traffic forecasts. We also recommend that research be undertaken to clarify the connections between road goods traffic and alterations in transport policy.

COST-BENEFIT ANALYSIS

7.46 Basic human needs have a first claim on society, which should ensure that projects are formulated so that, so far as possible, these needs can be met. Cost-benefit analysis is concerned with the assessment of projects, not with their elaboration. Yet the way in which projects are drawn up is critically important, since a sophisticated method of assessment is of little use if all alternatives are inferior. Imagination is required, and a systematic method of analysing the problems which will ensure that all the relevant considerations are identified and taken into account. In matters of transport these include problems of personal mobility, goods movement, safety, social justice, environment and resources.

7.47 Cost-benefit analysis is a method of assessing alternative investment projects by techniques based on economic criteria. Often there is only one alternative to the mooted project, namely that of continuing without it. The investment project analysed need not be one involving large expenditure. Cost-benefit analysis is equally applicable in the economic assessment of managerial innovations such as the introduction of separate bus lanes or the introduction of more stringent safety precautions.

7.48 From the moment of construction, any project will incur resource costs and will generate over the future a range of economic effects (benefits and "disbenefits"), to each of which, in principle, a monetary value can be attributed. Although the costs, benefits and disbenefits will occur at different periods in time, they can be directly compared once they have been discounted to the present (or to any agreed reference year) at some appropriate interest rate. If the sum of the (discounted) benefits, after the (discounted) disbenefits are subtracted, is expected to exceed the (discounted) resource costs, the project is said to meet a cost-benefit criterion. If several such projects meet the criterion, they can be ranked according to their respective benefit-cost ratios.

7.49 Ideally, the items that enter a cost-benefit calculation are to include all those that affect the welfare of any person in the particular society for which the calculation is to apply. Effects on each person's welfare arise not only from the more tangible goods and services but also from the less tangible goods or "bads" produced by the project. And the money values, positive or negative, placed on each of these items are not chosen arbitrarily by the economist, but are intended to be those put on them by the individuals directly affected.

7.50 There is, of course, nothing to prevent the government, representing society, from directing that the values placed on particular items be other than the relevant individual valuations. Indeed, some economists have suggested that such "intervention" be systematised to the extent of putting a larger weight on a pound gained or lost by members of a particular group deserving of preferred treatment, say "the poor", contrasted with the weight put on a pound gained or lost by another group, say "the rich". Others have gone so far as to propose sets of weights for different income groups derived on some political or ethical principle. But the advisability of superimposing these "noneconomic" weights on a cost-benefit analysis is a controversial issue which we need not enter here.

7.51 In normal circumstances, the most a person will pay for a good (or to avert a "bad") is a smaller amount than the least he is willing to accept to go without the good (or to put up with the "bad"). The greater the welfare impact of the good or "bad" in question, the larger the difference between the two sums becomes. Therefore it is important for the economist to decide which of these two sums he should be calculating. The tacit convention of cost-benefit analysis is that benefits to be received by a person are valued at the maximum sums he is willing to pay for them, and the dis-benefits at the minimum sum he is willing to accept in order to put up with them. If it is generally conceded that citizens have natural rights to a specific range of environmental amenities (and these rights could indeed be confirmed in law), then the particular benefit of a project designed to improve, say, air quality, should be calculated at the larger sum—that is, the minimum compensation adequate for forgoing the potential benefit of the scheme.

7.52 The people affected by an investment project are not necessarily limited to those directly benefiting or suffering from the activities associated with it. If a beautiful area of natural beauty is spoilt or a historic monument destroyed in order to make room for a new development, many who never expect to visit it may feel a sense of loss or of outrage. For example, a number of people will subscribe to a fund to prevent a historic building from falling into disrepair, or to preserve wild animals, even though they never expect to see the building or the wild animals. A properly conducted cost-benefit analysis requires that this legitimate concern of the wider community be represented as a subtraction from the more tangible benefits; and the sum subtracted should be large enough to compensate all concerned for the sense of loss they will experience if the scheme goes through. This crucial consideration has been neglected in all official cost-benefit studies.

7.53 Before the method can be applied, however, alternative possibilities of investment must first be formulated. There may, on occasion, be no difficulty in drawing up precise formulations of alternative investments to be considered; but there usually will be difficulties in transport problems, since they tend to have many interactions and side effects, especially in towns, where the number of possibilities can become very large. To draw up a sensible set of alternative investment plans for detailed scrutiny requires not only imagination but also a systematic method of ensuring that all the relevant considerations are identified—including personal mobility, goods movement, safety, environmental impact, and the depletion of irreplaceable resources.

Problems of cost-benefit analysis

7.54 Some of the criticisms of cost-benefit analysis apply more to the rather crude calculations which have passed under that name than to the principles that inform the techniques. Other criticisms seem to arise from a fear that cost-benefit calculations ignore important areas of public concern. There is also a belief that quantitative assessment cannot be a substitute for experience and judgment. The Commission does not dispute the role of experience and

172

judgment. The question is at what stage they are to be exercised. It is virtually impossible for anyone faced with a multitude of various effects arising from a large project to reach a reasoned conclusion on the basis of judgment alone whether, on balance, the project is good or bad. It follows that the greater the number of considerations that can be taken into account formally, and reduced to a common measure, the less is the burden on the judgment of the decision-maker. Nonetheless, cost-benefit analysis has limitations.

Complexity of economic relationships

7.55 Interrelationships enter cost-benefit analysis in two ways. The more obvious difficulty is isolating the value to be attributed to one particular effect from those of other effects that tend to accompany it. The economist might, for example, wish to examine the response of numbers of individuals who were at different times faced with opportunities for saving travel time, or increasing their comfort during travel, or reducing the risk of accidents, by spending more money in each case. But it is not easy to find situations that are in every respect the same save for a difference in travel time alone, or in travel comfort alone, or in risk of accident alone. Each individual response that is observed might be to a situation in which all three factors were different, and possibly others too. From a statistical relationship embracing all these factors, the economist can proceed to isolate the required relationship between the magnitude of the effect and its valuation. This procedure, however, is not always satisfactory, and questionnaires and experiments are sometimes used to elicit more detailed information and to check other statistical findings.

7.56 The second way in which economic interrelations complicate a cost-benefit analysis arises from the fact that the valuation of any particular good depends on the distribution of income, and also on the qualities and availabilities of alternative and complementary goods that are expected to prevail in the foreseeable future. An environmental improvement that reduces the average noise level from aircraft may be worth little if other noises from transport are to remain and possibly in time to increase. If however the level of all engine noises is to be reduced simultaneously by this

173

improvement, it would be worth more to people than the aggregate of the sums they would be willing to pay for the reduction of each type of noise on its own. Again, an improvement in air quality without any reduction in the level of noise might be worth, say, £1 million to the beneficiaries. A reduction of all forms of engine noise, though without any improvement in air quality, might be worth say £2 million to them. But if both these improvements were to take place simultaneously, people might be prepared to pay very much more than £3 million.

7.57 Again, the benefits expected to accrue over time from the construction of a highway for private traffic will depend upon the fares and the efficiency of the existing public transport. If therefore private transport is already highly subsidised (as we believe it to be, in the sense that the environmental and social damages it incurs are not paid for by the motorists), an increase in the number of private vehicles might cause a drastic reduction in the efficiency of public transport; and this, in its turn, would increase people's dependence upon private vehicles. In this way the apparent value of the highway scheme would be raised.

7.58 If motorists were actually required to pay for each and every highway or road project, the money values they would be able to place on successive projects would tend to diminish. Certainly those values would be smaller than those attributable to them under existing methods of finance, in which the costs are borne by taxpayers as a whole.

7.59 The competent economist is aware of the complexity of these relationships and the problems they pose in evaluating alternative projects. Where he is unable, through lack of data, to arrive at reliable figures for particular benefits or disbenefits, the conscientious economist will draw attention to his guesswork or omissions. He will also describe the incalculable effects, in terms of physical units wherever possible, along with information or surmises about the number of people involved.

Limitations of cost-benefit analysis

7.60 *Risk and uncertainty.* Sometimes neither the probability of one or more untoward events occurring over the future, nor even the severity of their consequences, can be known in advance. There may be no known way of guarding against such contingencies. There may be no way of acquiring dependable statistical information without a decision to proceed with the scheme and expose society to a number of accidents, some of which may have catastrophic and possibly irreversible ecological consequences directly affecting human life: for example, accidents associated with large-scale nuclear reactors. It is clearly not possible in such cases to reduce this uncertainty to a figure by any technique. In the last resort a decision to take an unknown risk that could have grave social consequences is a moral one, and one that should not be taken without prolonged public debate.

7.61 *Posterity*. The Commission recognises an obligation of this generation to generations yet to come. In particular, it affirms that this generation does not have the right to spoil the natural or man-made environment of which it is not only the inheritor but the custodian. Nor has it the right to squander the world's non-renewable sources of energy so as to impose hardships on future generations or impel them to take risks they might otherwise avoid. Some economists believe that inter-generation issues of this sort can be circumvented by recourse to a social rate of discount which reduces expected benefits and costs of future generations to present values. This discounting procedure can be justified by reference to the expected future growth in the social value of the alternative (and possibly private) investigations that have to be forgone when a project is undertaken. But this device by itself takes no account of the changes in the relative values, over a period of time, between, say, manufactured goods on the one hand and environmental "goods" (that were once free) on the other. Such changes are caused by gradual changes in taste and growing relative scarcity. And so, if continued expansion of population, the continued spread of industrialisation, and rising per capita income intensifies the demand for the limited and diminishing endowment of natural beauty, its value may rise steeply in relation to the prices of the sort of industrial goods that might be expected to become increasingly available over the future. If current trends were to continue our grandchildren would be wealthier than we are in industrial capital but poorer in natural assets. This consideration bears on the evaluation of investment projects having significant impact on the environment.

7.62 *Equity*. Even if a cost-benefit calculation were in all respects ideal, it could not by itself be accepted by society as final. If the cost-benefit criterion is unambiguously met, this reveals only that, given the economic principle of evaluation, the gains expected to be generated by the project exceed the losses. And this information is not sufficient, perhaps not even necessary, to warrant social approval. Since those who, on balance, lose by the project are not compensated by those who, on balance, are made better off, there is no ethical force in the statement that society "as a whole" is better off. For the outcome of an "approved project" can be highly inequitable in distribution. The vital needs of a small number of people can be swamped in a cost-benefit analysis by the less urgent desires of a much larger number. In connection with transport investment, the benefits of some small time-savings to a large number of people may come to a sum that exceeds the calculated losses of a few who are compelled to sell their homes and settle elsewhere. The inequity is compounded wherever the chief losers from a scheme are to be found among the less wealthy members of society. Examples of this sort of inequity are to be found in road projects that contribute to the destruction of the existing amenities and sense of neighbourhood in working-class areas in the attempt to provide better travel facilities for the motoring public.

Particular problems concerning cost-benefit analysis

7.63 There are, finally, a number of specific points we would raise in connection with current practices in cost-benefit analysis.

(i) *Travelling time*. Studies undertaken for the purpose of ascertaining the values travellers place on savings in journey time have been proceeding for some years and considerable progress has been made, but there are still some important unresolved difficulties. These include the valuation of leisure time, of time spent by children and housewives in travelling, and of very small time savings gained by a large number of travellers.

(ii) *Noise*. The costing of noise nuisance began to receive attention within the Department of the Environment after the Third London Airport inquiry. This inspired further studies on the social costing of both aircraft and road traffic noise. However, satisfactory methods for the economic estimation of noise nuisance are still in early stages of development, and both property price and social survey techniques of estimation are subject to criticism. Such assessments also largely ignore the possible health hazards of noise.

(iii) *Aesthetics*. Difficult as it is to evaluate an increase in noise, the value to be attached to a fine building or a beautiful landscape is yet more difficult. The general principle is straightforward enough. The loss suffered from the spoliation or destruction of some cherished part of our heritage is to be reckoned as equal to the sum of money that (if invested today) would suffice to compensate all existing and future generations for its loss. No one imagines that such a sum is easy to calculate. But the difficulty of the calculation hardly constitutes a reason for continuing to neglect it in cost-benefit studies, especially as transport investments undertaken by governments and local authorities often have an aesthetic impact on the area sufficient to raise doubts about their economic feasibility when judged in the light of more searching cost-benefit analysis.

(iv) *Accidents*. We discussed in Chapters 3 and 4 the methods in use for estimating the money costs of road accidents (including fatalities). The intangible elements of grief and suffering are inevitably a matter of judgment rather than of economic analysis, and these costs should be determined by the responsible Minister after public and parliamentary debate.

(v) *Design of road projects*. Recognition that there will be significant effects on the environment will also influence the choice between alternative plans for investment. Both natural and man-made beauty, if it is likely to be endangered by transport plans, should be appreciated at the first stage, and appreciated as a whole. It is absurd for the planner to pride himself on choosing, say, to put his ring-road through the lowlier, less glamorous, of two eighteenth century streets if both are essential to the character of the quarter. If it appears necessary to choose one or other of two remarkable features to be annihilated, the planner should be compelled to reconsider his whole

177

transport strategy for the area. For the planner's concern and his sense of place should be tested by the resource, imagination and foresight he can bring to bear in reassessing the very terms of a problem before designing plans which may turn out to conflict with aesthetic and conservational needs. Preservation of the organic integrity of an area of great charm or beauty should be recognised as one of the chief constraints in the design of road plans and transport strategies generally. Clearly, that constraint is not absolute. There can be other vital considerations also. But strategies that avoid damage should be the first to be sought, and if a particular plan involves some sacrifice of the organic integrity of an area in exchange for substantial benefits of a more mundane nature, it should be accompanied by one or more alternative investment plans, perhaps more costly, which entail smaller aesthetic sacrifice.

Concluding remark on cost-benefit analysis

7.64 In consequence of the inherent limitations of cost-benefit analysis and of the well-known difficulties in its consistent application, the Commission cannot regard it as an adequate technique for decision-making on its own. However, for most of us it is an important component of the social process of decision-making. The Commission recommends that it be used more consistently and with a wider frame of reference, and that more work be done in the attempt to refine the measurement of intangibles, because of the advantages in making explicit the weight and incidence of these factors in the decision-making process. However, the Commission is of the opinion that cost-benefit techniques are unlikely ever to become so sophisticated as to dispense with broad judgment on aesthetic and environmental effects. Nor should their application be independent of other moral or political considerations.

REFERENCES

[1] Buckles, P.: *Stevenage Super Bus Experiment*, paper given to a symposium at the University of Newcastle upon Tyne, Department of Civil Engineering, April 1972.
[2] Duff, J. T. (Assistant Chief Engineer, Department of the Environment): "The effect of small road improvements on accidents.' *Traffic Engineering and Control*, October 1971.

[3] From *Urban Transport Planning*, House of Commons Paper 57, Session 1972–73, presented to Parliament by the Secretary of State for the Environment, July 1973.

[4] *Local Transport Grants*, Joint Circular from the Department of the Environment and the Welsh Office, August 1973. (DoE circular 104/73, Welsh Office circular 193/73.)

[5] *Report of the Committee on Highway Maintenance*, HMSO, 1970.

[6] *Public Expenditure 1969/70 to 1974/75*, HMSO, 1972, p. 28. *Public Expenditure to 1975/76*, HMSO, 1971; p. 38. *Public Expenditure to 1976/77*, HMSO, 1972; p. 51 and Table 2.9.

[7] British Road Federation: *Basic Road Statistics 1973*, p. 22.

[8] Tulpule, A. H.: *Forecasts of Traffic and Vehicles in Great Britain*, TRRL Report LR 543, 1973.

[9] Tulpule, A. H.: *Trends in the Transport of Freight in Great Britain*, TRRL Report LR 429, 1973.

CHAPTER 8

Policy Changes—Urban

8.1 The traditional approach to transport problems contains serious defects, some of which still remain in spite of recent improvements. But how important are these defects in practice? Would a more rational approach lead to substantial changes in policy, or are the advantages of present policies so great as to outweigh the defects in the way in which they were produced?

8.2 The Commission is obviously not in a position to put forward detailed plans for any particular place. But we are in no doubt that substantial changes should be made in present policies. These are best examined under the headings of urban, rural and long-distance transport. This chapter is concerned with urban transport.

8.3 As such a large proportion of the population lives in towns, it is here that the effects of present traffic levels are most serious. The main effects are well known, and have been covered in Chapter 4. They include noise, pollution, delays and danger to pedestrians, vibration, and so on. Many of these factors can be directly measured and related to discomfort actually felt by people living near busy transport areas.

ROAD BUILDING

8.4 Roads have always been the main concern of urban transport planning. To some extent this preoccupation resulted from the prevailing arrangements of finance and legal powers; but, as has been seen, most of these institutional constraints have now been removed. The emphasis on roads has been increasingly attacked, not least by the House of Commons Expenditure Committee in its report on *Urban Transport Planning* [1]. In a few towns, notably London, Nottingham, Edinburgh, Southampton and Oxford, there have been second thoughts about road plans, amounting sometimes to complete reversals of policy. Nevertheless urban transport planning is still geared to the task of road building. As shown in Chapter 3, an increase is planned in total road expenditure, and the proportion for urban roads is expected to rise to over half the total; before the cutback in public works announced last autumn, expenditure on urban roads was expected to rise to over £600 million annually within the next decade. Most towns still have ambitious road schemes at various stages of planning, many of them first drawn up twenty or thirty years ago. The Commission takes the view that this emphasis on road building is excessive for a number of reasons.

Road building and personal mobility

8.5 The main reason put forward for road building in towns is to accommodate the growth in traffic expected to arise from the increase in car ownership and use brought about by rising incomes. (A subsidiary reason is to facilitate freight movement; freight is discussed below.) In our discussion of personal mobility in Chapter 5, we pointed out that most people do not have, and never will have, cars available for the daily journeys they want to make. These are the people whose mobility has declined very considerably in recent years, to an extent that causes them difficulty and even deprivation in their daily lives. Priority should be given to their problems, and that is not done by providing more road space for cars.

8.6 It may be said that road building will help such people, since new roads will reduce congestion and allow the introduction of bus priority schemes and schemes to help pedestrians and cyclists. This would need to be demonstrated to be true in each individual case. It would usually be necessary to carry out trials of such schemes without new road building to see whether they were adequate or not. But it might sometimes be possible to demonstrate in advance of physical trials that even the greatest reduction in traffic that these schemes might bring about would not suffice to restore civilised conditions or to permit effective management measures to be implemented. In any case the possible need for limited road building to improve particular local conditions has nothing to do with the more general case for an increase in the total capacity of urban roads.

Long term and short term

8.7 One difficulty about road building is that, even if it is a solution, it is only a very long-term solution. This is acknowledged in the design of the "transportation studies" used to assess road building plans; these studies concentrate attention on the problems expected to arise in twenty or thirty years' time, and completely disregard present difficulties. But the problems are with us now, and it is wrong to concentrate on very distant problems while urgent short-term problems go unsolved. The orthodox view is that rising car ownership will create problems of a different scale from those that face us now. But, as shown in the last chapter, no one knows how far car ownership and use are affected by the quality of public transport, by rising fuel prices or by parking difficulties. It is hazardous to plan for the distant future when big doubts surround the central assumption on which the planning is based. The least that should be done is to improve the alternatives to cars—a necessary step in any event—to see what effect they have on car ownership.

8.8 Moreover, even if car ownership were to reach the predicted levels, it still does not follow that road building, especially in towns, should keep pace with this increase. There is now general agreement that there must be discrimination in the use of cars in towns: their use must be limited where they can only be accommodated at great cost and where a satisfactory public alternative can be provided. The main use for cars in towns, apart from business purposes, is for local trips longer than convenient walking distance. Since these trips are short and random in pattern and may take place at any time of day, it is impossible for any public transport system to compete with the instant availability of the car and its ability to go direct from door to door—though this does not apply to the central areas of cities which have strict parking controls. For local trips, or for longer trips in towns made at off-peak times, new road capacity may not be required to accommodate the traffic that increasing car ownership would cause. Another common use of cars is for out-of-town trips, particularly of a

182

recreational character; but these would seldom justify extensive road building within towns.

8.9 If the need for discrimination in the use of cars is accepted, it must be questioned whether the right roads to build in towns are motorways (or other high-speed, high-capacity roads). Such roads do nothing directly to facilitate the use of cars for the short local trips for which public transport is not generally suitable. Their access points are usually too far apart; and travel on local roads is impeded by traffic going to or from the motorways. The journeys served by urban motorways are longer journeys which a well-developed public transport system could often handle.

Cost, damage and inflexibility

8.10 Other difficulties of urban road building have been mentioned in earlier chapters. Road building is expensive anywhere; in towns it can be many times as expensive as in the country. If benefits can be obtained from managing existing roads better, it becomes harder to justify the expense of new building. Road building and traffic on new roads damage the environment. Even if it were true that new roads brought environmental advantages in the form of relief to other streets, and that this relief could not be achieved in other simpler ways, it would still have to be shown that the indirect beneficial effects were greater than the direct deleterious effects. In fact major new roads, because they generate new traffic, are at least as likely to intensify the environmental problems on other streets as to relieve them. New roads are inflexible. If they do not achieve the intended benefits there is no easy way of getting rid of them or adapting them.

Conclusion on road building

8.11 The arguments for a large urban road-building programme rest on the belief that there is a general need to increase the capacity of town road networks. For the reasons just given, the Commission does not accept that more road capacity is necessary for a solution to the problems of personal mobility or for dealing (in ways discussed below) with freight problems. We therefore recommend that there should be a moratorium on urban road building until management measures have been implemented and their

183

effects assessed. There would be three exceptions to this moratorium:

(i) road building required for new development, whether in New Towns or in the physical expansion of existing towns;

(ii) road building which is still essential to environmental improvement or the implementation of management measures, even after the effects of all other appropriate policy changes in reducing traffic are taken into account.

(iii) road schemes now in progress which it would be more damaging or expensive to stop than to allow to go ahead.

IMMEDIATE MEASURES IN URBAN AREAS

8.12 It has been seen that the most urgent problems of personal mobility are those of people without access to a car. To help them, public transport and conditions for walking and cycling must be improved by whatever measures (as described in Chapter 6) can be brought into effect most quickly and suit the town best. The same measures will ease the problem of unwanted car use and will be generally conducive to improving the environment. These are likely to include parking controls, traffic restrictions and the expansion of the bus system by means of subsidies.

Pedestrians

8.13 For pedestrians, most attention has been paid to schemes for the creation of precincts in shopping streets or city centres. Such schemes are important and have often worked well, but there are other important problems for pedestrians elsewhere. There is a need to create good facilities for pedestrian movement generally over a town, not just in small areas where people walk about once they have arrived there by other means. Although most journeys on foot are short, and would still be relatively short even if conditions were improved, pedestrian movements overlap in a way which makes it impossible to tackle them in confined areas; what is required is a network of pedestrian facilities over an entire town or large parts of it. This does not mean building a new network at an upper or lower level, a solution which is hardly ever convenient or suitable in existing towns and which takes years to implement. Pedestrians ought to be able to walk about at ground level. This means widening pavements, supplying more pedestrian crossings, being more generous to pedestrians in the phasing of lights at crossings, and using traffic management measures to limit traffic speeds and flows. Attention should be paid to the possibility of improving pedestrian conditions in the detailed design of facilities. For example, in central areas, pavements might be raised at road crossings so that the pavement, rather than the road, forms a continuous level; and cover can be provided in pedestrian streets and ways. The laws against parking on pavements should be strictly enforced, and the practice of providing parking spaces in houses and other buildings to which access can be obtained only by driving across the pavement should be discouraged. Other valuable measures are the retention of existing rights of way through new developments, as was done in many Victorian towns and cities in the north of England, and the creation of new walkways separate from the road system, perhaps passing areas of parkland or open space, to create attractive and useful pedestrian routes.

8.14 Although these measures may be justified in the first instance by the benefits to those who now walk, they would have other desirable effects. They would relieve the problems of disabled or handicapped people who now find it impossible to travel at all because of poor conditions for pedestrians. Some people now drive even quite short distances because conditions discourage them from walking. This is particularly true of people accompanying children or old people, but it applies to the able-bodied on their own as well. Better conditions would encourage them to walk when they wanted to and would in consequence reduce traffic. Better conditions would also increase the length of the journey which people consider it reasonable to make on foot rather than by motorised means, hence again reducing traffic. Since the use of public transport almost always involves a walk at each end, whereas the use of a car usually does not, to make walking easier would encourage the use of public transport rather than cars for the longer journeys which people would still wish to make.

Cyclists

8.15 For cyclists, too, it is desirable to work towards the creation of some kind of special network. The problem is much less urgent than for pedestrians, since this is not a universal mode of transport. It is also a more difficult problem to tackle since, although pavements exist everywhere in towns, cycle tracks are found only rarely. It is possible to create cycle routes, if not an elaborate network, by providing paths through parks, by introducing cycle lanes on some roads, by incorporating certain streets into the cycle network or by allowing cyclists into some pedestrian streets. Cyclists can also share streets with motor vehicles with tolerable safety and convenience so long as the motor vehicles move slowly. The use of ramps and other devices to slow down traffic in residential streets, which is desirable on grounds of amenity and safety, also helps to make them safe for cyclists. It might be possible, by such means, to create reasonable conditions for local movements by cycle, for example to schools from the houses in their catchment area.

8.16 Cycling should also be encouraged by providing cycle stands at stations, in shopping centres and in office blocks and similar buildings.

Protecting buses from congestion

8.17 There are two broad ways to protect buses from congestion. The first is to give them priority on the streets, by the means (such as bus lanes, exemptions from turning restrictions and so on) which were discussed in Chapter 6. The second is to limit the volume of other traffic so that the buses can move with reasonable freedom. This is tantamount to restoring the conditions that prevailed twenty or thirty years ago. These alternatives are not exclusive, and sometimes the same measure may serve both purposes simultaneously. For example, bus lanes not only give priority to buses but also reduce the capacity available to the rest of the traffic. This may have a more than proportionate effect in reducing traffic volumes, especially if the bus lanes so improve the general quality of the bus service as to attract some former car users.

8.18 One of the most powerful measures to limit total traffic volumes is parking control. However, as seen in

Chapter 5, the existence of many uncontrolled private spaces limits the present scope of parking control, in some towns at least. Another limitation is that through traffic escapes parking control altogether. In many towns this does not matter, since the volume of through traffic will never be great in any event. In large towns, where it is unlikely that tight parking control can be applied outside the centre, the effect of reducing the volume of traffic destined for the centre may only be to create an additional route for through traffic. Parking control may then be supplemented by other forms of control which do impinge on through traffic. In the longer term, some form of payment for entry may be the most appropriate. In the meantime, various traffic management measures can be employed to limit the total volume of through traffic and also to keep speeds down so that the central streets do not form a quicker route, except for buses and any other privileged traffic, than they did in their previous congested state.

Expanding the bus system

8.19 Congestion is not the only problem that faces buses; indeed, in many towns congestion is not yet a serious problem for bus operation except at peak hours. But few if any towns have escaped the reductions in bus mileage that were chronicled in Chapter 2. The grounds for restoring this mileage are first to improve the position of people without cars available, second to cut down unwanted car travel with all its adverse side effects, and third to check the vicious circle that was described in Chapter 5. This restoration should be thought of as a transport investment alternative to road building. There is no reason why it should *necessarily* pay its way or should not be subsidised, so long as the costs can be justified on considerations of social justice and the widest form of cost-benefit analysis. What is dangerous, however, is the idea that, where congestion is a problem, subsidies can be a substitute for the measures to protect buses that have been described. Some people, deterred by the difficulties or supposed unpopularity of imposing such measures, have turned to the idea of subsidised or free public transport instead. It is unlikely that even free public transport on its own would attract enough car users to ease congestion to the extent required to solve the problems of bus operation. It is also undesirable that the users of a service should be relieved of all inducements to keep costs down; and, in the longer term, fares that bear no relation to the costs of providing transport are likely to add to the problem.

8.20 New bus services and the protection of buses from congestion will need to be accompanied by many improvements in the bus services themselves. The responsibility for this improvement largely falls upon the bus operator. Operators need to obtain a far better understanding of the markets they will be able to serve in the changed circumstances we propose. This will necessitate a good deal more attention to market research and the marketing of bus passenger services than is generally given at present. It should lead to a re-examination of fares policies (including family group fares), the routeing and frequency of services, the design of vehicles and the provision of ancillary services. Once the "product" is improved in this way, it will require promotion by far more effective methods than are used at present.

8.21 Improved and increased bus services will not be achieved if there are insufficient staff to operate them. The staffing difficulties of the bus industry are well known and are not of a temporary nature. Their solution is unlikely to lie solely in improving the wage level. Attention will be necessary to such difficult problems as worker status, "unsocial" hours of work, and the long-term career prospects.

8.22 We know that many bus operators are aware of these problems and are exploring remedies for some. However, for the reason stated above, we consider that a sense of urgency in dealing with them should be encouraged throughout the bus industry. One way of facilitating this would be to establish a Working Party on Bus Services consisting of representatives of the bus industry and the Department of the Environment with outside experts on marketing and personnel problems. The Working Party would be expected, within a twelve-month period, to produce guidelines on the aspects of marketing and personnel policies which have been listed. It might continue in being to monitor progress, and the continuation of subsidies to individual operators might become conditional upon satisfactory performance.

Control of lorries

8.23 Local authorities, as noted in Chapter 1, already possess powers under the Dykes Act to control the movement of lorries over 3 tons; they should be encouraged to use them.

LONGER TERM MEASURES

8.24 The measures just described are the only ones that can be used in the short term; they are also likely to be the most effective in the long term, especially if enhanced legal powers fill the gaps in parking control and permit local pricing measures to be employed. Other long-term measures of supreme importance are planning controls over the size and location of particular facilities and over the shape and density of the town. These also were described in Chapter 6. They should be used with the aim of keeping journeys short wherever possible, and of ensuring that the facilities which attract longer journeys are so sited and designed that the use of public transport is encouraged and the use of cars is discouraged.

Light rail systems

8.25 Where conventional railways, on the surface or underground, are not suitable, there may be an opportunity for a light rail system. As a recent OECD report says, such systems "fill a gap between the high-capacity, high-cost underground rapid transit and the low-capacity and slower buses and trams operating on city streets. Combining, as it does, extensive coverage in the outlying areas with fast, unobstructed access into the city centre, and providing capacities able to service passenger flows in all but the densest urban corridors, the light rail transit is among the most promising service innovations in urban transport that have emerged in recent years. It represents a major breakthrough in the search for less expensive, environmentally compatible transport systems that could serve economically the relatively dispersed travel patterns of today's urban areas" [2].

8.26 Light rail transit is being successfully operated or developed in many cities in Europe (for example in Brussels,

Munich, Cologne, Gothenburg, Rotterdam, Frankfurt, Stuttgart, Essen, Vienna, Mannheim, Nurnberg, Hanover and Bonn). Tyneside is the first urban area in the UK to include a light rail network as the core of its transport system. We recommend that other areas should examine similar systems.

Recreational needs

8.27 Some of the recreational needs of town dwellers can be satisfied only by journeys to the country; others ought to be satisfied in the towns themselves, if only because the time available for them may be too short for travel out of town. A considerable number of other recreational activities could in principle be satisfied in towns, but not in the towns we have; indeed, as was pointed out in Chapter 3, some of the desire to travel out of towns may arise as much from the wish to escape from their unpleasantness—an unpleasantness often caused by traffic—as from the desire to enjoy the facilities that only the country can provide. From every point of view it is desirable that towns themselves should satisfy as many as possible of the recreational needs of their citizens, so reducing the demand for travel outside. Once again, it is also desirable that facilities should be provided locally as far as possible, so as to reduce the demand for travel within towns. This may require large investment; but if it does, the sums involved should be seen in relation to those spent on transport generally and roads in particular. Most of the expected increase in the "demand" for car travel, the satisfaction of which is the main aim of current transport policy, is for social and recreational purposes. If it is in order to spend public money to improve the means of travel to the appropriate facilities, especially on modes which not all citizens can use, it should also be in order to spend the money on other ways of satisfying the same underlying needs.

Freight

8.28 Freight vehicles account for about 20% of vehicle miles travelled on urban roads. In terms of passenger car units, i.e. the relative road capacity requirements of vehicles of different sizes, they amount to about 25%. The latter figure may still underestimate the extent to which freight vehicles cause traffic problems, since it takes no account of the difficulties caused by parked vehicles during loading and unloading. The share of road maintenance costs attributed to freight traffic is much greater than its share of mileage. The environmental disturbance is also disproportionately large. The weight of a heavy vehicle not only affects the road pavement, but also may cause a vibration hazard for nearby buildings. Its size makes it unsuitable for certain roads, especially but not only in town centres. It is noisy. Its size and weight are an accident hazard to other vehicles. At the moment goods vehicles are the chief focus of public discontent about traffic and the environment, both in towns and elsewhere. For all these reasons goods traffic is an important part of the total problem, even though it is free from many of the complexities that affect personal travel. But any attempt to find solutions must take into account the technical problem of goods movement itself and the desirability of keeping costs down.

8.29 The Commission believes that policy towards freight movement in towns should be based on three ideas: segregation of freight traffic in both time and space; the design and style of the vehicle itself and of associated handling equipment; and better land use. The first two can be applied in the short term as well as the longer term. Better land use is a longer-term solution. Whereas it has been recognized for some time that to seek a rational pattern of personal travel requires study of the causes of movement of people and cannot be found simply in an examination of vehicle movements, policy for freight transport still operates largely at the level of the vehicle. There has been little examination of the flow of goods and there are no direct powers to influence their movement. We recommend that this should be investigated. Freight problems should be thought of in terms of the flow of goods—and this in relation to the use of land and the means of movement available. Each of the main points in this paragraph is discussed below.

Segregation of freight traffic

8.30 Segregation may result from rationalisation of the use of vehicles. In economic terms rationalisation may take two distinct forms, which bear differently upon amenity. The first consists of grouping traffic of like kind for a number of

191

towns, giving an economy of scale in size of unit (the groupage effect) and saving vehicle mileage (by optimising the number of journeys run). The foodstuffs industries have widely adopted this "milk-run" system, working from warehouses placed so as to serve a number of towns economically. In amenity terms there is an inter-urban mileage saving, but the large vehicles must enter the towns to make delivery. Some of the multiple grocery and meat companies have invested in rear access to premises as part of their policy. This has the amenity advantage of relieving main street congestion, but the practice is not universal.

8.31 The second form consists of transferring goods from a trunk vehicle at an urban warehouse for town delivery by other vehicles more suited to the purpose. An economic benefit arises where the cost of transfer is more than offset by the saving in overall ton-mileage inside the town resulting from better performance by the local vehicles. The potential advantages to urban amenity of this second method are considerable. The vehicles will be smaller and eventually perhaps powered in a quieter, less polluting way than at present. The distance travelled will be less. The opportunity arises to segregate traffic in time—as opposed to space—by means that are administratively practical. One reason is that a single operator will control a considerable number of drops, and action by that operator will have a significant effect. Secondly, it will be easier for local authorities to manage traffic if they can work with a limited number of operators.

8.32 These two forms of rationalisation are in conflict in the sense that a "milk-run" operator would not wish to use a town warehouse, but to supply a number of towns from one depot; they are complementary in the sense that they may both be able to contribute to amenity. The "milk-run" method may be suited to large distribution chains in foodstuffs with a premium on speedy delivery. The town warehouse method may be suited to general goods, for delivery to smaller retailers. At present, the second method is less obviously a commercial proposition than the first, but the trend towards consolidation of freight is universal and warehouse and lorry operators should be able to achieve some results. To the extent that social benefits remain uncovered by economic cost, and in the absence of a road pricing system, we recommend local authorities to act themselves both by subsidy and by direct intervention. Subsidy of freight would require local authority powers to be increased. The Commission has not investigated what other opportunities the law does now permit; for example, offering cheap sites for a town depot.

8.33 It is not suggested that the "town unit" system could be applied to all goods movements in any town. Some goods movements are not physically suited to such a system, either because it is impossible to re-handle them (bulk liquids might be an example) or because there is no benefit from doing so (a furniture removals van). Nor is it desirable to deprive shippers of all freedom in their choice of service. Local authorities might find it better to encourage larger operators to rationalise their own activities and to run some sort of shared service for others than to try to set up a district scheme; there is a variety of possible arrangements.

8.34 Segregation by time, by means of day off-peak delivery (an administrative restriction) or night delivery, also has amenity advantages in reducing congestion and aiding traffic management. Night delivery must be secure if it is to be commercially practicable, and quiet if it is to be acceptable on amenity grounds. The night safe system, whereby small containers or cages can be dropped at premises to await unloading by the day staff, provides security. Improved handling techniques exist for getting goods out of vehicles and across the pavement.

8.35 A limited use of weekend working would also be helpful. A particularly fruitful area is the collection and delivery of international freight containers, which are working to a round-the-week schedule of port movements. Many industries are reluctant to extend their reception facilities beyond the five-day week. Local authority influence might be able to improve the situation for international and other suitable traffic, the desirable extent of weekend working being a matter of local judgment in relation to the amount of other traffic arising at the weekend and the degree of disturbance caused.

8.36 Under the Dykes Act local authorities are ascribed a positive duty to consider the rationalisation of traffic flow and to propose schemes. Administrative restriction is one aspect of this. Pedestrian precincts, total bans on a limited number of streets or areas, discriminatory bans on certain types of traffic like heavy lorries, and bans on freight movement at certain times, are all instruments of policy which authorities will need to consider. The ban on heavy traffic merits special attention. It is administratively easy to ban through heavy traffic, but this in itself may cause a distortion of flows, canalising the traffic through streets unsuited to carry it. Subject to what we have said in paragraph 8.5 on urban road building, bans on through traffic should have regard to the quality of the route prescribed and the status of road improvements thereon. Bans on traffic wanting access in the town present a different problem. We have acknowledged above that the "town unit" idea of rationalisation is not suited to all traffic. Some factory and warehouse traffic and some types of goods need direct access for inter-urban vehicles. Time and route restrictions may still be feasible and helpful to amenity. The best solution (though a long-term one) concerns land use, discussed below in para. 8.38.

Vehicle and equipment design

8.37 The design of heavy vehicles and limits on their size constitute a key problem. It is discussed later in Chapter 10 as part of inter-urban policy. Attention may also need to be paid to the types of vehicles suited for urban delivery. It could be that fewer vans (which still proliferate) and more purpose-built lorries in the 1 to 3 ton category (currently on the decline) would assist rationalisation. Equipment for transferring goods across the pavement has been mentioned in para 8.34. Transfer of goods in the depot between trunk and local vehicles is also important. The large container is an obvious example of an "inter-modal" unit. There are other methods; for instance, a double unit which can work in tandem on a trunk journey and separately (as two articulated units, each with its own tractor) in the town. At the other extreme in size, a handy trolley unit needs to be devised for people to use in shopping precincts and between shops and car parks, too big to steal, small enough to handle easily. The supermarket trolley may already be close to the ideal unit. All these are areas for further research, none involving high technology.

194

Land use

8.38 In the long term the pattern of goods movement does not have to be taken as fixed, but can be influenced by the use of planning powers to locate industry and commerce more rationally. This does not necessarily mean the continuing removal of industrial and commercial uses from predominantly residential areas of inner cities. In order to provide as wide a range of jobs as possible and to keep work journeys to a minimum it may be desirable to allow such "non-conforming" uses to continue; each case would have to be considered on the basis of traffic and other effects on its neighbourhood, and the suitability of the site for other transport modes. In retail distribution, shopping precincts use land effectively and segregate the shopper from the delivery van or lorry. We do not advocate the use of out-of-town hypermarkets (see para 5.41), since these must tend to increase the number of urban journeys and cause travel difficulties for those without cars (who might be forced to use the hypermarket if it caused the demise of nearer supermarkets and shops). Lastly, are trans-shipment depots and warehouses better located near the town centre or on the perimeter? If they are placed in the centre the big lorries will come in; at the periphery, the number of journey-miles travelled by the smaller feeder lorries will be increased. This should be examined further as one aspect of the value of trans-shipment.

8.39 Better use of land will improve the ability of rail, and in some places of water transport, to carry urban freight in the conurbations and perhaps in large towns. Rail transport is not necessarily unsuitable for short hauls if there is direct access to premises. In some cases this would have to be provided, in others improved. Many British cities still possess extensive but partly disused networks of surface railways and abandoned freight depots which would provide a framework for such developments and would be suitable for integration with novel distribution systems for industrial traffic, particularly light industry. There should be further research into such systems, for example freight tripping by computer-controlled individual wagons. They would represent a logical extension of short-haul experiments which have produced some good results in West Germany and in the United States (e.g. Bee Line). If successful, such systems could themselves influence the location of industry in the conurbations. Lastly we have already stressed the importance of rail access for new industrial estates.

Environmental traffic management

8.40 Traffic restraint in an urban area should be part of a general policy designed to help those who suffer most from the effects of excessive traffic. The ultimate aim must be to improve the environment at home, school, work and shops and to improve the ease and safety of movement for the people as a whole. To achieve this, the capacity of urban roads must be limited to the more essential traffic. Bus lanes and lorry routes should be designated along main roads and the displaced traffic prevented from transferring to unsuitable minor roads. It is suggested that many existing four-lane roads which now have buses running along them could be so designated. Pedestrians too should benefit from the resultant reduction in traffic volumes and by the provision of regular crossings at ground level, pedestrian light phases, and other improvements such as pavement widening and traffic islands, especially along shopping streets. The areas between these designated roads should be protected from the non-essential traffic which would otherwise be transferred to them. Where possible this should be done by discouragements such as "sleeping policemen" or discriminatory bans such as "no entry except for access"; but the pertinacity of motorists and the shortage of police will often leave barriers as the only effective control.

8.41 Some local authorities have introduced large environmental traffic management schemes before anything has been done to limit the capacity of the potential bus/lorry routes which often make up the surrounding roads. This is clearly unfair (as it would be the other way round) and many people have understandably suggested that such schemes should be abandoned. But to re-open roads that have been closed will increase road capacity and hence the volume of traffic. A better course would be to restrain non-essential traffic by adopting the policies of environmental traffic management outlined above.

8.42 Some management measures can be introduced immediately and if necessary adjusted later in the light of experience. It may not be possible to predict with any precision how they will work. Their effects must be assessed by before-and-after studies, which will themselves suggest what course future action should take. We recommend that the Department of the Environment should not give financial support or planning approval to the investment proposals of any local authority where management measures have not been thoroughly examined.

8.43 We also recommend that certain towns or districts within towns should be selected for more intensive experiments to observe the effects of supplying very high levels of service to non-car-users and very high standards of amenity. Such experiments should be treated as part of the nation's research programme into urban transport, the costs being borne by the central government. The best towns to start with would be the historic towns which have most to lose from traffic and road works and most to gain from the restoration of civilised conditions, e.g. York, Bath and Chichester. Historic quarters of large towns should be selected for similar experiments, e.g. Covent Garden.

Research and monitoring

8.44 To guide and keep a check on a continuous programme of transport improvement will require the development of new research techniques. Social surveys will be required to monitor consumer satisfaction. These surveys should collect factual information about trips made, as is done at present; but instead of very large surveys at long intervals, the need is for smaller surveys conducted more frequently. These should cover journeys on foot and by cycle, which are omitted from most recent surveys, as well as journeys by motorised means. Enquiries should also be made into frustrated travel, (i.e. the journeys that people would like to make, but are deterred from making by unsatisfactory conditions), unwanted travel and quality aspects of travel.

8.45 These consumer studies should be accompanied by monitoring of the quality of service offered to travellers by different modes. This will require the development of new techniques to measure attributes such as the reliability, frequency, comfort and convenience of public transport, and the convenience of walking and cycling, as well as the more familiar measure of traffic speed. Such monitoring will require the application of statistical techniques developed in industry as an aid to quality control in production.

8.46 Finally, particular innovations should be appraised by before-and-after studies. Some systematisation of present studies is required, especially so that their results can be presented in the cost-benefit terms discussed in Chapter 7.

REFERENCES

[1] *Urban Transport Planning*, Second report from the Expenditure Committee. House of Commons Paper 57, Session 1972–73. HMSO, 1973.
[2] Organisation for Economic Co-operation and Development: *Environmental Implications of Optimum Urban Mobility*. OECD, Paris, September 1973, pp. 19–21.

Chapter 9

Policy Changes—Rural

9.1 The most pressing problem of personal mobility in the country, as in towns, is to provide for the needs of people without cars and by doing so to make it possible for car owners to become less dependent on their cars. The same measures may help the country dweller to satisfy his daily needs, and the townsman to obtain access to the countryside, without a car. There is, however, one problem which cuts across the distinctions between those with and without cars and between the countryman and the urban visitor: it is the problem of providing for pedestrians and cyclists.

Pedestrians and cyclists

9.2 Everyone needs to walk at some time. Not everyone would wish to cycle even if conditions were improved. But cycling is potentially even more important in the country than in towns, since it can serve some purposes which in towns may be more easily accomplished on foot or by public transport. To provide safe and convenient conditions for pedestrians and cyclists should therefore be a high priority for local authorities. Ideally it is desirable to provide facilities segregated from motor traffic, in the form of separate paths or tracks or of pavements and cycle tracks alongside roads. It may also be possible to set aside minor roads or country lanes for the exclusive use of pedestrians and cyclists. It may be desirable to establish a class of minor roads which are primarily for the use of pedestrians and cyclists, and where motor vehicles are permitted only at very low speeds, rather as delivery vehicles are permitted in some shopping precincts. Effective means would be needed to enforce very low speeds. The use of ramps or grids in the road, and the design of roads to a standard which obliges motor vehicles to keep to low speeds, should be investigated.
9.3 The Commission draws attention to the dense network

of footpaths and bridleways in most parts of Britain, which can provide traffic-free routes for walking and riding, usually taking a more direct line than the road system. These rights of way require adequate maintenance and signposting; if some additional lengths of path were created where necessary, the network could make a very effective contribution to the problems of pedestrians. We also draw attention to the high cost of carrying bicycles on trains; this may be discouraging self-help in solving some problems of rural transport both by townspeople and by country people.

Public transport

9.4 Much less can be done by traffic management to help public transport in rural than in urban areas, except where there is congestion, for instance, in small market towns or villages, or in areas attracting weekend recreational traffic. The basic problem is to provide services on an adequate scale at a reasonable price, which is a matter of finance. Since the problems have mostly arisen from the decline of formerly established services, both train and bus, and since most other solutions are beset with difficulties (as discussed below and in Appendix 6), the obvious remedy is to restore or expand the scheduled public transport services.

9.5 In practice this solution is not usually the first to be considered. For example, in a recent official report on rural transport problems in Devon the virtual disappearance of railways and the considerable decline in bus services were noted ([1], paras. 3.8 to 3.14), but the possibility of restoring those services, even partially, was not suggested as any part of its solution. On the contrary, a further decline in the National Bus Company's services was regarded as inevitable, because more than half their vehicle mileage (five million miles annually) was unremunerative ([1], para. 5.8). The assumption was that the costs involved in supplying scheduled bus and train services on an adequate scale would have been prohibitive, but no calculations were given in support of this.

9.6 Is this assumption in fact well founded? Before answering this question we must decide what level of service would count as "adequate" to meet the needs for work and leisure of rural dwellers. To give a satisfactory definition of "adequate" would require research into the social consequences of providing or not providing different levels of access to facilities such as employment, health, shops and social and leisure activities; and the Commission is not aware of such research. Most of the present hardship has been caused by the cuts and reductions in services over the last fifteen years or so. If these services were restored, the level of service might then be fairly regarded as adequate. We do not suggest that all the lost services should, or even could now, be restored, but it is useful to consider what the cost of this might be, simply to find out whether the sums involved are excessive.

Buses

9.7 The most recent official attempt to calculate what subsidies would be necessary to keep rural bus services going was contained in the report of the Jack Committee in 1961 [2]. It was estimated that withdrawals and reductions in service during the years 1957–1960 had caused the loss of some 18·5 million bus miles annually, or 5·8% of the total rural bus miles performed in 1956. The Jack Committee took the figure of one shilling per bus mile to indicate the support needed to restore the lost mileage, and calculated that it would have cost about £1m a year initially and perhaps twice that sum later if the trends of that time were to continue.
9.8 Some rough estimates made for the Commission suggest that between 1960 and 1972 the annual bus mileage in rural areas has been further reduced by a total of some 120 million bus miles. Meanwhile operating costs have risen sharply. In 1969, the last year for which figures were published in the annual publication *Passenger Transport in Great Britain*, costs per bus mile of all operators were 16·9p. The National Bus Company has informed us that the cost per bus mile of their own operations rose by 35% between 1969 and 1972. On this basis, the costs per bus mile of all operations would have been some 22·6p in 1972. This average relates to both urban and rural operations; since urban operations are more expensive, because speeds are lower, it can certainly be taken as a high estimate if applied to rural operations only. (Other estimates for rural operations which the Commission has examined suggest that the cost per bus mile may sometimes be well under 20p.) Maintaining rural bus operations at the 1956 level would

therefore have cost by 1972 at most an extra £31·3 million per annum.[1] Some of this extra cost would have been recovered from fares, so that the bill in terms of grant from the government or local authorities would have been less, perhaps by a substantial amount.

Railways

9.9 It is not possible to make the same kind of calculation for railways as for buses, since unfortunately in many places it is not a question simply of restoring the services, as for buses, but of physically replacing the track and infrastructure as well. The Commission has no information about the cost of replacement. It would vary very much from area to area. There is, however, information about the present costs of unremunerative rural rail services; and from this it may be calculated how much might be the cost of restoring services where conditions are favourable.

9.10 In 1972 a total grant of £67 million was paid to BR for unremunerative services. Most of this was paid for urban or commuter services in London and other conurbations. The remaining services, which may be roughly defined as rural, accounted for £29·4 million. But the grant paid for an unremunerative service is not intended to equal the loss to British Rail for maintaining the service rather than closing it down. The Cooper Brothers' formula used for the calculation of grant is officially said to overstate this shortfall, and, if used as an estimate of the loss, would exaggerate the saving which BR could make by withdrawing the service. It includes provision for overheads not escapable by closure, and it does not take into account that when a service is withdrawn BR tends to lose revenue not only on that service but on others as well, because some journeys made on the withdrawn service are part of a longer railway journey. It is true that some travellers continue to use the railway for part of their journey when a service is withdrawn, but most of this "contributory revenue" is lost.

9.11 If however the reforms in railway administration which we recommend later in this chapter and in Chapter 10 are implemented, it will then be possible and appropriate to make the grants correspond to the shortfall. The bill to local authorities (and it is the local authority rather than the

[1] 138·5 million bus miles at 22·6p per bus mile.

central government which is likely to decide in future whether or not a grant should be paid) would then be smaller. It is not possible to state exactly how much of the £29·4 million is properly due to the shortfall, since the necessary calculations, which are unavoidably lengthy, are made only when the future of some particular service is in question and not for unremunerative services as a whole. But the figures for some particular services provide useful indications. For example, the annual cost of keeping open the services on the Bedford to Bletchley line, if calculated in terms of the shortfall to British Rail arising from their existence, is estimated at £40,000; the annual grant payable for this service according to the Cooper Brothers' formula is £143,000.[1] For the Bradford–Keighley and Leeds/Bradford–Ilkley services, the grant was calculated in 1972 at £304,000, of which the shortfall to BR accounted for £212,000.[2] (The Bradford services are not rural services, but nevertheless the figures illustrate the difference between the grant payable under the formula and the amount needed to keep unremunerative services going.)

9.12 These two examples show that, given suitable changes in the rest of railway finances, the costs to local authorities of keeping the present rural rail services going might be very much less than £29·4 million a year—perhaps less than half that amount. If the system of subsidies which we advocate in Chapter 10 is implemented, the costs for local authorities might again be further reduced, since these subsidies, which would be paid by the central government, would provide BR with an incentive to reduce fares, particularly on more marginal services, in order to achieve a higher passenger mileage.

9.13 Another hazard in the calculation of the cost of rural railways concerns the correct treatment of staff costs. If a service is closed down, British Rail's wages bill is reduced. But this saving to British Rail may not signify a real gain to the economy. Where the local employment situation is buoyant, so that the staff made redundant can be quickly

---

[1] These figures are taken from the Minutes of the meeting of Bucks County Council of February 22nd 1973 and are agreed by the Department of the Environment.
[2] Figures supplied to the Commission by the Department of the Environment.

re-employed, the saving is genuine. But if staff cannot be re-employed locally and because of age or other reasons are unlikely to move elsewhere their dismissal from the railways does not represent a genuine saving to the economy. Similarly, if to re-open a service would mean creating work for people who would otherwise be unemployed, the true costs to the economy are less than the wages paid. Local authorities should consider carefully whether this situation obtains in their areas. If it does, it should be made possible for them to reclaim from the central government some part of the grant which they pay to maintain rail services, since it is on the central government that the responsibility of dealing with those who would otherwise be unemployed would fall.

9.14 The costs of running rural rail services of the present type are therefore much less than the amount paid in grant may suggest. It may also be possible to reduce costs by offering a different type of service. Basic railways on the model of the "pay train" pioneered in East Anglia by Gerard Fiennes ten years ago, now operate in most rural areas. One reason that the incorrect idea that rural railways are very expensive still maintains its hold may be that people have not fully realised what economies the institution of basic railways has brought about. Mr. Fiennes has claimed (in *I Tried to Run a Railway*, Ian Allen 1967; see also Rural District Review, January 1969) that he was able to reduce costs on the East Suffolk line from £250,000 annually to £84,000 and so make the line profitable. One can only speculate how many other rural lines closed in the 1960s might have been saved if these methods had been more speedily adopted elsewhere. It is also possible that some branch lines could be run more profitably (or less unprofitably) by private companies than by British Rail. A private company has two advantages. The fact that it is a local concern is a source of pride and interest to many people in the neighbourhood and to visitors, and this encourages custom. In addition, the companies attract voluntary labour, especially in the summer when the services are likely to be most used by tourists. It is therefore possible for them to run with a small permanent staff during the winter months, when the line must be kept open to serve the basic needs of local communities but frequent services are not required, and to make use of cheap voluntary labour to handle the peak summer periods. To facilitate private operation, some change in the present law is required (see para. 9.23 below). Local authorities should also consider that to pay grants for railways will reduce the amounts which they would otherwise have to pay for bus operation, or for unconventional means of public transport, and may even, in some areas at least, be a means of reducing expenditure on road maintenance and construction.

Rural subsidies

9.15 Are the sums of money that have been discussed an impossible price to pay for regular public transport services?

Table 9.1: Expenditure on roads in Great Britain
County Council areas for the financial year 1970/71

	£ million
Trunk roads	
New construction and improvement	237
Maintenance and cleansing	19
Administration	5
Lighting	2
Other construction and improvement	
Principal roads	82
Other roads	35
Other maintenance and cleansing	
Principal roads	25
Other roads	84
Other administration	
Total	30
Other lighting	
Total	18
Car parking	
Total net of receipts and other income	7
Total	544

Source: *Highway Statistics 1971.*

Once it is accepted that the transport problems of an area should be considered as a whole and that the budget should be regarded as being available for any transport use, it is legitimate to set them in the context of the total transport spending in rural areas, and in particular of the expenditure on roads. Table 9.1 shows the expenditure on roads in Great Britain for the financial year 1970/71 in county council areas (i.e. areas outside London, county boroughs and the equivalent urban authorities in Scotland). It will be seen that £544 million was spent on road purposes of all kinds. If trunk roads are completely excluded on the grounds that they are a national asset and the money involved should not be regarded as being available for local purposes, the total is £281 million.

9.16 It is also instructive to compare the money now being spent, or that would be required, on grants for public transport in particular counties with what is spent there on roads, car parking and other transport purposes. For buses, Hampshire is probably the county council that pays the largest grant under Section 34 of the 1968 Transport Act: in 1972/73 it paid £95,000 and in 1973/74 £145,000 [3], these sums would have been matched by equal payments from the central government. The amount spent in Hampshire for road purposes other than trunk roads in the year 1971/72 was £10,045,000, of which £514,000, net of receipts, was spent on car parking alone. The County Council of Lincoln, parts of Lindsey, recently refused to pay an annual subsidy of £33,000 [4] towards the retention of thirteen services in the eastern part of the county, a part where as recently as 1971 further substantial rail cuts took place. It is noteworthy that in 1971/72 £202,000 was spent on subsidising car parking, and £465,240 was budgeted for schools transport for the year 1972/73. One wonders how many of the school services could have been provided by improved scheduled services [5]. It has been mentioned that the shortfall suffered by BR in keeping the Bedford to Bletchley line open is £40,000 a year. In the year 1971/72, £7,880,000 was spent in the counties of Bedfordshire and Buckinghamshire on road purposes other than trunk roads; of this £118,000 net of receipts was spent on car parking.

9.17 It is not suggested that simply to contrast the amounts required to subsidise rural rail and bus services with the amounts spent on rural roads is enough to justify the subsidies. There is no substitute for a detailed appraisal in each area of the costs and benefits of alternative ways of providing public transport. It might turn out that to restore services to the level obtaining before the growth of car ownership could not always be justified. All that this comparison is intended to show is that the costs are not so great that the possibility of paying grants to maintain and restore services can simply be dismissed from the outset. The assumption that the costs would be excessive is simply a carry-over from the time when it was thought that public transport should operate commercially even though roads did not. This fallacious view is no longer embodied in the law, which now enables local authorities to consider the transport problems in their area as a whole. Nonetheless the old attitude dies hard. It is nowhere better exemplified than in the Department of the Environment's Devon study, to which reference has already been made. The statement "that there is now very little money to be made in stage bus operations of the traditional sort in rural areas" ([1], paras. 3.13 and 1.2) seemed to be taken as a sufficient reason for their withdrawal.

Other forms of public transport

9.18 Various schemes have been suggested over the years, in response to the increasing difficulties and decline of the regular rural public transport services, to make use of other less conventional means. These suggestions usually involve either allowing the public to use services supplied for the benefit of some special group, for example making school buses available to fare-paying passengers, or making provision for passenger and goods facilities to be shared, as for example with Post Office buses which also carry the mail. Such schemes have operated in other European countries for many years and there is certainly room for imaginative schemes of the same kind here, particularly in the more sparsely populated parts of the country. The Commission notes with interest the successful expansion of the Post Office bus services even in the last year to a total of over thirty [3]. But any special services of this kind mean that routes and timetables for public transport operation have to be geared to other requirements rather than designed to suit the customer's convenience. In addition, if the special services are used to supplement conventional bus services rather than as a substitute where no conventional services exist, the frequency of the conventional service is reduced; and this weakens the entire operation and makes it harder to co-ordinate different bus services with each other and with trains. For this reason, the Commission recommends that these possibilities should be considered only after the potential of conventional services has been fully investigated; the maintenance or restoration of scheduled bus and train services should always be the first option to be considered. In fact, the possibilities of replacing restricted bus services (such as school bus services, or buses serving the employees of particular workplaces) by regular scheduled services should be examined wherever possible. This would not only strengthen the regular services but would often suit the interest of the customers of the specialised service better too. For example, a school child who is tied to the time of the school bus to make his journey home may be prevented from taking part in the school's extra-curricular activities.

Cars as a substitute for public transport

9.19 In the Department of the Environment's view, although the bus still has a limited role in rural areas and other schemes such as postal buses also have a part to play in some localities, the right way to deal with the requirements of those country people still without cars is to devise ways in which their car-owning neighbours can supply their wants. "The great and increasing amount of private transport in rural areas must be made the basis of dealing with these scattered needs" [6]. Country people have always helped each other by giving each other lifts, as in other ways, and naturally such neighbourly acts should continue. But to institutionalise this practice so that it becomes the main way of meeting people's fundamental mobility needs has aroused the impassioned hostility of all the women's groups and other organisations representing those whose needs it is intended to satisfy in this way. They fear that it could lead to assaults on women and children, or to men being blackmailed by unscrupulous passengers. They object to the principle that people should have to be beholden to their neighbours for their basic necessities. They also doubt, these moral points apart, whether it would ever be possible to devise a convenient system based on the synchronisation of different people's journeys. The Commission endorses these views. On moral grounds alone the principle is unacceptable. The sentence quoted above from the DoE Press Notice is also misleading in that it suggests that the people without cars available to them are a small residue only. It was argued in Chapter 5 that those in this position are now and are always likely to be a majority of the population, and the DoE's own studies did not in fact support the view that this was a small residual problem. The situation is examined more fully in Appendix 6.

The role of urban local authorities

9.20 To restore public transport in the country will generally serve the interests of the townsman anxious to use public transport to travel into the countryside as well as those of the countryman himself. There will be particular cases, however, where a service which helps the townsman to reach some particular park or other attraction in the country is of little value to country dwellers. Urban local authorities will now have the power to subsidise such services, and should look at possible schemes with great sympathy, as they help to fulfil a basic need of their citizens, particularly the poorer ones who might otherwise be deprived altogether of access to fine countryside.

Changes required in railway finance and administration

9.21 It has been pointed out that the grants paid to BR to maintain rural services amount to more than BR could in fact save by closing them down. The Commission believes that the present system of calculating the grants to be paid for unremunerative services is unfortunate and should be changed to a system whereby the grant is equivalent to the loss that BR actually incurs. (This reform would have to be accompanied by a new way of supporting BR's "commercial" services; our suggestions are given in Chapter 10.) An important defect of the existing system is that it creates a misleading impression of where BR's losses occur, and therefore gives rise to political pressure to improve BR's financial position by closing down rural lines where closures would not in fact have the hoped-for effect. The Cooper Brothers' formula is also inequitable because it places too great a burden on local authorities rather than on central government. One result is that some local authorities have concluded that the only type of public transport which they can afford to subsidise is the bus, even though in the long term the bus has not the same potential for complete automation as the train, and even though the disadvantages have become evident of replacing the former system of complementary buses and trains by a "bus-only system". Bus replacements have in practice found the regular patronage of the former service halved. In many cases they have been unable to make transits quickly enough for country people to get into town and back again in one day, and they are often unsuitable for long journeys. On the other hand, at peak periods (e.g. summer weekends when extra buses are hardest to muster) buses have been unable to carry everyone who wished to travel. The Commission does not therefore subscribe to the idea that the deficiencies of buses which are intended to replace trains are to be altogether blamed upon their operators. In many cases, for example between Skipton and Carlisle through Yorkshire and Westmorland, or between Alston in Cumberland and Haltwhistle in Northumberland, the geography of the area makes a replacement bus service almost impossible even in good weather conditions. On other routes the length and discomfort of the journey have deterred almost all regular travellers. Notable examples are the replacement buses which now take more than twice the time of former rail services between Dumfries and Stranraer, or along the former Waverley route between Carlisle and Edinburgh via Hawick. It was found on a trial run in 1973 that a planned replacement bus for the Inverness–Kyle of Lochalsh railway could not maintain even the generous schedule allowed. And many other examples could be quoted from many parts of the country where, because of local geography, or congestion,or the pattern of settlement, a replacement bus service cannot be expected to play the part which trains played in the network of public transport.

9.22 Another defect in the Cooper Brothers' formula is that it calculates costs on a long-term basis although the grant is paid only for three years at a time. The Commission's view is that, whatever system of grants operates in the future, the period for which they are paid should be lengthened to ten years. Short-term grants result in constant insecurity about their jobs for BR's staff. This is unfair to them and bad for morale. Executives from BR and the local authorities are in an almost continuous state of negotiation. The uncertainty hampers co-ordinated planning of other transport and land-use policy in the area.

9.23 We also recommend a change in procedures which

would make it easier for private companies to take over unprofitable branch lines. Whenever BR cannot operate a branch line profitably and the line therefore becomes a candidate for grant aid, it should be possible for the local authority to invite any soundly constituted company to tender for it and to accept an offer which would be more advantageous than paying to BR whatever sum would be necessary according to the revised formula. The private company would have to demonstrate that it had the necessary technical competence and financial support. The land, track and works would be leased, not sold, so that the line would remain in public ownership.[1]

Co-ordination of rural public transport services

9.24 Too often in the past rural bus and rail services have operated in almost total isolation from each other, with bus and rail stations situated widely apart, and trains failing to connect with country bus services. The Commission notes the new powers given to the new county council authorities to co-ordinate services, and recommends that these powers are used to bring about a much more carefully integrated pattern of road and rail services, with a common timetable available indicating connections at railheads (see para. 10.28).

Traffic management in the country

9.25 It was said at the beginning of this chapter that the traffic situation is simpler in the country than in the towns, and that there is correspondingly less need or scope for traffic management measures in the country. This is true in the sense that traffic management will not often aid the problems of personal mobility in the countryside, but there is both scope and need to use it to protect and enhance the environment, particularly in National Parks, Country Parks and Areas of Outstanding Natural Beauty. Some of the schemes that have already been tried in such places were mentioned in Chapter 4. All such schemes so far have taken for granted that people will travel to the area by car, even though on arrival they may be prevented or dissuaded from using their cars by the provision of car parks and alternative

[1] In France a rural line of 33 kms was recently transferred for the nominal sum of 1 franc (*Le Monde*, 7.6.70).

means of transport. Access to the parks and to popular beauty spots and "stately homes" by public transport should be improved in the interests of those without cars, and more publicity should be given to existing possibilities of travel by public transport to these places. This would help to avoid saturation by cars in some areas. Any car owner who would prefer to use public transport for such journeys would be free to do so; and this would ease the environmental problems. It would also open the way to implementing more ambitious schemes of limiting entry into certain parks to pedestrians, cyclists and travellers by public transport. There ought to be some places in the countryside available to people who particularly value the complete absence of traffic and are prepared to put themselves to some personal inconvenience to find it. The objection to this idea is that it would bear hard on people who, because of some physical handicap or disability, find it difficult to travel without a car. It might be possible to make some special provision for them; but, even if it is not, the Commission recommends that some such schemes should be tried as experiments. At the same time, the more conventional traffic management schemes should go ahead in selected areas, as envisaged in the Countryside Commission's programme.

Freight

9.26 The proposals for rationalising urban goods transport by organising it on an area basis, which were put forward in the last chapter, would not apply in the country. But to control the speeds and routes of heavy goods vehicles is at least as important in the country as in towns, especially in order to safeguard minor roads and country lanes. Our suggestions for rail freight subsidies (see Chapter 10) will help to relieve the countryside of heavy through traffic on the roads and will also enable more freight originating in country areas to be carried by rail, especially if there is also a more favourable policy towards rail passenger services. Provision should also be made to allow special rail subsidies to be granted over and above those suggested in the next chapter so as to limit the use of heavy lorries in particularly sensitive areas, for example for the transport of stone quarried in National Parks. Discussions are already taking place between the National Park authorities, quarry operators and British Rail in the Yorkshire Dales National Park to encourage the transport by rail of the maximum amount of stone in place of the present use of the Park's overloaded road system. At present, however, only trainload traffic is "economic" in the narrow sense of the Government's present remit to BR, and some system of controls or subsidies will have to be introduced to encourage wagon-load traffic. The Peak Park Planning Board, faced with similar environmental problems, is both encouraging rail travel to the Park and developing in part of the Park a system by which lorries are limited to particular roads. This policy is developed from the Board's recent report [7].

Experiments and research

9.27 The recommendations under these headings for towns apply in the country too. It is not possible to find out what the public wants, or what the practical problems and effects of different possible arrangements are, without conducting trials in particular places. Where extra expenditure is involved the central government should again contribute all or part, since these experiments are a part of the nation's research and development programme.

9.28 Further experiments in National Parks and other selected areas have just been mentioned. Another desirable experiment would be to subsidise rural transport in some particular county or district so as to provide a level of service higher than the basic level required to satisfy the inhabitants' basic needs. The object would be to investigate the relationship between car ownership and use and the quality of the alternatives supplied, and more generally to gain an understanding of what people's attitudes are when they are presented with options not usually open to them. Such trials would have to be maintained for several years; the localities would have to be carefully chosen, and other similar areas selected as controls.

9.29 More ambitious regional experiments in restraining car use and providing a high level of alternatives should be undertaken, first of all in areas where by common consent the car is already a threat to amenities. The problems are particularly severe in Cornwall (see Chapter 4). Since Cornwall is also a self-contained peninsula, it seems an ideal choice for experiment.

REFERENCES

[1] *Study of Rural Transport in Devon*. Report by the Steering Group, Department of the Environment, 1971.

[2] *Rural Bus Services*, Report of the Committee, HMSO, 1961.

[3] White, Peter R. "A review of developments in British rural transport since November 1972, in *Proceedings of a seminar on Rural Transport*, Polytechnic of Central London, November 1973.

[4] *Report of Special Sub-Committee on Rural Transport for the General Purposes Committee of the County of Lincoln, Parts of Lindsey*, February 1973. The recommendations were adopted by the County Council later in the same month.

[5] *Rural Transport Problems in Lincolnshire and East Nottinghamshire*, The Open University, 1973, part 2, p. 13.

[6] Department of the Environment Press Notice 468, July 1971.

[7] Peak Park Planning Board: *Routes for People*, 1972.

CHAPTER 10

Policy Changes—Inter-Urban and Long-Distance

INTRODUCTION

10.1 Inter-urban and long distance transport depend essentially on road and rail. It has been assumed in official policy and in the public mind that the railways can make only a relatively small contribution, and that road travel and transport must provide most of the nation's growing needs. We have shown that if road building is to cater for this assumed growth it is bound to cause great environmental problems, by the use of land and resources for road building, by generating new road traffic, and by damaging the urban and rural environment when these vehicles enter towns and villages or use country roads.

10.2 We believe it is desirable from many points of view to ensure that the growth of road traffic and of road space slows down. We shall therefore examine two sets of arguments: the first, that road and rail transport are complementary rather than competitive and have little interaction one with the other, so that policies to transfer traffic are valueless; the second, the case for a national network of new roads, especially the national roads programme.

10.3 In order to see whether other means of transport, besides rail, might be able to take some of the traffic and do less harm to the environment than the car and the lorry, we shall examine the potential of other available modes. These we deal with first and conclude that they will be able to make a useful but limited contribution. We then discuss the road/ rail relationship and the roads programme. After that we look at the specific problems of British Rail, and in the last section we consider the heavy lorry.

10.4 Information on long distance travel is surprisingly limited. It is for this reason that this chapter largely consists of a discussion of official proposals and of the arguments given in their support, and so differs from the last two chapters which started with our own analysis of the problems. But some useful background information on personal travel is given in Tables 1 to 3 and on freight in Table 4.

ALTERNATIVES TO RAIL, CAR AND LORRY

Long-distance buses

10.5 Long-distance buses and coaches play an important part in long-distance travel, carrying about half as many passengers as are carried by rail (see Table 10.2). The National Bus Company plans to improve its long-distance services, taking advantage of the motorway and trunk road

Table 10.1: Long-distance travel by length of journey and purpose
Units: Journeys

Purpose	Length of journey				All journeys 25 miles or more	
	25 to 100 miles		100 miles or more			
To and from work	1063	14%	41	4%	1104	12%
In the course of work	1303	17%	190	17%	1493	17%
Shopping and personal business	871	11%	90	8%	961	11%
Recreational	2413	31%	211	18%	2624	29%
Social and visiting	1727	22%	165	15%	1892	21%
Holiday	325	4%	431	38%	756	9%
Other	57	1%	2	*	59	1%
All purposes:	7759	100%	1130	100%	8889	100%

* Less than 0·5%.

Source: National Travel Survey.

Notes

1. The journeys represented were all those made by people living in private households in Great Britain over the age of three during the year April 1972 to March 1973.
2. The category "shopping and personal business" includes journeys made for educational purposes and journeys made to escort other people. A trip is classed as a "holiday" if at least one night is spent away.
3. These figures are taken from a preliminary analysis of the National Travel Survey and are subject to some modification. In particular, the category "recreational" is slightly over-stated and the category "holiday" correspondingly under-stated.

network. The question arises what effect this development is likely to have on rail services and whether wasteful competition will develop.

10.6 Bus services provide many cross-country links not easily provided by rail. Even if some cross-country rail links were restored, the bus is often more convenient. Buses can also feed the railways, e.g. by linking East Anglia to the East Coast main line. Bus services may sometimes be more convenient for people living on the periphery of the large conurbations, obviating the need to make a back journey to the rail terminus in the city centre.

10.7 Express bus services on motorways and other main routes are cheaper than rail services. The Commission would like to see lower rail fares, which would make the two forms of service more competitive in price. If, for this or other reasons, competition increased to the point of wasteful duplication of services, Government intervention might be required, but the Commission would not wish to see an end to all competition between the two modes.

Table 10.2: Long-distance travel by length of journey and main mode used
Units: Journeys

Mode	Length of journey 25 to 100 miles		100 miles or more		All journeys 25 miles or more	
Rail	712	9%	168	15%	880	10%
Stage and long distance buses	440	6%	83	7%	523	6%
Other public transport	94	1%	18	2%	112	1%
Private car	6454	83%	843	75%	7297	82%
All others	59	1%	18	2%	77	1%
All modes:	7759	100%	1130	100%	8889	100%

Source: National Travel Survey.

Notes:

1. See Note 1 to Table 10.1.

2. The category "rail" includes a very small number of journeys made by London Transport rail services. The category "other public transport" includes coach hire, private bus, taxis, planes. The category "private car" includes vans and lorries when being used for personal travel only.

10.8 Another possible danger in the development of the long-distance bus network is that this more glamorous and profitable service may distract the attention of NBC's top management from the more humdrum but socially essential local bus services. NBC's structure of local subsidiaries may constitute some safeguard against this; and, in theory at

Table 10.3: Long distance journeys by main mode of travel and purpose

A. Journeys 25–100 miles in length
Units: Percentages

| Purpose | Mode | | | | | |
	Rail	Bus	Other public transport	Private car	All others	Total modes
To and from work	54	1	34	10	—	14
In the course of work	7	2	17	19	7	17
Shopping and personal business	9	10	10	12	3	11
Recreational	14	63	28	31	54	31
Social and visiting	12	18	3	24	22	22
Holiday	3	6	9	4	10	4
Other	1	—	—	1	3	1
All purposes	100 (712)	100 (440)	100 (94)	100 (6454)	100 (59)	100 (7759)

B. Journeys of 100 miles or more
Units: Percentages

| Purpose | Mode | | | | | |
	Rail	Bus	Other public transport	Private car	All others	Total modes
To and from work	10	1	6	3	6	4
In the course of work	23	1	67	16	—	17
Shopping and personal business	13	—	—	8	6	8
Recreational	18	43	6	16	33	19
Social and visiting	11	7	—	17	11	15
Holiday	26	47	22	40	39	38
Other	—	—	—	—	6	—
All purposes	100 (168)	100 (83)	100 (18)	100 (843)	100 (18)	100 (1130)

Source: National Travel Survey. See notes to Tables 10.1 and 10.2.

least, dissatisfied county councils could, with the agreement of the Traffic Commissioners, turn to another operator to supply local bus services.

Table 10.4: Freight carried by road and rail in 1971
Units: thousands of millions of ton miles

Road vehicles: unladen weight (tons) over	not over	Length of haul Under 25 miles	25–49 miles	50–99 miles	100 miles and over	Total
–	1½	1·45	0·45	0·25	0·15	2·3
1½	3	1·20	0·45	0·25	0·30	2·2
3	5	3·40	1·50	2·00	2·70	9·6
5	8	3·75	3·20	3·50	6·45	16·9
8	–	3·10	3·50	3·70	9·10	19·4
Total		12·9	9·1	9·7	18·7	50·4
BR Rail Freight		1·0	1·7	3·2	10·0	15·9

Source: The rail freight figures were supplied by the British Railways Board. The road figures in the Total column are taken from *The Transport of Goods by Road 1970–1972*, Directorate of Statistics, Department of the Environment, December 1972. The detailed road figures are derived by extrapolation of the results of the corresponding survey carried out in 1967/68 and are approximate only.

Air

10.9 Air travel accounts for only a small share of long-distance domestic travel and, as was shown in Table 2.6 of Chapter 2, passenger mileage by air has not increased over the last few years. Nevertheless, air is an important competitor to rail on certain routes. The development of inter-city train services has enabled rail to compete more effectively with air, and has brought about a drastic reduction of the London–Birmingham air service. It is generally believed that the introduction of British Rail's High Speed Diesel Train and Advanced Passenger Train will win back more traffic from air to rail, particularly since rising fuel prices are likely to have their greatest impact on the cost of air travel. Because of rail's advantages over air in using less fuel and causing less environmental damage, the Commission welcomes this likely development; but it would not want to see the end of all competition between rail and domestic air services, unless a worsening in the fuel crisis compels it. The Government should retain powers to decide which air services may be operated and should be prepared to use them to avoid unnecessary duplication of facilities, particularly of subsidised services. But the course that events are expected to take without government intervention does not suggest that intervention will often be necessary.

10.10 Air at present accounts for only a minute share of domestic freight and, even though this share may grow, the impact on road and rail will never be significant.

10.11 Many, if not most, airports in the UK are currently receiving financial support from municipal funds. For instance, in 1972, subsidies were paid to Liverpool, East Midlands, and Birmingham airports of £765,000, £440,000 and £290,000 respectively. The Commission sees no valid reason for the subsidisation of airports and urges the Government to take steps to prevent or discourage this practice.

Coastal shipping freight services

10.12 The role of coastal shipping around the mainland of Great Britain is confined to the carriage of bulk cargoes in shiploads. In 1971, coastwise carryings totalled approximately 48 million tons, of which some 34 million were of petroleum, 8 million of coal and 6 million of other bulk cargo, principally stone, slag, cement, china clay, fertilisers and grain. In the peak year of 1957, 29 million tons of coal were carried on coastal routes; it is the rapid decline of the coal trade that chiefly accounts for the fall in the ton-mileage by coastal shipping which was recorded in Table C of Appendix 1. But coastal shipping still makes an important contribution to long-distance freight movement in Britain.

10.13 Coastal shipping has great advantages as a mode of transport: it is unobtrusive, safe, and, when ships are fully loaded, extremely economical in fuel and cheap per ton-mile. A substantial difficulty in extending its use beyond those trades where it is now employed is that it would require a great many consignments of the size usually carried by road to make one full cargo. In addition, unless loads are moving between two waterside premises, the cost of the extra handling and the road or rail journey at each end is likely to negate the saving on the trunk journey. For these reasons, it is hard to envisage any expansion of coastal shipping of a

220

kind likely to make an impact on the problems associated with land freight transport, unless there is a deliberate national policy to encourage industrial development on the coast. Such a policy would also enable the transport costs of imported raw materials to be reduced. But substantial environmental, economic and social problems would have to be investigated before any such policy could be recommended, and in any case its effects could only be felt in the very long term. For these reasons, the Commission has not investigated this matter any further.

10.14 An important exception is the carriage of abnormal, indivisible loads. These are, by statutory definition, too large to be transported by rail and are usually carried by special road vehicles. The harm done to the road surface by these vehicles, and the cost of congestion and necessary police supervision, are often very considerable but are not borne by the consignors. Some manufacturers are siting their heavy manufacturing works at or near coastal sites in order to be able to use coastal or direct ocean services. The Commission believes that this practice could be encouraged and recommends that permission to transport abnormal loads by road should be subject to a charge commensurate with the costs imposed on the community.

Inland waterways

10.15 As shown in Table C of Appendix 1, inland waterways now account for only a minute proportion—a fraction of 1%—of ton-mileage in Great Britain. The cargoes carried are the same sorts of bulk commodities as are carried by coastal shipping: coal and other solid fuel, liquids in bulk, and solid bulk cargoes including timber, grain, metal, alloys, ores, paper, pulp, fertilisers and foodstuffs.

10.16 The main commercial waterways are linked to estuaries and ports. Some people have claimed that there is scope for more use to be made of these waterways as an extension of coastal and short sea shipping, or even of deep sea shipping, taking advantage of the development of barge-carrying large cargo ships (LASH). Canals which were improved for this purpose might then also be able to serve other more local freight traffic.

10.17 Some of these possibilities appear promising enough in themselves to warrant investigation; among the schemes brought to the Commission's attention were the improvement of the Grand Union Canal between Warford and the Thames at Brentford, the improvement of the Sheffield and South Yorkshire Navigation Canal to enable 400-ton barges to ply as far as Rotherham (which has since been approved), and the proposal to build an inland transshipment terminal at the head of the Weaver Navigation Canal at Winsford in Cheshire. But, even if such schemes were successful, their impact on the wider problems of freight transport would be confined to a few localities. The Commission has therefore not inquired further into these suggestions.

10.18 If inland waterways were to make a significant national contribution to the problems of freight transport, large investment would be required, coupled with planning policies to encourage suitable industries to expand and locate at the waterside. Such a policy could only be of long-term effect and would be hard to reconcile with the recreational use of inland waterways. The traffic that might be transferred from roads to canals is much the same as could be attracted to the railways, given suitable encouragement. A drive to attract freight traffic to the railways will be necessary in any event and could show results much more quickly. In the Commission's view, no prima facie case for a general expansion of the inland waterway system has been made out, nor indeed could it be until the policies—which we discuss below—to encourage greater use of the railways have been implemented.

Pipelines

10.19 Pipelines have long been used in water and town gas supply and sewage disposal, and are indispensable for these purposes. But these operations are not normally regarded as freight transport, and we have not considered them. Measured in ton-miles, pipelines also account for 2% to 3% of freight transport, as usually defined, within Great Britain. With trivial exceptions, the commodities transported by pipeline are all oil or natural gas, and the use of pipelines for these purposes is expected to grow. It is technically possible to convey material in semi-liquid or slurry form by pipelines and even to carry containers in them. However, the capital cost and inflexibility of a pipeline system make it unlikely that in a small country like Britain there will be a significant development of pipelines for solid commodities.

Financial policy towards freight modes

10.20 Although the Commission does not believe that coastal shipping, inland waterways or pipelines have a major part to play in the solution of the domestic freight transport problems that are now causing so much public concern, it is nevertheless important that financial and institutional arrangements should enable them to make what contribution they can. In Chapter 6 it was argued that subsidies to freight transport are a legitimate instrument of transport policy, and, in the absence of a fully effective charging system, an instrument that should be used. Later in this chapter we discuss subsidies to encourage rail freight transport. We recommend that these should also be paid to encourage the use of water transport or pipelines wherever it can be demonstrated that a net benefit to the community would result.

THE RELATIONSHIP BETWEEN ROAD AND RAIL TRANSPORT

10.21 The idea of a comprehensive approach is now accepted in local transport planning. But at a national level, road and rail are treated separately. Plans are formulated by different agencies, predictions of traffic take no account of the effect on the other mode and quite different investment criteria are employed. This separation is officially defended on the grounds that road and rail serve quite different markets and are not substitutes for each other. If this were true, it still would not justify the use of different investment criteria, since whether or not the two modes compete for custom they certainly compete for resources; we have already discussed this anomaly in Chapter 7. The Commission is not convinced by the arguments, which are set out below, that the interaction between the two modes is negligible.

Personal travel

10.22 According to British Rail, new road developments do not generally affect the level of personal rail travel very much even though some motorway building has had a discernible effect. They find that the new custom brought by new and improved services is mainly generated by these services and not diverted from the roads. For instance, journeys that might have been made to local destinations to shop or to seek professional services are extended to a wider range of opportunities at a greater distance. British Rail also believe that they cannot satisfy the needs of many long-distance road travellers, especially families on holiday or on other social and recreational journeys. It is claimed that even their own executives tend to prefer car travel on such occasions, despite their entitlement to free rail travel.

10.23 According to the Department of the Environment, traffic studies suggest that many car journeys made on motorways are of a length and pattern that could not easily be accommodated by rail, since the average distance travelled on motorways is probably about twenty miles; and, even if there were car journeys which British Rail could reasonably hope to attract, they would amount to such a tiny proportion of total road traffic that the case for road building would be almost unaffected.

10.24 The Commission does not find these views convincing. Whatever the effect of marginal improvements to the road network, the road programme *as a whole* must have an effect, especially in the long term, on the rail system *as a whole*. The effects of road building on location and car ownership, described in Chapter 5, may possibly be ignored in the context of individual schemes, but not at the overall, national level.

10.25 British Rail's observations are drawn from a fairly narrow range of circumstances. Different conclusions might result from more radical policies. For example, restraint on cars in towns and in vulnerable country and coastal areas, together with improvement of other modes, would diminish the popularity of car travel for inter-urban journeys; and lower prices for rail travel, in conjunction with other policy changes we have suggested, would induce some travellers to switch from road to rail.

10.26 The figure of twenty miles for the average length of the motorway sections of car journeys includes urban and suburban motorway travel, which is irrelevant to the long distance problem. It may well be true that the pattern of origins and destinations of many other car journeys is not well suited to the rail system, but this pattern should not be regarded as fixed, even in the short term. Table 10.3 shows that most car journeys of over twenty-five miles in length are made for leisure purposes. For such journeys, travellers do not first decide where to go and then how to get there; their decisions where, when and how to travel all depend on each other and are very much affected by the quality of the available travel facilities. It is true that the destinations of some leisure journeys, for example journeys to visit a particular friend or relation, can be taken as fixed. But even this holds only in the short term, since people will choose where to live partly with regard to the ease with which visitors can reach them. For example, people about to retire who might formerly have chosen to live in a resort which their children could reach by rail may now be more concerned to find a house close to the motorway. In the long term, very few destinations are fixed; travel desires develop in response to the facilities offered.

10.27 The fact that there are fewer long-distance trips (i.e. over 100 miles) by rail than by car is no reason for ignoring the impact of the road building programme on rail; nor does it mean that rail could not serve a useful proportion of those long-distance car trips for which the national road programme is intended, especially between towns.

10.28 If the railways are to compete with door to door travel, attention must be paid to the interchange between the railway and other modes of travel. Because interchange is not the direct responsibility of any one mode of travel, planning authorities should pay particular attention to it. We recommend that County Councils should ensure that proper provision is made at all railway and bus stations for interchange between all the motorised forms of transport concerned—the train, bus, taxi, hired car and private car—and should also ensure that pedestrians and cyclists are properly catered for. We recommend that County Councils should not give grants to public transport operators until they are satisfied with the interchange arrangements; and that the Department of the Environment should also satisfy itself in this respect before approving councils' transport plans or making grants to transport operators or to the County Councils.

10.29 In recent years it has been made much easier for

travellers to hire cars at railway stations. We recommend that the British Railways Board should extend these arrangements further and should itself provide cars for hire as well as enabling car-hire firms to do so. The French Railways (SNCF) already follow that policy.

10.30 European railways also make better provision for cyclists than do British Railways at present. In Britain, the charge for taking a bicycle by train is half the adult fare; this adds considerably to the cost of day trips which form the biggest potential market. The policy of the German Railways, in contrast, is to encourage the cyclist by making a very small charge for the machine and even carrying it free if one of certain types of tickets (e.g. the "roundabout") is purchased. In Upper Bavaria bicycles can be hired at the station of arrival and returned at the end of the day to one of a number of specified stations in the area. The Commission recommends that, as a first step to encourage cyclists to make greater use of the railways, British Railways should markedly reduce the present half-fare for bicycles, at least in conjunction with day return tickets.

Freight

10.31 The Department of the Environment believes that for freight as for passengers there is only a small area of competition between road and rail. Most freight movements are short, the average haul by lorries of over three tons being only 30 miles. Railways, it is said, cannot perform short hauls cheaply, especially when delivery by lorry is required at one or both ends of the rail journey. Road transport, it is said, often gives greatly superior service to the customer: shorter door-to-door journey times, less risk of pilferage, higher standards of reliability, and greater flexibility in meeting customers' special requirements. Furthermore, it is argued, even if British Railways were to increase its freight tonnage by (say) 50%, the consequent reduction in road vehicle mileage would be very small. Even after allowing for the high road capacity requirements of heavy lorries, the Department of the Environment has calculated that the reduction would be equivalent to only 1·5% of total road traffic, or six months' normal growth. Moreover, it is claimed that the transfer of goods traffic from road to rail would not substantially help the environment, because

226

collection and delivery by lorry would still be necessary and, since freight depots are often located near town centres, the environmental damage caused by lorries serving them is large.

10.32 Although the great advantages of road transport for many types of goods are undeniable, the Commission nevertheless believes that the interaction between rail and road is important and that there are some valuable gains to be made by transferring traffic from road to rail.

10.33 Road haulage may seem cheap, but its charges take no account of external costs: congestion, accidents, police costs and environmental damage. Even for internal costs, freight charges do not necessarily reflect the inherent capabilities of the two modes. We believe there are still ways in which BR should be able to reduce its labour costs and, by modernisation of its wagon fleet and automation of some wagon movement, further reduce its operating costs.

10.34 As shown in Table 10.5, the railways are still in the short haul business. Where trans-shipment costs can be averted by door to door journeys through the provision of direct access to factories and warehouses, rail transport should be able to compete in short haul work. Between 1959 and 1970 freight depots decreased from 5,786 to 646 (see Table 2.2). Additional access points, including private sidings, are required. In any case the number of road-to-road trans-shipments is increasing, thus diminishing this particular disadvantage.

Table 10.5: Length of haul of freight carried on British Railways, 1973
Units: million tons

| Type of traffic | Length of haul (miles) | | | | |
	10–25	26–50	51–100	Over 100	Total
Trainload:					
Coal: M.G.R.*	19·6	13·6	5·5	3·9	42·6
Other	18·3	11·2	4·6	4·3	38·4
Freightliner	—	—	0·4	6·0	6·4
Other traffic	15·7	12·5	18·5	17·5	64·2
Wagonload	14·4	6·5	9·9	17·9	48·7
Total	68·0	43·8	38·9	49·6	200·3

* Merry-go-round, i.e. continuous train movement without shunting.
Source: British Railways Board (based on 1973 budget estimates).

Table 10.6: Effects of a possible transfer of 100 million ton miles from road to rail

Length of road haul (miles)	Share of road traffic which might be transferred to rail	Million tons transported by road in 1971	Million tons involved in transfer	Million ton miles accounted for by road in 1971	Million ton miles involved in transfer
Under 25	Nil	1,230	Nil	12,900	Nil
25–49	Nil	245	Nil	9,100	Nil
50–99	30%	145	43·5	9,700	2,910
100–149	40%	63	25·2	8,200	3,280
150 or more	60%	52	31·2	10,500	6,300
Total		1,735	99·9	50,400	12,490

Sources: Survey of the Transport of Goods by Road, 1967–68.
Survey of the Transport of Goods by Road, 1971–72.
Notes. See notes to Table 10.4. A further assumption made for the purpose of this table is that the traffic of 100 miles or more in 1971 could be split between the 100–149 miles range and the 150 or more miles range in the same ratios as were observed in 1967/68.

10.35 The DoE calculation that the maximum likely transfer from road to rail would reduce road traffic volumes by only 1·5% rests on several questionable assumptions, including one that the average length of haul of the transferred traffic would be 75 miles. This figure was chosen because it is the average for all hauls by road of over 25 miles. Hence if 100 million tons were transferred to the railways (i.e. if the tonnage they carried increased by 50%) the ton-mileage involved would be 7,500 million. But the longer the haul, the more chance the railways have of capturing the traffic. If the railways were to capture 60% of the road traffic in the 150 miles and over range, 40% in the 100–149 miles range and 30% in the 50–99 miles range, this would amount to a total of 100 million tons but 12,490 million ton miles (see Table 10.6), which represents about a quarter of all ton miles performed by road vehicles and one third of ton miles performed by road vehicles on journeys of over twenty-five miles. A transfer of this magnitude would be of real significance.

10.36 The Commission accepts that for many types of traffic industry generally gets a better service by using road haulage (often in its own lorries) than by using the railways. For this reason we do not advocate control policies which would deprive customers of all choice. Nevertheless, it is important to see if the rail service to the freight customer can be improved. We return to this subject later in this chapter.

THE INTER-URBAN ROAD PROGRAMME

10.37 The road programme announced by Mr. Walker, then Secretary of State for the Environment, in the House of Commons on 23 June 1971 is still the basis (at the time of writing) of the present administration's plans. Mr. Walker announced the intention of completing by the early 1980s a "primary" or "strategic" continuous inter-urban network of about 3,500 miles, of which about 2,000 miles were to be motorways and the rest high-standard trunk roads. In addition, many improvements were planned to sections of other trunk roads not forming part of the primary network.

10.38 At the time of Mr. Walker's announcement, nearly 800 miles of motorway were in use. At 31 October 1973, of a planned total of 2097 miles of motorway, 1118 were in use, 282 were under construction, 316 were at the programming stage and 381 at the preparation stage.[1] Mr. Walker said that in addition to motorways there were expected to be nearly 1000 miles of all-purpose, dual-carriageway trunk roads by the end of 1972. The roads are not all new routes; many consist of existing roads up-graded.

10.39 According to the White Paper on Public Expenditure, December 1973, the cuts in Government spending announced in May 1973 and the changes in transport policy announced by Mr. Peyton in November 1973, involving more support to the railways, will have the effect of putting back the expected date of completion of the programme but not of altering the programme [1]. The effects of the further cuts in government spending announced in December 1973 and not taken into account in the White Paper will further postpone the programme, but still have not altered it.

10.40 Road programmes take a long time to formulate. Mr. Walker's programme of June 1971 closely resembled that announced by Mr. Mulley, then Minister of Transport of the Labour Government, on 27 May 1970. Mr. Mulley's programme incorporated many schemes planned much earlier. At least until 1971, there was no significant difference in the thinking of the two main parties on inter-urban roads. We have therefore looked at the reasons advanced over the years for building inter-urban roads, and not only at those of the recent Conservative Government, or the present administration.

10.41 The prime reason has been *to serve economic growth and to maintain our competitive position in the world*. As stated by Mr. G. R. Strauss, Labour MP for Vauxhall:

"Every Hon. Member must agree that our present road system is hopelessly inadequate and if allowed to grow worse or even to continue as it is will gravely threaten the nation's welfare. It does not need statistics to prove that our economy is being damaged by the present inadequacy of our roads. It is plain to anyone who drives on a route frequented by heavy industrial traffic" (*Hansard*, 22 July 1957).

[1] Information supplied by the British Road Federation.

Mr. Harold Watkinson, then Minister of Transport and Civil Aviation, said on the same occasion:

"The more quickly they (the civil engineering industry) get on with it (road building) the better I shall be pleased and the more economic benefit shall we get at a time when we shall need it very greatly—over the next few years when our competitive power in the world will, perhaps, be the one thing which stands between us and complete and utter disaster."

Again, in the Green Paper *Roads for the Future*, HMSO 1969 (para. 3(1)):

"The establishment of a much needed basic network of high quality routes—mostly motorways—(will) provide the vital access between regions and between the major cities."

Mr. Peter Walker, then Secretary of State for the Environment, repeated the call:

"To complete by the early 1980s a comprehensive network of strategic trunk routes to promote economic growth."

10.42 It is implicit in these statements that the lack of good communications is or may shortly become a crippling handicap to industry and that roads are required rather than any other facilities. These suggestions do not appear to be based on any analysis of the problems of industry; at any rate, no such analysis appears in the documents. We have suggested above that a substantial amount of goods traffic could go by rail; so, if there is a problem of the dimensions suggested, or even a smaller problem, rail should be considered as one of the alternatives. The economic evaluation of individual road schemes in the last three years suggests that the proportion of the total benefit accounted for by work travel (i.e. heavy lorries, other commercial vehicles, and personal trips made on business) usually lies within the range 25–50%. This suggests that a smaller programme, especially if coupled with some form of restraint on less essential traffic, might be adequate to serve the needs of industry; its extent would depend on the peaking characteristics of the essential traffic.

10.43 The second reason for the roads programme is *to eliminate or reduce congestion and to meet future demand*. As stated in the White Paper, *Roads for the Future*, 1970:

"The aim is to provide a comprehensive national system of trunk roads on which commercial traffic and private cars can move freely and safely and on which congestion and the frustration and economic costs it creates will have been virtually eliminated . . .

"For many years traffic has been rising faster than the provision of new road capacity to meet it. But the continuing expansion of the effort on road building, and the forecast of some slackening in the rate of growth of traffic in the late 1970s and 1980s, does now offer the possibility of first checking and then progressively eliminating the congestion on our trunk road system. It is this possibility that the Government plans to turn into a reality."

According to Mr. Mulley (*Hansard*, 27 May 1970):

"This programme will enable us to plan and provide a primary network serving all main centres of population and, by the end of the period (i.e. by 1985 or 1990), to eliminate serious congestion on all inter-urban roads, despite the continuing rapid growth of traffic."

Mr. Peter Walker added, in June 1971:

"The total number of vehicles on the roads is expected to rise from 15 million at present to about 22 million by 1980. The plans I have announced today are designed to meet this challenge."

These figures were revised in the White Paper *Public Expenditure to 1976–77*, HMSO, December 1972:

"The number of road vehicles in Great Britain is expected to increase from some 15½ million to over 20 million by 1980. That is the background against which the programme for new construction and improvement of roads has to be set. Without an expanding programme, there would inevitably be greater congestion and delay on the roads and, for many places, increasing damage to the environment."

10.44 Relief of congestion is the basic inspiration of the national roads programme. In the Commission's view there are three weaknesses in this approach. First, the traditional philosophy, as we have noted, has been to predict and provide for the free demand for road space. In Chapter 7 we pointed out that although this might have been understandable in former days, it would not do in modern conditions, when the costs run into thousands of millions of pounds, to say nothing of the other consequences. Secondly, as also stated in Chapter 7, factors producing the demand for road transport have been over-estimated. Hence the traffic "needs" are exaggerated. Thirdly, on the other hand, there is a tendency for new roads to generate new traffic of marginal value, which is likely to cause local congestion, especially on the approaches to large towns.

10.45 Another reason given for the roads programme is *to serve ports and assist exporters*. Mr. Alfred Barnes, then Minister of Transport, said in 1947:

> "I propose to direct such resources as may be at my disposal to the following purposes: . . . improvements to assist development areas in particular and industrial development generally, including better access to ports and markets." (*Hansard*, 6 May 1947.)

And Mr. Peter Walker in June 1971 claimed the need

> "to design the network so that it serves all major ports and airports, including the new Third London Airport at Foulness."

Mr. John Peyton, Minister for Transport Industries, repeated the point on 30 April 1973:

> "The road system is still far from adequate for our needs. We still lack, in many instances, proper means of access to the ports . . ."

10.46 If the problem is seen as how to find ways of facilitating Britain's international trade, and our exports in particular, improvements to the trunk road system should not figure prominently on the list of likely measures. Such was the judgment of the Chairman of the National Ports Council, speaking at the Royal Society of Arts on 5 February 1969. The haul to the ports accounts for only a small proportion of the costs or transit time of exports, even exports to Europe. Improvements in the ports themselves, or on those roads immediately adjacent to them, provide more scope for improvement and are likely to be more cost effective.

10.47 Port traffic is one of the elements of the industrial traffic discussed in paragraphs 10.31 and 10.32. But it must be a small element on most roads. The proportion of the total benefit from inter-urban road schemes which is accounted for by heavy lorries usually falls in the range 5–20%; only a fraction of this will be port traffic. So even if there were no other ways of facilitating port traffic, it would scarcely justify much expenditure on road building.

10.48 Longer port hauls could be carried by rail more than most goods traffic, since the flows are concentrated at one end of the journey at least. It is also particularly advantageous to the community that heavy consignments should go by rail, since they are among the largest and most awkward loads on the road.

10.49 Yet another reason given for the roads programme is *to provide assistance to development areas*. Thus Mr. Alfred Barnes, in May 1947:

"I propose to direct such resources as may be at my disposal to the following purposes ... improvements to assist development areas in particular and industrial development generally ... the redevelopment of devastated areas."

The Green Paper, *Roads for the Future*, 1969, stated:

"A national highway strategy must be considered in the light of the important contribution it can make to national and regional economic growth. Wherever major routes are built they provide an economic stimulus to the areas through which they pass and to those distant areas brought into closer contact with the nation's main economic centres ... In particular, roads can substantially reinforce the major measures which the Government are already taking to ensure a better balance of economic development throughout the country."

Mr. Peter Walker said in June 1971:

"The proposals are also designed to cater for the needs of the less prosperous regions. These areas of special concern will benefit both from the new roads within their boundaries and from the whole of the new network. By the early 1980s high quality roads will link all the major industrial centres in the development areas to the primary network."

10.50 The effect that new roads have on solving the problems of depressed areas is variable. New industries need adequate roads, but new roads could expose weak industries to still greater competition from outside. Other measures of regional planning, particularly grants and development permits, help depressed regions more directly and with less risk of unfortunate side-effects. Where transport investment does appear to be essential, needs should be considered as a whole, embracing all modes of transport. A case in point is the current development of the Scottish oil industry. It is argued in Appendix 8 that the lack of a single department capable of looking at Scottish transport needs as a whole has led to a mistaken concentration on road building.

10.51 *Road safety* has always been one of the aims of road planning. It was the first objective mentioned by Alfred Barnes when introducing his plan in 1947. He proposed that a programme of tackling "black spots" on the roads should go ahead concurrently with a programme of new road building; the new roads themselves were not designed to reduce accidents except where towns would be bypassed. Mr. Strauss in his speech in 1957 (referred to above) explicitly claimed that a main reason for building motorways was that they reduced the number of road accidents. Mr. Mulley, introducing the Labour Government's inter-urban road programme in Parliament on 27 May 1970, made only a passing reference to safety, and Mr. Walker did not include safety among his six aims for the programme in June 1971. More recently, however, Mr. Keith Speed, Under-Secretary of State for the Environment, said:

"It is worth emphasising that, for all the publicity given to serious accidents on them, motorways are by far the safest roads we have. Thus, while carrying over 5 per cent

235

of traffic, only 2·7 per cent of deaths, 1·3 per cent of serious injuries and 1 per cent of slight injuries, occur in road accidents on them." (*Hansard*, 14 May 1973.)

10.52 It is demonstrable from the statistics that motorways are safer than other roads, measured in casualties per hundred million vehicle miles; but this is the wrong comparison. The right comparison is between the estimated number of casualties on the road network as a whole with and without motorways. The motorways generate additional vehicle-miles and also affect traffic on other roads. It is difficult to assess these effects. How much traffic is actually created by a motorway? What is the precise effect on safety on other roads? What kind of drivers tend to use motorways most? A motorway may reduce the traffic on other roads, at least for a time, but there may be offsetting effects such as faster speeds on the relieved roads or failure by drivers to adjust to non-motorway conditions after leaving a motorway. The official publication *Road Accidents in Great Britain 1971* [2] is cautious about the effect of motorways: "It is not possible to assess precisely the contribution of motorways to road safety, since the traffic using them is partly diverted from other roads and partly newly generated traffic."

10.53 If motorways do lead to fewer casualties, this is a welcome benefit, but it does not follow that they (or other new roads) are good value for money in road safety terms. They are not. There are many other safety measures that could be introduced with great effect at relatively little cost.

10.54 Another reason given for the roads programme is *to provide local relief and environmental improvement*, particularly to towns through which major routes now pass. This argument has a long history, but it has not always meant the same thing. Alfred Barnes's statement, quoted below, is one of the few that refer to pedestrians and cyclists, but does not refer explicitly to any other form of environmental relief. The Green and White Papers, *Roads for the Future*, mention environmental improvement only in passing. Mr. Mulley's statement of May 1970 does not mention environmental improvement as one of the reasons for the inter-urban road plan. Mr. Walker's statement of June 1971 gave pride of place to environmental improvement, and this argument has figured prominently ever since.

Mr. Alfred Barnes said:

"If Parliament sees fit to grant the necessary powers, it would be my intention to start on a further number of motor roads where that course is found to be preferable to the widening or by-passing of the existing roads. The latter, freed from fast-moving through traffic, would then remain available for pedestrians, cyclists and local motor traffic, which would use them in greater comfort and security." (*Hansard*, 6 May 1947.)

The White Paper, *Roads for the Future*, 1970, stated:

"In selecting routes for new and improved roads full account will be taken of environmental and amenity questions including the conservation of historic areas. New roads do improve the total environment although, inevitably, amenity is reduced in some areas and for some people. The aim will be to safeguard and, indeed, to enhance both amenity and environment to the maximum possible extent."

Mr. Peter Walker said in June 1971:

"In selecting these schemes (for inter-urban roads), which are listed below, I have had in mind the totality of my responsibilities for the environment and in particular the following six aims:
    1. to achieve environmental improvements by diverting long-distance traffic, and particularly heavy goods vehicles, from a large number of towns and villages, so as to relieve them of the noise, dirt and danger which they suffer at present.

. . . .

    6. to relieve as many historic towns as possible of through trunk traffic."

10.55 To bring environmental relief to towns is important. It is a benefit not included in economic rates of return as calculated at present. But this argument cannot be used to justify the national programme and should be treated with great caution in the context of any particular scheme.
10.56 It is first necessary to consider how much relief would in fact come about. The extent to which environmental

problems in towns are caused by through traffic varies considerably, and new motorways or trunk roads will not necessarily remove all the through traffic. The growth of local traffic, which the removal of through traffic will itself stimulate, will reduce some of the relief gained; it would again be necessary to consider in each individual town how serious this effect might be. Secondly, where the environmental relief to towns near the route would be substantial, the environmental harm which all new roads do must also be considered. New roads damage the countryside through which they pass and by encouraging traffic growth they contribute to the environmental problems of the places to which the traffic is destined, whether these are towns, coast or countryside. Thirdly, it is necessary to consider other possible ways of bringing the same relief. Mr. Walker's statement just quoted referred particularly to long distance heavy goods vehicles. We have already shown that a reasonable transfer of freight to rail would bring about a significant reduction in such traffic and we discuss below the means by which this transfer could be achieved. Where road building would be desirable as a way of bringing relief to towns and villages, a by-pass or series of by-passes may be more effective than new motorways or trunk roads. It is usually possible to locate by-passes so as to attract more of the through traffic than would take some other trunk road. They are unlikely to generate so much traffic and they may well do less harm to the countryside through which they pass, although they can create an awkward barrier between towns and their immediate hinterland.

10.57 The Commission does not dispute that road building to relieve towns of through traffic may sometimes be appropriate, and accepts that new trunk roads may sometimes be more suitable than by-passes. But each scheme would have to be justified individually: there are no grounds for the confident generalisation of the White Paper that "new roads do improve the total environment."

10.58 Finally, the roads programme is intended *to connect important centres of population*. According to the White Paper on *Roads for the Future* (1970).

"The strategy has three main elements—
(a) to concentrate a substantial part of resources for

238

new road construction on the comprehensive improvement of a national network of trunk routes to which all important centres of population—existing and projected—would, or could easily, be connected."

Mr. Peter Walker, June 1971, stated the objective:

"to ensure that every major city and town with a population of more than 250,000 will be directly connected to the strategic network and that all with a population of 80,000 will be within about 10 miles of it."

10.59 It is a truism that good communications are essential to a developed society. It is also a laudable aim that no city or major town should be far from access to a national network; but it does not automatically follow that the present motorways, dual carriage trunk roads and railways are inadequate for the purpose and that a new strategic network must be created. The argument really comes back to capacity, which we have already considered.

10.60 The documents on which the above discussion is based contain little or no reference to several important points which ought to be considered before the road programme is accepted. Little is said about the purposes of the car journeys likely to be made on the new roads or the sort of journeys likely to be stimulated by them. The impression is given that roads are primarily required for purposes of work or transport of goods. It appears from Table 10.1, however, that work trips are relatively small in number and importance. Most long-distance car journeys are for holiday, recreational and social purposes. Of course, those purposes are important: they contribute to people's welfare, just as does the possession of material goods. But it is doubtful whether in the longer term it is desirable to *encourage* people to make longer leisure journeys than they need, or to make them by car. Commuting is not a major cause of long-distance car travel at present, but it is another type of journey which the provision of a fast inter-urban road system will stimulate, with long-term consequences of very doubtful advantage. It is also questionable whether society is justified in devoting large resources to these ends while so many people live in bad housing conditions and in squalid and depressing surroundings.

239

10.61 The problems which long-distance traffic causes at each end of the journey are also scarcely mentioned. In London, one of the reasons given for the proposed urban motorways was to accommodate traffic coming off the inter-urban network. The force of this argument is open to question, but the fact that it was used illustrates the need to think of the urban problems caused by building inter-urban roads. Similarly, if the inter-urban road network generates an influx of traffic into certain holiday areas, this too should be taken into account when planning the network.

10.62 Although it is incidental to their purposes, motorways also induce a lot of local travel; this is evidenced by the fact that the average distance travelled on motorways is only 20 miles, which means of course that many journeys are much shorter than that. It is hard to see how this local generation can be prevented. It may have serious consequences for congestion, the environment, the viability of urban public transport services, and urban form.

10.63 Six-lane, dual-carriageway motorways and trunk roads form permanent, divisive barriers in the countryside through which they pass. Farms which are fragmented are paid compensation but communities are divided and social intercourse may no longer take place as formerly. Perhaps the least studied and most destructive effect is on the normal pathways of wildlife through the countryside. To a certain extent, as cosmetic treatment of motorways begins to appear, wildlife may adapt itself; but the casualties will still be great and the biological effect on the variety of the infrastructure of the countryside is permanently at risk. This is a matter which can probably not be treated in any cost-benefit analysis but it is nonetheless of great importance to the balance and variety of country life, both human and animal.

10.64 Finally, it should be noted that the inter-urban road programme as a whole has never been subjected to any economic appraisal (notwithstanding the hopes held out in paragraph 19 of the Green Paper *Roads for the Future*). Methods have been developed to assess individual sections of it, which (on the basis of traffic predictions that we have criticised) often show very favourable rates of return in terms of benefits to road users. But it cannot be argued from this that the network as a whole is justified, since neither the short nor the long-term effects of building the entire network are taken into account. The methods are only of value on the assumption that the underlying strategy of providing a new or much developed inter-urban road system is sound. They can then be used to check the validity of a particular scheme within this strategy or to compare alternative ways of achieving similar ends.

Conclusion on the road programme

10.65 The Commission draws the following conclusion from the preceding arguments:

(i) It has not been shown that the benefits expected from the inter-urban road network, if they all came about, would justify the expenditure involved, even if there were no other ways of achieving them.

(ii) It is doubtful whether some of the benefits would in fact be achieved; and there are alternative ways of achieving them which might be both surer and simpler.

(iii) Many of the problems associated with the programme, especially the less immediate effects, have not been recognised.

(iv) Too much emphasis is given to the concept of a strategic or primary road network, especially now that the main cities have been linked. It is more important that the remaining schemes should be assessed in a regional context than as part of a national road network.

10.66 The Commission believes that, because of the expense involved in the programme and its profound and irreversible character, the burden of proof must lie with its proponents, and that this burden has not been discharged. We therefore recommend that the national motorway and trunk road programme should be reappraised in the light of the arguments set out above. In the reappraisal, roads which now form part of the national programme (including bypasses) should be considered as only one of the possible means of solving particular local or regional problems. They should be compared with alternative schemes, including more modest road schemes, rail improvements and subsidies, and regional planning measures. In this comparison, the changes in transport policy which we have recommended elsewhere in this report, and their likely effect in reducing traffic volumes, should be taken into account. All proposals should be assessed on the basis of revised methods of prediction.

RAIL PLANS

10.67 The British Railways Board's most recent proposals are contained in the document *The Board's Review of Railway Policy* published in June 1973 [3]. The Government has not finally pronounced on the ideas put forward, so they cannot yet be taken as firm plans. The Board assumes that, although support will be necessary, most railway operations will have to be justified commercially as at present. In assessing its proposals, we have tried to consider whether they are sound in the context of the Board's commercial remit, and to what extent they would have to be altered if different criteria were applied on account of the wider economic, environmental and social considerations. 10.68 The Board's proposals are put forward as commercially sound, but it should be explained what this means. It does not mean that the proposals would make the railways financially self-supporting, even with the continuation of present grants for unremunerative but socially desirable services. Some support will be necessary for the railway system in any case; but, given that support, it is claimed that each of the Board's proposals is profitable in its own right and would help to reduce the total deficit. 10.69 The Commission's assessment has not gone into great detail. We have not, for example, been able to check any of the Board's estimates of costs, traffic, revenues, etc. We have only been able to question the Board on some major issues. Understandably, even the Board cannot say exactly how its proposals might be affected by a change in its remit. 10.70 The Board's proposed investment expenditure between 1972 and 1981 amounts to £1,787 million. The breakdown between the purely commercial services and the grant-aided services and between passenger, freight and shared facilities is shown in Table 10.7. The greater part of the expenditure on shared facilities is necessitated by improvements to the passenger services. 10.71 The commercial passenger services are almost the same as the Inter-City services, the development of which is the main theme of British Rail's passenger strategy. The

242

Table 10.7: Proposed railway investment 1972–1981
Unit: £ million

	Commercial services	Grant-aided services London and south east	Passenger transport executives	Other	Total
Passenger	284	203	92	3	582
Freight and parcels	71	—	—	—	71
Systems and operations	705	250	93	45	1093
Office services, computers etc.	40	1	—	—	41
Total	1100	454	185	48	1787

Source: British Railways Board's Review of Railway Policy, June 1973.

Note: Owing to a delay in the planned introduction of the High Speed Diesel Train and the Advanced Passenger Train, these figures and those in Table 10.8 are likely to be reduced.

introduction of the High Speed Diesel Train and later the Advanced Passenger Train, together with other improvements, is expected to produce an increase on Inter-City services of some 50% in passenger miles and over 100% in (real) receipts compared with 1971. Passenger miles and receipts are also expected to increase in London and the South East and in the other conurbations. Table 10.8 shows the expected position.

10.72 On freight services, the Board expected a slight fall in both tonnage and receipts between 1971 and 1981, mainly

Table 10.8: Passenger miles and receipts in 1971 and 1981

	Passenger miles (thousand million)		Receipts (£m at 1972 prices)	
	1971	1981	1971	1981
Inter-City	7·6	11·4	115	240
London and south east	8·4	9·9	114	146
Passenger transport executives	1·4	2·0	16	26
Other grant-aided	1·3	1·2	16	15
Total	18·7	24·5	261	427

Source: British Railways Board Review of Railway Policy, June 1973.

because of the fall in the tonnage of coal carried, which reflected their expected decline in the use of coal. This decline would mask an expected increase in the tonnage of other commodities. The Board has deliberately made a conservative forecast, within the terms of a purely commercial remit, in order to avoid the charge of over-optimism. Tables 10.9 and 10.10 show the Board's forecast.

Table 10.9: Freight tonnage and receipts in 1971 and 1981

How carried	Year 1971 million tons	1981 million tons
Freightliner	5	11
Other train load	121	156
Wagon load	69	24
Total	195	191
Total receipts (1972 price levels)	£202 million	£185 million

Table 10.10: Freight tonnage by commodity, 1971 and 1981
Unit: million tons

Commodity	Year 1971	1981
Coal and coke	107·5	76·0
Iron and steel products	12·3	14·3
Iron and steel raw materials	21·1	25·4
Earths and stones	14·0	18·1
Chemicals	4·1	6·3
Building materials	4·6	5·5
Petroleum products	19·2	27·8
Freightliner Ltd.	5·0	10·6
Other traffics	7·5	7·2
Total	195·3	191·2

Assessment of passenger plans

10.73 From a purely commercial point of view, the Commission was concerned whether passengers would be willing to pay the fare increases apparently required for the sake of faster trains, and, even if they would, whether a more modest investment programme might not be preferable.

British Railways Board pointed out, first, that the increase in fares will be less than is suggested by the fact that passenger receipts are expected to rise faster, in real terms, than passenger mileage. There will be some increase in fares, but the difference is also explained by a bigger growth of traffic on routes where fares are relatively high than on other routes, and also more growth in first-class than in second-class travel. Experience in this country and abroad suggests that passengers are prepared to pay quite a lot for faster travel times. British Rail usually adjusts its predictions downwards before using them, in order to be on the safe side in appraising an investment. Its investment plans are predicted to show a profit on each successive step in the programme; this suggests that a smaller programme would have been wrong. It should be noted that the costs of providing high speed trains are largely offset by the increase in track capacity which arises from their use.

10.74 Although the Commission is not in a position to pass judgement on these matters, it is satisfied that they have been carefully considered with the aid of sophisticated predictive techniques. Socially, the high cost of long-distance rail travel is disturbing, since some people may be deterred from travel altogether and others, who might prefer rail if it were cheaper, may be diverted to cars. The Board pointed to the very substantial reductions for off-peak travel, which on some routes amount to 40% of the regular fare. It agreed that a different approach to long-distance travel as a whole might lead to a different policy for rail fares, but this would not affect the proposals to improve quality and speed.

10.75 The Commission would wish to see added to British Railways Board's appraisal an equally sophisticated analysis of the effect of all the proposals on the overall accessibility of the railway system to people in all socio-economic groups (including implications for fares and the diversion of investment from the secondary and suburban routes, etc.) and of the overall effect of the proposals on the system's usefulness for the less spectacular basic needs of moving people and goods for everyday purposes, including any operational difficulties the Advanced Passenger Train might cause for traffic on lower speed bands.

10.76 The Commission also considered the possibility of operational conflict between the proposed new passenger services and other services which might be operated if the Board's terms of reference were changed. If the railways were expected to run more freight trains and more slow passenger services, in order to meet more local travel needs, problems of capacity might arise, but according to the Board these would not necessarily require the provision of new track. The extent of the problems and the costs of possible solutions would, of course, depend on the scale of new services and the timing of their introduction.

10.77 Better long-distance rail services tend to generate new traffic rather than attract traffic from the roads, and this raises some doubt about their social desirability. The implication is that people are going to distant cities to satisfy certain purposes such as shopping, entertainment, professional advice and so on which would otherwise have been satisfied (to some extent) locally. For the travellers themselves, in the short term, this is a benefit, since it extends their range and quality of their choice. But in the longer term the effect may be unfortunate if it reinforces the position of the bigger cities, and of London in particular, as the hub of the rail system, and inhibits the development of comparable facilities elsewhere. No one is in a position to assess how big a danger this is. The contrary position could be argued, that faster services to London and other big cities reduce the disinclination of business firms or their staff to set up in development areas. In the Commission's view, this possible danger is not a reason to reject BR's Inter-City strategy, but it may be a reason to improve the links between cities other than London before improving connections with London.

10.78 In conclusion, therefore, the Commission has not been able to make a full appraisal of BR's proposals for long-distance passenger travel. The Department of the Environment will clearly satisfy itself that BR's costings are accurate and its predictions sound. In the Commission's view, two of the other points discussed above should also be considered before approval is given:

(i) the extent of any capacity problems which would arise if these plans were pursued concurrently with plans designed to increase other passenger and freight traffic, and the costs of dealing with such problems;

(ii) the possibility and desirability of modifying BR's

plans so that priority is given to services not involving London.

Concerning (i) the Commission would not wish to see APT given priority over measures, considered below, for winning freight back on to the railways. Subject to satisfactory answers to all these points, we recommend that BR's proposals be approved.

Assessment of freight plans

10.79 The British Railways Board's forecast of a decline in the amount of freight carried by rail is disappointing, even allowing for a decline in coal and the fact that the Board has deliberately pitched its estimate on the cautious side. The Board maintains that so long as it is obliged to treat freight as a purely commercial business, substantially different estimates would be unrealistic. We have already referred to the fact that BR's service to customers appears to be less good than it should be. Reliability and customer contact are the most important elements of service: local traffic offices should be in much closer contact with customers, and should play a more prominent part in securing traffic and in bridging the gap between customer and the BR senior management.

10.80 The Commission would like to see a firmer policy towards increasing freight traffic. An important factor in the decline witnessed in the past ten years or so has been the continuing uncertainty as to whether the remit from the Ministry of Transport required BR to retain or discard certain types of traffic; this led to further uncertainty on costings and commercial policy, and caused discouragement at local level. As a result, freight has been turned away which could have been carried by rail. The Commission believes that positive policies to increase freight traffic, coupled with some subsidy, would dispel this particular trouble. We do not doubt that a large increase in freight requires something more than commercial policies; hence our subsidy proposal. But it would be unwise to advocate subsidy without itemising areas where improvements could reduce costs and increase traffic. Further, attention should be paid to types of traffic suitable for rail carriage (for a variety of reasons), substantial volumes of which are carried by road. Social, environmental and some economic advantages could be expected if these traffics were transferred to the railways.

10.81 There is no doubt that for general traffic road transport provides a better service than do the railways. However, there may be ways in which rail service to freight customers can be improved. For example, a new branch of management science known as "Physical Distribution Management" (PDM) could assist BR. Many manufacturers are becoming more aware of the importance of distribution, and they recognise that the "unit of product" in distribution is the total journey of a consignment and not simply that part of the journey which belongs to one mode of transport. In international traffic the combined transport operator manages the traffic for the customer throughout the whole journey, whatever the mode of transport; he offers the total journey of the consignment as the "unit of product". In a sense the railways have treated it as such in the past through their road collection and delivery services. They could, however, exercise closer control of consignments through professionals in PDM.

10.82 The road haulage industry has flexibility in providing a door-to-door service without trans-shipment, which increases cost and reduces performance. But many firms are rationalising distribution with larger depots to obtain larger trunk hauls; and this increases the amount of trans-shipment. If trans-shipment is economic in this context, the railways could gain a share in this market with trunk hauls by rail and local hauls by road. This would require initiative by BR so that, when firms have decided where to locate a depot, a site is chosen which can be served by rail.

10.83 The marine container and the freightliner container have permitted a smoother and more reliable transfer at trans-shipment points, usually at reduced cost. The freightliner system was conceived as a highly rationalised system, with high throughput on a limited number of routes and using a gantry loading system which is expensive in capital but cheap to operate at high throughput. The inability of the Freightliner Company to capture an economic share of the medium-haul market suggests that more access points are needed. These may require cheaper loading systems, like side-loaders or even the piggy-back system using low loader (small wheel) trailers and rail flat wagons.

248

10.84 BR's market for passenger and freight traffic will be enlarged if the Channel Tunnel is built and their plans for through trains are permitted. In contrast to traffic from Asia, Australasia and the Atlantic, the European freight traffic is generated in comparatively small amounts and is preponderantly road traffic. The Channel Tunnel will be well placed for markets in Eastern France, Southern Belgium, Switzerland and Northern Italy. A large part of that traffic could be carried direct through the Tunnel without trans-shipment.

10.85 Although there is a substantial volume of freight traffic which, on general economic, social and environmental grounds, should be transferred to rail, it is only possible to present a case in general terms. There ought to be detailed calculations of the differences in road maintenance costs, traffic congestion, accidents, noise and other environmental intrusion, as well as the more obvious resource costs which are reflected in the charges made by road hauliers and the railways, if some of the more obvious goods flows were transferred from road to rail. But no such exercise has ever been done, and the Commission lacked the resources to undertake it itself. Our calculation in lieu of such an exercise must necessarily be only approximate.

10.86 The traffics which should be considered first for transfer are the longer-distance road traffic and those commodities which lend themselves physically to rail handling. The railways should first aim to obtain traffic with a haul of over 300 miles, then traffic in the 250–300 miles range, then the 200–250 miles, and so on. It would probably be found that a declining proportion of traffic could reasonably be transferred down to a haul of somewhere around 150 miles.

10.87 In *A Study of the Relative True Costs of Rail and Road Transport over Trunk Routes*, published in 1964, the British Railways Board found that true costs by rail become cheaper than by road at around 150 miles. A study by independent consultants reached the same conclusion in respect of traffic in East Africa. Recently, the Swedish Government has decided that, through the licensing system, heavy freight traffic with a haul of over 160 miles should gradually be transferred from road to rail. The aim is to reduce accidents, pollution, congestion and the expenditure on roads. It is reasonable to infer that the future maximum haul by road in Sweden has been fixed at the point where true costs by rail become lower than by road. As fuel constitutes a higher fraction of costs by road, recent rises in fuel prices (with more increases to come) will reduce the distance at which rail costs should be less than road costs. It so happens that the 1967/68 *Survey of the Transport of Goods by Road* gives a break-down of the length of haul by road only up to 150 miles. As shown in Table 10.6 above, if a modest 60% of the traffic moving over 150 miles were transferred to rail, this would add 6,300 million ton-miles or 39% of the present total rail freight, even on the conservative assumption that the transferred tonnage was drawn equally from all goods travelling more than that distance instead of being drawn principally from the longer hauls.

10.88 An important class of traffic which should where practicable be transferred to rail—almost irrespective of distance—is the substantial volume of bulk liquids, powders and granular or similar material which can be loaded and unloaded by gravity or by mechanical means. These can usually be carried most economically in tank cars or similar specially designed vehicles. The aim should be to obtain train loads where possible, but wagon-load traffic (and wagons can have a capacity in the 65 to 70 tons range) should also be transferred. Most of this traffic will originate and end on the rail system (suitably adjusted). If one end of the journey is not on the rail system, transfer can often be made economically direct from or to rail by handling equipment used in the particular industry. Each traffic flow requires detailed examination to decide on the best transit arrangements.

10.89 We suggest that a reasonable target for the first five years would be to increase the present ton mileage on the railways by 50% by transferring some road traffic. This should not strain railway capacity and it would give time for customers and hauliers, as well as BR, to adapt.

Rail subsidies

10.90 The British Railways Board has argued, and the Government has now accepted, that there is no commercially viable railway system, that is to say, a system that would require no subsidies. The Commission's argument is rather different. It holds that, since there is no fully developed charging system which takes account of all the costs involved in journeys by all modes, subsidies are necessary to achieve the best solution for transport problems taken as a whole. The only question therefore is the right form and size of subsidies.

10.91 Subsidies should be in a form which is simple to understand and operate, easy to extend or adapt in the light of experience, providing an incentive to management to be efficient, and likely to produce the most desirable results from the point of view of the community as a whole.

10.92 The form of subsidy we recommend is that BR should be paid a given amount for each passenger mile above a specified minimum and a given amount for each ton mile above a specified minimum. The subsidy could begin by being a blanket subsidy (i.e. non-selective between types of traffic), so as to achieve simplicity of administration and thus make immediate implementation possible. It could later become more selective in order to encourage particular routes and/or particular traffics, e.g. traffic to development areas or wagon-load traffic between rail-connected premises. The levels at which the minima were set, the rate per passenger and per ton mile and the nature and degree of selectivity would be subject to periodic review.

10.93 The size of the subsidy should be determined in the light of a fairly detailed study of the kind mentioned in para. 10.85. In the absence of such a study, our recommendations can only be tentative. We propose that for passenger traffic the subsidy should initially be 0·5p for each passenger mile above a floor of 18 thousand million, and for freight 0·5p for each ton mile above a floor of 15 thousand million.[1] In 1971 the number of passenger miles on British Rail was 18·7 thousand million; on this total the amount of subsidy paid would have been £3·5 million compared with passenger receipts of £261 million. However, if this subsidy had been in force it is likely that a much greater effort would have been made to attract passengers. The average fare paid per passenger mile in 1971 was 1·38 pence. Without the subsidy, an increase of 5% of passenger miles, i.e. an increase of 935 million passenger miles, would have increased revenue by some £12·9 million. But with the subsidy, the increase in revenue from the same increase in passenger miles would have been some £17·6 million. Similarly, the

[1] See Note of Reservation on p. 279f.

amount of subsidy paid on the ton miles of freight achieved in 1971, 15·9 thousand million ton miles, would have been £4·5 million, as compared with receipts of £194 million. Receipts per ton mile average about 1·34 pence. A target of 50% additional freight traffic would, if achieved, produce additional revenue of £106·5 million without subsidy; with a subsidy of 0·5p per additional ton mile the additional revenue would be £146·25 million.

10·94 The payment of these subsidies would itself ease the situation on some of the more marginal passenger services. But in addition the scheme whereby local authorities could pay British Rail the shortfall (correctly calculated) for keeping open otherwise unremunerative services should continue, as suggested in para. 9.22 above.

Government control of British Rail

10.95 One of the causes of the unhappy state of the railways since nationalisation has been the uneasy relationship that has existed between the British Railways Board and the Ministry of Transport or the Department of the Environment. To some extent, this has been due to uncertainty on both sides about the role which the railways should play and the support it was legitimate and appropriate for them to expect. These points are now being clarified, and we hope that our report assists the process of clarification. But another problem has been that government appears to have been content to meet each successive crisis as it came, while between crises the responsible Minister appears to have taken little interest in the progress (or otherwise) of the railways. This was never satisfactory, and certainly the situation must be changed if the railways are to run on a permanently subsidised basis. Some much more continuous form of supervision is required. This is not a role that the civil service normally fills, and because of changes in staff and lack of practical experience in transport operations it is unlikely that the civil service would be well suited to it. We put forward the following proposals as the basis of a possible system.

10.96 We recommend that the Government should propose attainable but difficult targets for BR to achieve in terms of traffic carried, revenue earned and expenditure. These would be discussed and agreed (after modification if necessary) with the Board, and would be the basis of its planning over the period for which targets were set (say five years). We recommend that a small but skilled management audit team (directly responsible to the Chairman and quite independent of the executive staff) should be appointed to review, at regular intervals, progress in the various activities and in particular to examine productivity, utilisation of equipment and results of capital expenditure. The Chairman would submit reports on these subjects to the Minister. In this way it should be possible to ensure that difficulties could be resolved before crisis point was reached.

HEAVY LORRIES

10.97 The increasing numbers of heavy, and yet heavier, lorries on the roads causes great public disquiet. The small lorries have declined in number absolutely while the large lorries, above 5 tons and especially above 8 tons, have grown in number dramatically in the last decade, as shown in Table 10.11.

Table 10.11: Number of commercial vehicles by unladen weight

Unladen weight	1961 ('000s)	1971 ('000s)	% change
Not over 1½ tons	793	941	+19
1½ tons not over 2 tons	84	65	−23
2 tons not over 3 tons	246	124	−50
3 tons not over 5 tons	212	221	+4
5 tons not over 8 tons	47	139	+195
Over 8 tons	13	65	+400

Source: Highway Statistics 1971, Table 6. Percentages added.

10.98 It would be unrealistic to think that we could live without the heavy lorry; nor would the environment be better served in some important ways, such as fuel economy and relief of congestion, if all the large lorries were replaced by small ones, of which many more would be needed. A sound policy for reconciling the heavy lorry with the environment must rest on route segregation and the design of an *amenity lorry*, i.e. one acceptable in environmental terms. Some of the problems have been discussed in Chapter 8 on urban transport. In this chapter there are three issues to be considered, of particular relevance to the inter-urban problem:

(i) the extent, if any, to which even heavier vehicles than are now accepted should be permitted;

(ii) the extent to which the use of heavy vehicles should be restricted;

(iii) the adequacy of the taxes imposed on heavy vehicles.

Constraints at these points would assist rail freight and further the policies which we have already advocated. But no massive transfer of traffic could be expected from them: their prime importance is the direct effect they would have on the environment.

10.99 The maximum permitted gross weight of a lorry is at present 30 tons for a rigid lorry and 32 tons for an articulated lorry, with respectively $9\frac{1}{2}$ and 10 ton axle loadings. "The Six" in the EEC agreed in 1972 to harmonise lorry characteristics by 1980, working to an 11 metric ton (10·826 English tons) axle loading and a 40 metric ton gross vehicle weight. However, the British Government is firm in its intention to retain a maximum 10 ton axle loading. Axle loading is important to any consideration of increasing lorry weights. Some important tests were carried out in the United States by the American Association of State Highway Officers (AASHO) to discover the relationship between axle loads and road maintenance and construction costs. On the basis of their findings, the extra 0·826 of a ton requested by "The Six" would increase wear, lorry for lorry, by 38% and construction costs to cater for the heavier lorry would be increased by 5%. The question is certainly complicated, for there is a body of opinion in Europe which regards the increase in wear under European conditions as 27%. The DoE has given a figure of £300 million as the cost of strengthening roads and bridges, but this is for an 11·5 metric ton axle.

10.100 The Commission sees some force in the arguments in favour of the heavier lorry. In amenity terms fewer (though heavier) lorries on inter-urban journeys would reduce congestion. Nonetheless we recommend that there should be no general increase in axle loadings or gross vehicle weights until the total costs and benefits can be more clearly defined. Research both into road wear and into vehicle design to reduce wear should be carried out as a matter of urgency, particularly in view of the position in the EEC.

10.101 International trade presents a particular problem. There have been two developments: the use of TIR lorries between Britain and the Continent, carried across the Channel and the North Sea on roll-on/roll-off ferries; and the use of international standard (ISO) containers designed to fit into the cells of a container ship, on to a rail flat wagon or on to the trailer of an articulated lorry. Containers are becoming increasingly used on the short sea route as an alternative to TIR lorries and are becoming universal on the most important deep-sea routes. The roll-on/roll-off ferries are not economic except for short sea routes. The Commission welcomes the moves that have been taken to prohibit the use of oversize and overweight lorries on the ferry routes. The eventual weight of such lorries is linked to the EEC proposals. The more difficult immediate problem concerns the carriage by road of ISO containers, which are of fixed sizes: the most widely used are 20 and 40 feet long, the latter being the largest permitted size. The 20 foot container can be carried economically now. The 40 foot container cannot always be fully loaded because of the weight restriction, and therefore may have to make the very long sea journey underloaded. Unilateral action would put the UK at a disadvantage. We understand that the restrictions in the UK are effectively greater than elsewhere. Safe loading of 40-foot containers would require a 10·826 ton axle and a gross lorry weight in the 40–44 ton range. The Commission recommends that such vehicles be permitted to operate, but only on a few specified routes between inland clearance depots and railheads, and to ports where there is no reasonably direct rail service or where hauls are short. Each specified road route should be approved by the Minister after necessary engineering work had been completed and after its economics had been justified. The container operators maintain that the development of container service has greatly increased the use of the railway for trunk hauls.

10.102 Public disquiet over the use of unsuitable routes by heavy lorries applies both to urban and to country roads.

Objections arise from the size and scale of the vehicles (in relation to narrow streets and country lanes), the physical damage to adjoining property from vibration, the congestion from the use of narrow roads and the physical damage to road surfaces and foundations not designed for high loadings. We have drawn attention (see 6.14 above) to the fact that local authorities have powers, under the Heavy Commercial Vehicles Act 1973 (the Dykes Act), to regulate the routes of heavy lorries, and recommend that these powers be used (8.14). In this way, heavy lorries on inter-urban roads can be confined to principal routes. Local authorities have a duty to formulate route plans by 1977. It is desirable that they (and the Department of the Environment in the case of trunk roads) consult with trade and industry at an early stage in formulating their plans. Through these means much more can and must be done to minimise environmental damage from heavy lorries over the next few years.

10.103 The taxation of vehicles is a complex matter because of their great variety. Users should pay their full share of the total costs of providing, maintaining and policing the roads, but the extent to which owners of vehicles should be taxed in the interests of general revenue is a matter for debate. However some factors can be clarified. In *Living with the Lorry* (Leicester University, 1973), Clifford Sharp draws attention to the serious shortcomings of the present system of basing the licence duty on the unladen weight of freight vehicles. In particular, the present duties tend to bear too heavily on smaller vehicles and too lightly on the large vehicles, which compete with rail for heavy long-distance traffic. The AASHO tests on road wear demonstrate that wear is a function of axle loadings. It is desirable therefore that licence duties should in some way take account of a vehicle's maximum permitted axle load. It will clearly take some time to evolve a more appropriate licence structure which takes account of axle loads and gross loads. In the meantime we recommend that licence duties be raised as soon as possible on vehicles with an unladen weight of 5 tons and over.

10.104 Sharp illustrates his findings with two sets of calculations. First, he took the 1970 yield of excise duties for heavy vehicles (£110·5m) and recalculated the excise duties on the assumption that they should vary as the fourth power of the axle loadings. The results are shown in Table 10.12. Second, he took for 1970 the maintenance costs of roads as attributed by the Ministry of Transport to heavy

Table 10.12: Calculations of excise duty

Unladen weight		4th power of axle load	Ratio of 4th power of axle load	Recalculated excise duty £	Present excise duty £
Over tons	Not over tons				
1·5	3	33·7	1	5·80	78·00
3	5	789·0	23·4	114·50	148·50
5	8	1187·3	35·2	305·50	283·50
8		1228·2	36·4	758·60	418·50

goods vehicles (approximately £50m of a total of £135m) and recalculated the excise duties to produce this amount. The results are shown in Table 10.13. Both calculations show that vehicles over 5 tons unladen weight are at present relatively more lightly taxed than the smaller vehicles. On the assumption that revenue from this source is to be maintained, the absolute level of tax on the two heaviest

Table 10.13: Calculations of excise duty

Unladen weight		Recalculated annual excise duty £	Present annual excise duty £
Over tons	Not over tons		
1·5	3	2·6	78·00
3	5	52·1	148·50
5	8	138·9	283·50
8		344·8	418·50

classes of vehicles is too low, and we recommend that it be increased proportionately to the road wear and maintenance costs involved. (It should be noted that Table 10.13 is based on an arbitrary fraction of maintenance costs, and no account is taken of current heavy expenditure on motorways and trunk roads.)

10.105 There are many different ways in which vehicles may be taxed, including road fuel tax. Commercial vehicles compete with other modes of transport and it is appropriate that they should be taxed to pay their full share of providing, maintaining, policing and lighting roads and also to cover all social costs arising from their operations. At present, while the future of the untaxed price of fuel is uncertain, the Commission does not wish to comment on the level of fuel tax desirable for commercial vehicles, apart from the general point that if the full costs of these vehicles to the national economy are to be recovered there is no case for reducing taxes.

CONCLUSION

10.106 We have examined the major problems of inter-urban and long-distance travel at some length, because the subject is large and complex, and we have found it necessary to question commonly accepted assumptions of far-reaching importance. As a result we have put forward some radical recommendations concerning the road programme (and in particular the completion of the motorway network), the heavy lorry, and railway passenger and freight traffic. If these recommendations are accepted, we are convinced that there will be considerable environmental improvement and greater social justice without attendant economic disadvantage or the loss of essential mobility.

REFERENCES

[1] *Public Expenditure 1977–78*. HMSO, December 1973.
[2] *Road accidents in Great Britain 1971*. HMSO, 1972.
[3] British Railways Board: *The British Railways Board's Review of Railway Policy*. June 1973.
[4] British Railways Board: *A study of the relative true costs of rail and road transport over trunk routes*. 1964.
[5] *Survey of the transport of goods by road 1967/68*.
[6] Sharp, Clifford: *Living with the lorry*. Leicester University, 1973.

CHAPTER 11

Summary and Recommendations

11.1 Our work has been a response to one of the conspicuous trends of our time, namely the growing consumption of transport. In less than twenty years, personal travel has doubled and goods transport has grown by more than a half. This growth has been almost entirely accounted for by cars and lorries, and in consequence the volume of road traffic has expanded nearly threefold. The trend is officially forecast to continue until at least the end of the century. The rapid growth of private road traffic has been accompanied by an expanding roadbuilding programme and a declining public transport system, both rail and bus.

11.2 This profound change in the nation's use of transport has been achieved at high cost. Between 1958 and 1971 household expenditure on transport rose by $3\frac{1}{2}$ times, and its share of the family budget went up from $8 \cdot 3\%$ to $13 \cdot 4\%$. Transport now consumes about one fifth of the nation's total output, nearly one fifth of its supplies of useful energy and nearly one quarter of its oil. It is a major contributor, directly and indirectly, to the spread of concrete and construction that in twelve years has swallowed up an area the size of Oxfordshire. During the same period over a million people have been killed or seriously injured in transport accidents, nearly all on the roads. One third of the population are now subject to a severe level of noise from road traffic, and some densely inhabited areas suffer from extreme aircraft noise. Transport also contributes towards air pollution, mainly through exhaust emissions, though in British conditions this problem does not seem insurmountable. The visual damage done by roads, railways and car parks to town and country is difficult to assess objectively but, in the Commission's view, this is something that society will increasingly regret.

11.3 Other important side effects of the trend in transport

developments include the growth of long-distance commuting, with its financial and social consequences, the growth of second homes and their impact on rural communities, and the very heavy concentration of visitors—and their cars—on places of outstanding beauty and interest.

11.4 Formidable though these diverse costs and disadvantages are, the benefits from the emerging new style of life are also impressive for those able to enjoy them. As expressed in the word "mobility", they confer a freedom and ease of movement, an independence and a wealth of opportunity, that the Commission fully appreciates. Sizeable communities have grown up on the basis of the private car. Holidays and weekend pursuits are often dependent on it. Social life in both town and country owes a vast amount to the convenience and versatility of the automobile. Similarly the convenience and flexibility of the private truck have freed many industrial and commercial firms from dependence on what some regarded as an inefficient and unreliable railway system.

11.5 Clearly we are witnessing a vast social transformation giving great convenience and pleasure to millions of people, but only at a huge sacrifice of some of the true riches of life and, indeed, of life itself. It is useless to take up a simple position for or against this process. Nor is it good enough just to accept the "march of progress" and try to mitigate its harsher aspects. The answer, in the Commission's view, must be to control the process, in order to enjoy its benefits where these can be gained without undue sacrifice. But this requires, first of all, an understanding of the complex relationships and interactions between the benefits and the sacrifices.

11.6 In particular, a clear understanding is needed of the concept of mobility. The real goal is not ease of movement, but access to people and facilities. Movement is desirable only to the extent that access requires it. People will seek, of course, to improve their power of access within the situation in which they find themselves. In present conditions they evidently choose to acquire and use more and more transport. This fact, sometimes presented as proof of "society's choice", is people's response to the options offered them. They do not control the options; nor can they, as individuals, affect the collective impact of their individual choices. The

Commission cannot accept the thesis that the sum of people's individual decisions necessarily equals what they really want.

11.7 A demonstration of this fallacy is the vicious circle of traffic growth. Everywhere, but especially in large towns, the advantages of private car ownership have reduced bus patronage and obstructed the streets, undermining the ability of public transport to give a good, cheap service, causing noise and pollution, creating danger and nuisance for pedestrians and cyclists, thereby increasing the *relative* advantages of owning and using a car, and creating the familiar vicious spiral. Road building and traffic management have accelerated the spiral. Attempts to escape congestion by shifting facilities to uncongested areas have increased dependence on private transport and added to the volumes of traffic. The eventual outcome of the process has been the run-down of public transport, the degradation of conditions for pedestrians and cyclists, and the growth of "unwanted" or "forced" car ownership and use among those cut off from adequate public transport. The position of people without cars has seriously deteriorated, and it is questionable whether all those with cars are really better off than they were before. To take an extreme case, the appalling rush-hour conditions in most city centres are the collective result of people's individual choices; yet it is impossible to accept that this is what people really want.

11.8 The Commission feels bound to conclude that present transport policies, far from letting people choose what they want, are forcing them into a new way of life which, despite its evident attractions, is in many ways needlessly ugly, brutal and inefficient. Above all, it is unjust. Those who chiefly suffer its deficiencies are the old, the young, the infirm and the poor, i.e. all those who do not have ready access to a car; and they comprise over half the population. If our report does nothing else we hope it will draw attention to the immensity of the injury inflicted by one half of the community upon the other. The interests of motorists and businessmen are strongly represented. Those of children, old people, housewives and others who make up the masses of pedestrians, cyclists and bus passengers, are not. It is right that we should speak up for them.

11.9 The problem will not wither away as car ownership

spreads, because the number of carless (who include many people within car-owning households) will never fall much below half the population; and, to the extent that their numbers do decline, so will their problems become more acute.

11.10 The continuation of the trend for the rest of this century could only intensify the pressures upon the nation's assets, both tangible and intangible. The spread of motorways, car parks and all the paraphernalia of the motorised society would continue. Urban congestion, oil consumption and the burden of supporting essential public transport services would all continue to grow. Remedial measures could, we believe, check the growth of air pollution and *slow down*—if not halt—the growth of traffic noise and accidents. Better planning could *help* to conserve the dwindling supply of undeveloped land, and better design and management could *soften* the impact of further traffic growth on pedestrian movement and the environment. But the prospect is nevertheless one of continuing deterioration in almost all these aspects, and nowhere is there any promise of improvement in an already dismal situation.

11.11 The Commission is convinced that the many serious transport problems confronting the nation, if it maintains its current course, cannot be adequately tackled by palliatives alone. Nothing short of a major change of course will suffice. Transport policies must be fundamentally re-examined. First, the transport system needs some basic reforms in its methods of management: it needs a legal framework that protects society from the worst side effects of transport, a new approach towards the regulation and control of traffic, a more efficient use of the price mechanism, a bolder use of taxes and subsidies in order to promote socially desirable transport systems, and a redirection of planning controls towards new transport goals.

11.12 Secondly, all major decisions need to be firmly and consistently based on a comprehensive analysis of the problem. We are glad to see that the old methods of making decisions, based on narrowly conceived profit criteria for public transport and engineering criteria for roads, are being largely superseded, but they still survive in some places. Moreover many current investment proposals were conceived and approved years ago on the strength of criteria no longer accepted. The Commission is also critical of the traffic predictions upon which most of these investment proposals are based. It welcomes cost-benefit analysis as an important component of the decision-making process, but believes that the principles of economic evaluation cannot be independent of other moral and political considerations.

11.13 Finally, the Commission has arrived at some major conclusions concerning the content of transport policies. In urban areas, the failure to maintain effective transport facilities demands immediate action. Improvements in public transport are needed urgently. The Commission believes that a moratorium on urban roadbuilding should be called until new management policies have been implemented and current investment proposals reviewed; the moratorium should not apply to roads forming part of new urban developments, or to environmental projects, or to road schemes already well advanced. Management policies should be designed for rapid implementation to help pedestrians and cyclists, to give priority to buses, to expand bus services and, where necessary, to restrain private traffic. In the longer run the use of goods trans-shipment depots may be justified as a way of reducing the number of heavy lorries in towns. The use of light urban railways should be investigated.

11.14 In rural areas the needs are not very different from those in towns. Restoration of buses and trains is urgently needed to give tolerable services for the carless population. The Cooper Brothers' formula should be revised and the opening up of closed railway lines under private ownership facilitated. Multipurpose vehicles—e.g. school buses carrying ordinary passengers, and buses carrying mail—should be encouraged. Minor design alterations to many smaller roads, together with traffic regulation, are required to provide acceptable conditions for pedestrians and cyclists.

11.15 As regards inter-urban transport the Commission, largely for geographical reasons, foresees only minor gains from the development of water transport and pipelines. Although a smoothly flowing main road network has an obvious role to play in long-distance transport, the Commission finds that the roads programme has not been planned or justified in a way that is rationally defensible. The country is being asked to accept an immense programme produced by outdated planning methods no longer accepted by the DoE itself. The Commission can only recommend a reappraisal of the main roads programme in the light of modern methods of transport planning and evaluation.

11.16 Our report dwells at length on the social priorities, value judgments and ethical questions raised by such a deeply human subject as transport. These matters cannot be summarised in tightly worded recommendations; they must remain embodied in the spirit of our report. But we also have a considerable number of specific recommendations which, for convenience, are extracted and set out below.

SPECIFIC RECOMMENDATIONS

Legal framework

1. Transport consumers' councils should be set up in each county to represent consumers' interests in public transport. They should be concerned with all surface passenger transport services (including taxis) within their areas and should have wide powers to investigate complaints and to take legal action on behalf of customers. They should have the power to appoint non-executive directors to the boards of local transport undertakings and non-voting members to the appropriate local authority committees. They should be elected or appointed in such a way as to guarantee their independence: the chairman and perhaps other members should be paid.[1] They should be financed from the rates or from taxes levied on local transport undertakings. County transport consumers' councils should elect members of regional or national councils with similar powers in relation to national transport undertakings and central government. (6.10–6.11).

2. Possible changes in the laws relating to the provision of cars by companies for their employees, and the payment of their motoring expenses, should be examined in order to prevent or discourage the use of these practices as a means of supplementing salaries. (6.47).

3. Penalties for those who infringe the road traffic laws should generally be made more severe and should be applied more uniformly throughout the country. (4.14).

[1] See Note of Reservation on p. 279.

4. There are more urgent claims on public expenditure than transport (housing, for example). Management rather than investment should be used to solve problems of personal mobility, safety and environmental protection. Local authorities should examine critically schemes now in the pipeline in the light of this principle (7.17).

5. In all towns, ways of increasing accessibility through locational and land use planning should be examined. A major aim should be to keep journeys short. The transport advantages of providing smaller and more numerous public facilities of all kinds rather than larger and fewer should be borne in mind, and any extra costs thereby incurred should be compared with the savings in transport. Facilities should be sited where possible within easy reach of their users by foot, bicycle or public transport. (6.53).

6. The scope for using locational and land use planning to ease the problems of goods distribution in towns should also be examined. Opportunities should be sought to relocate activities if they generate lorry traffic in unsuitable places. Future locations of activities that generate goods movements should be chosen with three aims in view:

(i) to avoid the creation of traffic and environmental problems;

(ii) to facilitate the use of town or district goods distribution schemes, either existing or planned;

(iii) to facilitate the use of rail or water transport, especially for goods movements that do not lie entirely within the town. (8.38–8.39).

7. Major applications for planning permission should be required to include estimates of traffic generation by vehicles of all types. The burden of proof should be on the developer to show that his application is consistent with the local authority's general transport policies. (6.52).

8. Before granting planning permission for activities on sites that generate goods movements which can only be served by road transport, planning authorities should satisfy themselves that there are no suitable alternative sites that permit the use of rail or water transport. (6.51).

9. The practice of making planning consent conditional on

the provision of a minimum number of parking spaces should cease and maximum numbers should be specified instead. These numbers should be specified by reference to the transport arrangements of the locality in question and not by reference to a standard formula. (6.50).

10. Planning approval for opening a pit or quarry for the purpose of extracting aggregates used in road building should be conditional on new procedures to ensure that contractors will back-fill the exhausted pit and finish off with topsoil, or to ensure by other means that the area is at least as attractive and productive as before. (3.79).

11. Cost benefit techniques should be used more consistently and with a wider frame of reference in evaluating transport decisions, but their application should not be independent of aesthetic, environmental, moral and political considerations. (7.64).

12. The indirect costs of land lost to transport activities should, as far as possible, be included in future cost benefit studies. These indirect costs should include environmental costs and the loss of food production. (3.80).

13. Demonstration experiments should be undertaken in selected areas, both urban (8.43) and rural (9.27–29), to restrict the use of private cars and lorries and to supply exceptionally high standards of service by other modes and very high standards of amenity. Only in this way can the problems and merits of the alternatives be compared and real choices made. These experiments should be financed by central government as national research projects. (8.43, 9.29).

Road building and maintenance

14. There should be a moratorium on urban road building schemes until management measures designed to improve conditions for public transport passengers, pedestrians and cyclists, and to restrain the use of cars during peak hours have been implemented and their effects assessed. This moratorium should have three exceptions: (1) road building essential for the development of New Towns or the expansion of existing towns; (2) road building still essential for environmental improvement or the implementation of management measures even after the implementation of appropriate policy changes; (3) road construction now in

266

progress which it would be more damaging or expensive to stop than to complete. (8.11).

15. The national motorway and trunk road programme should be re-appraised. For each road or by-pass in the programme, the burden of proof must lie with its proponents that it is the best means of solving particular local or regional problems. All proposals should be assessed on the basis of revised predictions of traffic demand. (10.66).

16. The decision to accept the Marshall Committee's recommendation for higher initial standards of road maintenance should be reviewed. (7.27).

17. In areas of scenic beauty which present engineering difficulties in road construction, standards of design should conform to lower speeds, and speed limits of 45 or 50 m.p.h. should be imposed over appropriate sections of motorway. (4.78).

Traffic control

18. Local authorities should pay greater attention to traffic management as a primary instrument of transport policy. There should be more experiments with different schemes. (6.18).

19. Legislation should be introduced to enable county councils to introduce local schemes of road pricing, such as toll gates and daily licences for entry into central areas, particularly suitable to local circumstances. (6.28).[1]

20. Laws which limit the use of ramps and other devices designed to enforce low traffic speeds should be revised. (6.19).

21. Local authorities should use the powers given to them under the Heavy Commercial Vehicles Act 1973 to regulate the routes of heavy lorries (8.23, 10.102).

22. More traffic management schemes should be introduced in country parks and similar areas of tourist attraction to limit the use of cars; and in some places experiments should be held in banning entry by cars altogether. (9.26).

Buses

23. Of the various ways of providing the required standards of mobility, in towns or country, the expansion or restora-

[1] See Note of Reservation on p. 279.

tion of scheduled bus and train services should always be considered first. Where possible bus services at present supplied for reserved classes of travellers (e.g. school children) should be replaced by scheduled services available to all. Where the expense of conventional scheduled services is shown to be too great, postal buses and similar schemes should be encouraged. (8.19, 9.4 ff.).

24. Local authorities in urban areas should improve conditions for bus operation, either by giving buses priority on the streets or by reducing the volumes of other traffic using bus routes. Priority is best given by the reservation of continuous routes of lanes or streets for buses, either exclusively or with limited provision for other classes of traffic. Other priority measures, such as traffic signals actuated by buses and exemption from turning restrictions, should also be used where necessary. The reduction of other traffic on bus routes should be achieved by a variety of means, including traffic management, parking control and direct restriction. (6.18, 8.17–8.18).

25. Local authorities in urban areas should consider subsidised extensions of the bus system. Experiments should be undertaken, with before-and-after studies based on considerations of social justice and the widest form of cost benefit analysis. Subsidies should not, however, be a substitute for other measures to protect buses from congestion and raise their quality of service. (8.19).

26. Lower fares (or free travel) in off-peak periods should be offered to the elderly provided that the facilities are available in any case. (6.30, 33).

27. A Working Party on bus services, consisting of representatives of the bus industry, the Department of the Environment and outside experts, should be established to produce guidelines on the improvement of bus services, with particular reference to marketing and personnel policies. (8.22).

Pedestrians and cyclists

28. Local authorities in towns should aim to make walking safe and convenient throughout the town, not in pedestrian precincts only. Pedestrian movement should normally be at ground level. Where necessary to achieve the desired standards, pedestrian networks should be extended by

pavement widening and the conversion of some streets to pedestrian use. Where the pedestrian and road networks intersect, a fair degree of priority should be given to pedestrians. Vehicle access over pavements to garages should be discouraged, and laws against parking on pavements should be strictly enforced so as to give pedestrians the right of way. (8.13).

29. Local authorities should set as a long-term aim the provision of a comprehensive network safe for cyclists, and a start should be made by designating linked cycle lanes, where possible, on inner and central area minor roads, and through parks and other suitable areas. Bicycling should be encouraged by the enforcement of very low speeds for motor traffic in residential and other selected streets, by traffic management measures, especially the control of parking, by the detailed design of streets and intersections, and by the provision of cycle stands and stalls. (8.15–8.16).

30. Highway authorities in rural areas should pay more attention to the safety and convenience of walking and cycling in the country. Facilities segregated from motor traffic should be provided wherever possible, either alongside roads or separate from roads. A new class of minor rural roads should be created in which pedestrians and cyclists are given priority and motor vehicles are limited to very low speeds. (9.2).

Freight traffic

31. Urban local authorities should investigate the possibility of town or district goods distribution schemes. The aim should be to reduce goods vehicle mileage and to control the timing of goods deliveries in order to avoid conflict with personal transport. In larger towns, the possibility of using specialised vehicles for goods distribution within the town should be investigated. More modest schemes along the same lines, involving the cooperation of local haulage operators and the use of existing depots, should be investigated either as an alternative or a preliminary to full town distribution schemes. Such schemes should be assessed by cost benefit criteria and should be supported financially by local authorities where this can be shown to benefit the community. (8.30–8.31).

32. No general increases in maximum axle loading or gross

vehicle weight of lorries should be permitted until the costs and benefits of such increases can be clearly defined. (10.100).

33. Exemptions should be made for lorries involved in international movements to permit some use of vehicles heavier than those currently allowed. These exemptions should apply only to specified routes between inland clearance depots and railheads or between depots and ports where there is no regular direct rail service or where hauls are short. Each specified route should require approval by the Minister of Transport Industries after its economics have been justified and subject to the completion of any necessary engineering works. (10.101).

34. Licence duties for vehicles with an unladen weight of 5 tons or over should be raised as soon as possible (10.103).

35. A goods vehicle licence structure should be evolved which takes account of axle loads and gross loads; in particular the level of tax on the two heaviest classes of vehicle should be increased proportionately to the road wear and maintenance costs involved. (10.104).

36. Permission to transport abnormal loads by road should be subject to a charge commensurate with the costs imposed on the community. (10.14).

37. Legislation should be introduced enabling central government or local authorities to subsidise goods transport operations including water transport or pipelines where this can be shown to be of economic or environmental advantage to the community. (10.20).

Railways

38. The government should pay subsidies to British Rail in the form of a payment for every passenger mile and every ton mile carried above a specified annual threshold. Our tentative recommendations for the size of the subsidies are 0·5p for each passenger mile above a threshold of 18 thousand million and 0·5p per ton mile for each ton mile above a threshold of 15 thousand million.[1] The form of the subsidies should be adapted as soon as possible to discriminate in favour of particular types of traffic and particular routes where the greatest social benefit in rail haulage is anticipated. (10.93).

39. Subject to its compatibility with other more important

[1] See Note of Reservation on p. 279f.

railway developments British Rail's proposals for APT should be approved. (10.75–10.78).

40. British Rail should provide better facilities for wagon loading traffic, use more imaginative marketing methods, and, where practicable, use automatic techniques for control of wagon movements. British Rail should attempt to increase its freight ton mileage by 50% within 5 years, first by gaining more freight traffic with a haul of 300 miles or more. (10.81–10.89).

41. Subject to a more suitable means being found of financing British Rail's main line operations the Cooper Brothers' formula for calculating grants for unremunerative services should be revised. The grant should correspond as closely as possible to the shortfall that British Rail would incur by continuing to operate the service rather than closing it down. Agreements to pay grants should run for ten years rather than three years as at present. (9.22).

42. In addition to the rail subsidies proposed in Recommendation 38 above, there should be provision for additional rail subsidies in order to limit the use of lorries in particularly sensitive rural areas. (9.26).

43. Government should repay local authorities part of the grant paid by them to British Rail for maintaining rail services, where it can be shown that closure would increase unemployment payments. The same principle should apply where branch lines are re-opened. (9.13).

44. When British Rail cannot operate branch lines without specific subsidies, local authorities should allow soundly constituted private companies to tender for the lines in question. Companies should produce proof of technical competence and financial support and should undertake to operate an agreed minimum schedule of services throughout the year. The land, tracks and works should be leased, not sold, to the private company. (9.23).

45. British Rail should improve the arrangements for car hire at stations and should itself provide cars for hire in competition with car hire firms. (10.29).

46. British Rail should markedly reduce the present half-fare for bicycles, at least in conjunction with day return tickets. (10.30).

47. The Government should propose targets for British Rail to achieve in terms of traffic carried, revenue earned

271

and expenditure, to be discussed and agreed with the Board. A management audit team, responsible to the Chairman but independent of the executive staff, should be appointed to review progress on these activities and to examine efficiency. The Chairman would submit reports on these subjects to the Minister. (10.96).

Interchanges

48. The new powers given to County Councils to coordinate rural bus and rail services should be used to bring about a much more carefully integrated pattern of services. Combined timetables should be available indicating connection at railheads. (9.24).

49. County Councils should not make grants to public transport operators unless they are satisfied with these and other interchange arrangements, and the Department of the Environment should also satisfy itself in this respect before approving local authority transport plans or making grants. (10.28).

Motor vehicle design

50. Legislation should be carefully considered governing the use of private cars and the size of engine and power-to-weight ratio of petroleum fuelled vehicles in urban areas. (6.22).

51. The DTI should impose on all vehicle manufacturers new standards of design to achieve inter alia:

(a) a reasonable minimum life time for each vehicle under normal usage;

(b) a significant element of protection from and inhibition of corrosion in the body shell;

(c) the elimination of all unnecessary bright work. (3.88).

52. The Department of the Environment's vehicle testing procedure should be used, in conjunction with appropriate legislation, to ensure that technical innovations which are both desirable and relatively cheap are incorporated into the existing stock of motor vehicles. (3.87).

53. The Department of Trade and Industry should establish a code of practice in the designing of motor vehicles to facilitate metals recovery. (3.90).

54. The Department of the Environment should promote

adequate consultation between all user interests and lorry manufacturers concerning the amenity aspects of lorry design. (8.37, 10.98).

Fuel

55. The amount of petroleum used in transport should be reduced. To this end the Commission makes a number of specific suggestions in addition to proposals for general policy changes (3.64-71). In particular:

(a) despite rising prices of vehicle fuels, taxation of fuel should remain, and be used as an instrument to promote fuel economy (3.69);

(b) changes in vehicle and engine design to promote fuel economy should be encouraged by a suitable taxation policy (3.69).

56. The Department of the Environment should take steps to ensure that there is no increase in the amount of lead dispersed in the atmosphere via petrol engine exhausts (4.58) even if this means a reduction in the lead content of petrol (4.65).

Airways

57. The Government should retain powers to decide which air services may be operated and should use them to avoid unnecessary duplication of facilities (10.9). Steps should be taken to prevent or discourage support from municipal funds for local airports. (10.11).

Noise

58. The Department of the Environment should promote legislation to increase the legal rights of residents to freedom from the nuisance of road traffic noise. (4.38).

59. Legislation should be undertaken to restore the right of the individual to take legal action under common law against nuisance from aircraft. (4.50).

60. Steps should be taken to procure the reduction of railway noise by the provision of adequate silencers on diesel-powered locomotives. (4.40).

61. The Department of the Environment should take the necessary steps to reduce the noise from road traffic by:

(a) incorporating noise tests in the requirements of

annual road vehicle tests; automatic vehicle testers should be made available to garages on lease;

(b) introducing regulations to reduce the permitted noise level of new motor cars sold in the UK to 80 dB(A), and of goods vehicles sold in the UK to 85 dB(A), by 1978;

(c) causing police officers and traffic wardens to report the registration number of any motor vehicle found to be emitting more than the permitted noise level to the Central Registry, which should require the vehicle owner to furnish evidence in the form of a certificate supplied by an approved garage within 21 days that the vehicle conforms to the regulations;

(d) withholding grants for the purchase of buses unless they conform to noise standards to be determined by the Department. (4.38).

62. Contracts for all (major) road works in built-up areas should contain provision for the control of noise levels and of vibration from heavy machinery; and during the course of the work the Public Health Inspector should inspect the site. (4.72).

63. The Department of the Environment should request the Noise Advisory Council to review the formula by which the Noise and Number Index is now calculated. (4.24).

64. Responsibility for control of civil aircraft noise should be transferred from the Department of Trade and Industry to the Department of the Environment. (4.46).

65. The Department of Trade and Industry and/or the Department of the Environment should take steps to improve the control of aircraft noise by:

(a) permitting public inquiries into the proposed introduction of new aircraft routes;

(b) allowing exceptions to the application of the Minimum Noise Route principle where the principle fails to take due account of the severity of noise imposed upon communities;

(c) introducing a noise tax on all passengers departing from UK airports, with exemptions for those flying on aircraft types with noise characteristics satisfying standards to be determined by the Department(s);

(d) introducing supplementary landing charges for night movements at UK airports;

274

(c) introducing stringent noise level standards for aircraft engaged in night movements at UK airports (4.47–4.49).

Other recommendations

66. A refundable deposit (of the order of £50) should be included in the initial registration fee for all private vehicles. This should be subsequently repaid to the eventual owner upon relinquishment of the vehicle (with log book) for recycling. In the absence of an identifiable owner (in the case of dumped cars) the appropriate local authority should collect the deposit on delivery of the vehicle. (3.90).

67. The Government should not attempt to eliminate competition between coach, rail and air services but should retain powers necessary to prevent wasteful duplication of services. (10.7–10.9).

68. Monetary values for death and injuries should be the responsibility of the Secretary of State for the Environment after parliamentary debate. (4.9).

69. The Department of the Environment should actively promote training schemes for local authority councillors and officers designed to improve their understanding of transport problems. (7.16).

70. Publicity should be given to the powers and responsibilities of local authorities contained in recent legislation concerning transport. (7.16).

RECOMMENDATIONS FOR RESEARCH AND DEVELOPMENT

Social and statistical

71. There should be extensive public opinion surveys of the real aspirations of people concerning transport. These surveys should cover both general concerns and particular schemes. (6.21, 7.34).

72. The measurement of less easily quantifiable aspects of transport decisions (noise, deaths and injuries, aesthetics, loss of amenity etc.) should be greatly refined. Refined measurements should be applied to transport cost benefit studies. (7.64).

73. Forecasts of future road traffic should be much more sophisticated. For private vehicles, they should be based on

studies of the causal and behavioural determinants of car ownership. For goods traffic, the connections between traffic and alterations in transport policy needs to be refined and clarified. There is a further need to use much more sophisticated statistical methods in forecasting. (7.32, 7.45).

74. There should be extensive research on the determinants of car ownership, with special regard to unwanted ownership. Account should be taken of variables such as town form and density, conditions for pedestrians and cyclists, and the quality of public transport. There should be experiments to see how changing such factors in a particular location affects car ownership and consumer satisfaction, while large surveys should monitor the growth of car ownership and its relationship to such factors. (5.38, 7.36).

75. Consumer satisfaction with transport should be extensively surveyed. Apart from collecting factual information about trips made, the surveys should study frustrated travel, unwanted travel, and quality aspects of travel (including fares, coverage, reliability, waiting time, comfort, and convenience). Ways of measuring these standards of service should be developed and used both to monitor the effects of transport policy and to indicate policy needs. (5.38, 7.36, 8.44–8.46).

76. Travel studies should always include movements by pedestrians and cyclists. They should attempt to measure suppressed or "would be" travel and the frustrations and fears experienced by pedestrians and cyclists, especially where traffic management schemes have been introduced. (5.37, 8.44).

77. The relationship between increased traffic and road building and the deterioration of public transport should be monitored continuously rather than over a single and short time span. These studies should concentrate on changes in personal mobility or access to facilities and not solely on motorised traffic flows. (5.46).

78. There should be a detailed study of the differences in road maintenance costs, traffic congestion, accidents, noise and other environmental intrusion, as well as the more obvious resource costs which are already reflected in pricing, that would result from the transfer of goods traffic from road to rail. (10.85).

79. Large scale studies of freight movements should be

made in which the emphasis is not on the flow of vehicles but on the flow of goods carried and the relationship between this flow and types of vehicle, types of route, and land use. (8.29).

80. The siting of warehouses and trans-shipment depots should be studied to determine the relative efficiencies of placing them on the edges or in the centres of towns. (8.38).

81. Studies should be undertaken to enable the value of road maintenance to be appraised in the same cost benefit terms that are appropriate in assessing other transport expenditure. (7.27).

82. Disused rail networks and depots in many cities should be examined with a view to potential freight use and there should be experiments with novel freight distribution systems such as "freight tripping" by individual computer-controlled rail wagons. (8.39).

Physiological and psychological

83. Research into ways of reducing stress in drivers should be increased. (4.16–4.21).

84. Research into the long term effects on the body of lead, nitrogen oxides and polynuclear aromatic hydrocarbons should be intensified, and the degree to which motor vehicles contribute should be examined more critically than at present. (4.56–4.60).

Technical

85. Techniques for reclaiming minor metal components from scrapped cars, especially copper wiring and chromium-plated fittings, should be improved. (3.82, 3.89).

86. There should be a development programme to create a quiet diesel bus. (4.37).

87. Studies of road wear by lorries of different axle weights should be intensified with a view to resolving present un-certainties and to designing vehicles which will reduce wear. (10.99).

88. A hand trolley for public use in shopping precincts should be developed. (8.37).

89. New lorry designs for urban delivery are needed. (8.37).

90. More experiments are needed to make roads safer for pedestrians and cyclists in towns and in the country. Apart

from providing separate routes for vehicular and foot/cycle traffic, the use of ramps or grids in the road should be investigated. (8.15, 9.2).

91. The potential for light rail systems should be examined closely. (8.25–8.26).

CHAPTER 12

Notes of Reservation

Payment of Chairmen of reconstituted Transport Consumers' Councils

Sir James Farquharson and Mr. Ralph Verney dissent from that part of Recommendation 1 which recommends the payment of Chairmen (and perhaps other members) of reconstituted Transport Consumers' Councils. (6.10-11).

Future energy availability

Mr. Frank Chapple dissents from the arguments in Chapter 3 about energy availability in the future, with special reference to the belief that informed public debate is necessary, through the normal political process, before substantially greater reliance is placed on nuclear fission (3.44).

Road pricing by local authorities

Mr. Frank Chapple dissents from the arguments in Chapter 6, paras. 27–8, embodied in Recommendation 19, proposing legislation to enable local authorities to introduce road pricing.

Type and level of interim rail subsidies

Dr. Norman Lee writes as follows:

"In Chapter 6 the Commission advocates that transport operators and private motorists should be charged according to the social costs for which they are responsible. In paras. 6.30–6.34 it indicates those circumstances where subsidisation is justified as an exception to this general charging principle. On both these counts I am in agreement with the Commission. However, I believe the translation of these principles into a new form of road user taxation for cars, buses and lorries and into a new subsidy system for public transport is a very complex matter requiring far more information than the Commission has at its disposal. I therefore cannot support the Commission's interim proposals, contained in para. 10.93 (and summarised in Recommendation 38) on the type and level of rail subsidies. These and other aspects of transport subsidies and road user taxation should be the subject of a specific Government investigation, conducted in accordance with a strict timetable which reflects the urgency of the situation."

Appendix to Chapter 2: The Scale of Transport Activity

Personal travel

Tables A and B: The growth of personal travel

The projections in Table B are based on the Transport and Road Research Laboratory's forecasts of vehicle mileage, and assume that current occupancy rates will be maintained. The rail figures assume that the passenger mileage targets for 1981 in the British Railways Board's Review of June 1973 will be achieved and that thereafter rail will maintain its share of total travel. The projections for the other modes assume that the passenger mileage achieved by each in 1971 will be maintained for the future. In other words, it is assumed that the downward trend in travel by modes other than car and taxi will be checked and, in the case of rail, even reversed. This may be a rather optimistic view in light of the recent record, but to alter it would make little difference to the forecast.

Goods transport

Tables C and D: The growth in goods transport

In 1971, air freight accounted for approximately 0·004 thousand million ton-miles. Domestic air freight has not been growing over the last four years. Coastal shipping has not maintained its position as well as these figures suggest, since the definition of coastal ton-miles was changed in 1967; by the old definition, coastal shipping accounted for only 10·8 thousand million ton-miles in that year. Estimates of future ton-miles by road have been taken from TRRL Report LR 429 for goods vehicles over $1\frac{1}{2}$ tons unladen weight; a small allowance has been made for ton-miles performed by smaller goods vehicles. The assumption made for rail is that the absolute ton-mileage achieved in 1970 will be maintained indefinitely. This is the same assumption as made in LR 429 and accords well with BR's own projections for 1981. All other modes, taken together, are also assumed to retain their 1970 ton-mileage.

Table E: Road goods transport by size of vehicle used

Vehicles

Tables F and G: The growth of vehicle mileage
Table H: The growth of motor vehicles in use
Table J: The number of goods vehicles in use by size

Table A: Growth of personal travel in Great Britain
Units: thousand million passenger miles

Mode	Year 1953	1955	1957	1959	1961	1963	1965	1967	1969	1970	1971
Air	0·2	0·2	0·3	0·4	0·6	0·8	1·0	1·2	1·2	1·2	1·2
Rail	24·1	23·8	25·9	25·5	24·1	22·4	21·8	21·2	21·6	22·2	22·1
Road											
Pedal cycle	12·9	11·3	10·0	8·4	6·7	5·0	4·4	3·5	2·8	2·6	2·6
Motor cycle	4·8	5·4	5·9	7·0	6·8	5·4	4·7	3·7	2·9	2·7	2·7
Car and taxi	37·3	48·9	54·0	75·1	90·9	110·1	140·0	164·2	181·1	193·5	208·6
Bus, coach, trolleybus	50·7	49·8	45·9	44·1	43·1	41·5	39·2	37·0	35·7	34·1	34·0
Road total	105·7	115·4	115·8	134·6	147·5	162·0	188·3	208·4	223·5	232·9	247·9
Total	130·0	139·4	142·0	160·5	172·2	185·2	211·1	230·8	246·3	256·3	271·2

Sources: Passenger Transport in Great Britain, HMSO.
Highway Statistics, HMSO.

Table B: Projected growth of personal travel in Great Britain
Units: thousand million passenger miles

Mode	Year 1980 Units	%	1990 Units	%	2000 Units	%
Air	1·2	0·3	1·2	0·3	1·2	0·2
Rail	28·2	7·5	35·1	7·5	39·3	7·5
Road	346·0	92·0	431·0	92·0	483·0	92·0
Pedal cycle	2·6	0·7	2·6	0·6	2·6	0·5
Motor cycle	2·7	0·7	2·7	0·6	2·7	0·5
Car and taxi	307·0	81·8	392·0	83·7	444·0	84·8
Bus and coach	34·0	9·0	34·0	7·3	34·0	6·5
Total	376	100	468	100	524	100

Table C: Growth of goods transport in Great Britain
Units: thousand million ton-miles

Mode	Year 1953	1955	1957	1959	1961	1963	1965	1967	1969	1970	1971
Pipelines	0·1	0·1	0·1	0·1	0·3	0·5	0·8	1·0	1·6	1·8	2·0
Inland waterways	0·2	0·2	0·2	0·2	0·2	0·1	0·1	0·1	0·1	0·1	0·1
Coastal shipping	9·0	9·0	9·8	9·5	13·5	14·9	15·3	15·2	14·8	14·2	13·1
Rail	22·8	21·5	20·9	17·7	17·6	15·4	15·4	13·6	15·3	16·4	14·9
Road	19·7	23·0	22·9	28·1	32·3	35·1	42·1	45·6	49·3	50·8	52·0
Total	51·8	53·8	53·9	55·6	63·9	66·0	73·7	75·5	81·1	83·3	82·1

Source: Annual Abstract of Statistics, HMSO.
Notes: 1. In 1971, air freight accounted for approximately 0·004 thousand million ton miles. Air freight has not been growing over the last four years.
2. Coastal shipping has not maintained its position as well as these figures suggest. The definition of coastal ton-miles was changed in 1967; by the old definition coastal shipping accounted for only 10·8 thousand million ton-miles in that year.

Table D: Projected growth of goods transport in Great Britain
Units: thousand million ton-miles

	1980	1990	2000
All other	16·0	16·0	16·0
Rail	16·4	16·4	16·4
Road	73·3	103·2	144·2
Total	105·7	135·6	176·6

Table E: Road goods transport by size of vehicle used
Units: thousand million ton-miles

Vehicle size (unladen weight)	Year 1962 Units	%	1967/8 Units	%	1970 Units	%	1971 Units	%
5 tons or less	21·9	65	19·8	42	15·7	31	14·4	28
Over 5 and up to 8 tons	8·2	24	16·6	35	18·7	37	17·5	34
8 tons or more	3·6	11	10·6	33	16·4	32	20·1	38
Total	33·6	100	47·0	100	50·8	100	52·0	100

Sources: Survey of the Transport of Goods by Road 1967–68, Department of the Environment, 1971.
The Transport of Goods by Road 1970–1972, Department of the Environment, 1972.

Table F: Growth of vehicle mileage
Unit: thousand million vehicle miles

Type of vehicle	Year 1953	1955	1957	1959	1961	1963	1965	1967	1959	1970	1971
Pedal cycle	12·9	11·3	10·0	8·4	6·7	5·0	4·4	3·5	2·8	2·6	2·6
Motor cycle	4·2	4·7	5·2	6·1	6·0	4·7	4·1	3·2	2·6	2·4	2·4
Car and taxi	20·7	26·3	28·1	38·6	46·7	56·8	72·0	85·2	93·8	100·3	108·1
Bus and coach	2·6	2·6	2·5	2·5	2·5	2·5	2·4	2·4	2·4	2·3	2·2
Light van*	5·6	6·1	6·3	8·4	9·8	10·5	11·2	11·0	11·2	11·7	12·2
Other goods vehicles	7·2	8·2	7·8	9·2	9·9	10·2	11·3	11·3	11·6	11·8	12·1
Total	53·2	59·2	59·9	73·2	81·6	89·7	105·4	116·6	124·4	131·1	139·6

* Not exceeding 30 cwt. unladen weight.
Source: Highway Statistics, HMSO.

Table G: Projected growth of vehicle mileage
Unit: thousand million vehicle miles

	1980	1990	2000
Pedal cycle	2·6	2·6	2·6
Motor cycle	2·5	2·5	2·5
Car and taxi	159	203	230
Bus and coach	2·5	2·5	2·5
Light van	13	15	18
Other goods vehicle	13	15	17
Total	192·6	240·6	272·6

Sources: Highway Statistics, HMSO.
Forecasts of vehicles and traffic in Great Britain, 1972 revision, TRRL Report LR 543, 1973.

Table H: Past and projected growth of motor vehicles in use
Units: millions

| | Actual | | | | | | | | Projected | | | | | |
	1946 Unit	%	1953 Unit	%	1960 Unit	%	1970 Unit	%	1980 Unit	%	1990 Unit	%	2000 Unit	%
Other vehicles	0·33	10·6	0·57	10·7	0·72	7·6	0·77	5·2	0·8	3·7	0·8	3·0	0·8	2·6
Motor cycles	0·45	14·5	1·01	18·9	1·80	19·1	1·05	7·0	1·1	5·1	1·1	4·1	1·2	4·0
Private cars	1·77	56·9	2·76	51·7	5·53	58·5	11·52	77·0	17·8	83·3	22·8	85·4	25·9	85·8
Goods vehicles	0·56	18·0	1·00	18·7	1·40	14·8	1·62	10·8	1·7	7·9	2·0	7·5	2·3	7·6
Total	3·11	100	5·34	100	9·44	100	14·95	100	21·5	100	26·8	100	30·2	100

Sources: Basic Road Statistics 1972, British Road Federation. TRRL Report LR 543, 1973.

Table J: Number of goods vehicles in use by size
Units: thousands registered vehicles

Size (unladen weight)	Year 1957	1960	1965	1970	1971
Over 8 tons	7	11	24	55	65
5–8 tons	29	41	76	132	139
3–5 tons	114	186	269	234	221
1½–3 tons	391	348	269	197	189
Not over 1½ tons	626	756	864	933	941
Total	1167	1342	1502	1552	1555

(See Fig. A.1 opposite.)

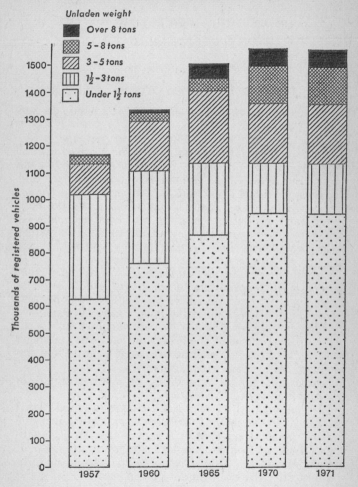

Fig. A.1. Number of goods vehicles in use by size.

Unladen weight

- ■ Over 8 tons
- ▨ 5 - 8 tons
- ▨ 3 - 5 tons
- ▥ 1½ - 3 tons
- ⋮ Under 1½ tons

Thousands of registered vehicles

1957 1960 1965 1970 1971

291

Appendix to Chapter 3: Resources For Transport

A2.1 TRANSPORT EXPENDITURE AND GDP

The expenditure figures set out in Table 3.1 were derived in the following ways.

Current expenditure on railways, road passenger transport and road haulage was obtained from a breakdown of figures in *National Income and Expenditure*, supplied by the Central Statistical Office. Capital expenditure in each case was obtained direct from *National Income and Expenditure* for the relevant years. The road haulage item includes both current and capital expenditure by "own account" (C licence) road haulage operators, but, as explained in Chapter 3, does not include capital expenditure by the road haulage industry on garages and other fixed plant.

Expenditure on cars and motorcycles was obtained from the consumers' expenditure tables in *National Income and Expenditure*. Expenditure on bicycles and prams came from a breakdown of one item in the *Family Expenditure Survey* for the relevant year. The tax element cannot be excluded, but it is probably trivial. The FES figure had to be multiplied by the ratio of total population over average household size to obtain the national expenditure.

Current and capital expenditure on roads comes from *National Income and Expenditure*.

The economic costs of road accidents was calculated according to the method developed by Dawson at the Transport and Road Research Laboratory [1], [2]. It includes the loss of output due to death and injury, costs of medical treatment, costs of damage to vehicles and the administrative costs of insurance companies and the police that result from accidents. The cost for 1970 was taken directly from published sources [3], but the 1963 figure given by the TRRL was increased slightly to make approximate allowance for a subsequent change in its method of calculation [2]. The 1959 cost had to be estimated. This was done by using the 1963 costs per death, injury and accident, reduced by the ratio of the GDPs in the two years, and applied to the 1959 accident statistics.

To avoid double counting of repair costs of private cars and motorcycles, the cost of insurance premiums was obtained from the FES, multiplied by the estimated number of households, and excluded from total expenditure on cars and motorcycles. Survey estimates of average expenditure on insurance premiums were used for the years 1963 and 1970, but no estimate was available for 1958. We therefore adopted the crude expedient of reducing the 1963 insurance expenditure according to the ratio of passenger miles travelled by private vehicles in 1958 and 1963; this ratio was observed to correspond closely to the increased cost of insurance premiums between 1963 and 1970. There is still an element of double counting, since most insurance companies require a motorist making a claim to pay a proportion of the repair costs resulting from any accident. This is offset to some extent by the fact that the overall calculation of transport costs excludes the general administrative costs and profits of insurance companies from the summation; these costs are those which arise not as the direct result of an accident, but simply in the general operation of the vast insurance industry which road transport needs.

A2.2 PRESENT ENERGY CONSUMPTION BY TRANSPORT

Primary and end-use consumption

The distinction between primary and end-use energy consumption is explained in Chapter 3. All published statistics are expressed in terms of end-use consumption. A conversion factor for each form of energy (coal, oil, electricity, etc.), representing the proportion of final useful energy which is used by the energy industry in extraction, transport and processing, must be applied to obtain the primary consumption figures. The conversion factors used are derived from Leach and Slesser [4] and are as follows:

oil, 1·12; coal, 1·04; electricity, 3·50; coke, gas and all other fuels, 1·30.

The conversion factor for electricity is the reciprocal of the average thermal efficiency of British power stations. On the basis of this figure alone, the use of electricity would appear to be a very inefficient way of consuming energy. However, so far as transport is concerned, it must be remembered that the thermal efficiency of a petrol engine is of the order of 20%, i.e. only about 20% of the energy supplied in a gallon of petrol is used in driving the wheels. The comparable figure for electric propulsion is about 85%. Hence the overall efficiencies of the two methods of propulsion are roughly the same.

Estimation of energy consumption in domestic air and water transport

Since this report is concerned with domestic transport, some modifications to the published statistics must be made in the case of air and water transport to obtain the energy consumed in domestic transport alone.

Water transport energy consumption figures in the *Digest of UK Energy Statistics* exclude international water transport but include the fuel used by the fishing industry. The latter can be identified and subtracted from the total to give accurate figures for total energy and oil fuels used by coastal and inland shipping. This has been done in compiling Tables 3.3, 3.4 and 3.5; The energy used by fishing vessels has been included under the heading of agriculture.

It is less easy to estimate the fuel used in domestic aviation because the relevant statistics are not published, on the grounds of commercial secrecy. We were told informally by one of the oil companies that about 6% of total UK sales of aviation fuel was sold for so-called domestic aviation, which is defined for this purpose as all flying from the smaller airports which have no scheduled international flights. This means that the 6% includes a small amount of fuel used in private international flights. A much more important point is that it excludes most of the fuel used on domestic flights by British Airways (formerly BEA) and its subsidiaries, which are responsible for most commercial domestic flying. By reference to the BEA annual accounts for the year 1971–72 and to the price of aviation turbine fuel at that time, it can be estimated that British Airways' domestic flights used about 2% of the total UK consumption of aviation fuel. Addition of the two figures gives an estimate of 8% of aviation fuel used in domestic flying. In 1971 this was equal to 135 million therms, or 300,000 tons of oil. Since there is undoubtedly some double counting in this addition, the estimate is very rough and almost certainly too large. No comparable estimate could be made for 1960.

A2.3 THE CONSUMPTION OF ENERGY BY VARIOUS TRANSPORT MODES

In para. 3.61 we discussed the possibility of reducing the amount of energy consumed in transport by making greater use of transport modes which use energy most efficiently. Table K sets out what might be termed the theoretical energy efficiencies of various forms of transport. These efficiencies measure the energy consumed by individual vehicles or trains under test conditions with a specified payload of passengers or freight. It must be stressed that energy consumption varies considerably according to the conditions, e.g. hills, frequent stops, heavy traffic congestion, etc. Hence these figures are not really precise and ideally all should be expressed as a range, as some of them are. All the figures are given in terms of a common unit, the load-miles performed on the energy contained in a gallon of petrol, although, of course, they do not all use petrol as a fuel. The figures for electric trains represent the amount of energy used at the power station to generate the electricity used by the train; for the other vehicles the figures are in terms of fuel in the tank. For aircraft, the measurements are made on the basis of a 576 mile trip.

For cars and motorcycles, and for walking and cycling, these figures represent quite well the energy used in actual operation over a number of journeys. However, for the public transport modes and for freight transport, these measured energy efficiencies do not give a very good idea of the overall efficiency achieved in practice because they take no account of the nature of transport operation. For example, the load factor on trains and buses varies greatly and is seldom 100% (full); road freight vehicles often make empty return journeys.

295

Table K: Theoretical energy efficiencies of various modes of transport, fully loaded

Passenger transport
Units: passenger-miles per gallon of petrol equivalent

*Bicycle	1650
*Walking	370
*Small motorcycle, 1 rider	130
*Large motorcycle, 1 rider	55
*Small car, 2 occupants	80
*Average UK car, 4 occupants	108
*Large car, 4 occupants	52
*Urban double decker bus	550
*Inter-city coach	510
†Inter-city diesel train	320–530
†Inter-city electric train	470–530
†Electric APT	190–220
‡Suburban electric train	410
§Narrow-bodied jet (BAC 111-500)	51
§Wide-bodied jet (A300B-10-1G)	49

Freight transport
Units: ton-miles per gallon of petrol equivalent

‖BACAT barge system, 420 tons	230
*Diesel train, 600 tons	310
*Electric train, 1000 tons	150
¶Ford minibus, 0·4 tons load	6–9
¶Ford parcel van, 5½ tons load	38–56
¶AEC Mandator, 21 tons load	77–137

Sources:
* Leach, G.: "Transport moves off oil", *New Scientist, 60,* 396–400, 8 November 1973.
† British Rail, Derby, personal communication.
‡ British Railways Board, personal communication.
§ British Aircraft Corporation, personal communication.
‖ British Waterways Board, personal communication.
¶ Everall, D. F.: *The effect of road and traffic conditions on fuel consumption,* Transport and Road Research Laboratory, Report LR 226, 1968.

We have attempted to overcome this problem by using statistics of overall fuel consumption, passenger-miles and freight ton-miles to estimate the overall energy efficiencies achieved by the railways, the bus system, the road haulage industry, and so on. The results are shown in Table L. These figures are rough estimates only, because of the need to make some rather sweeping assumptions in the course of their calculation.

For road transport the estimates are based on the passenger- and ton-mile statistics given in Chapter 2, and the

Passenger transport

Units: passenger-miles per gallon of petrol equivalent

All railways, 1971—high passenger: freight (see text)	91
All railways, 1971—low passenger: freight (see text)	61
London Transport, rail only, 1971	50
All buses in UK, 1971	117
All cars in UK, 1971	60
BEA and subsidiaries, domestic air services, 1971	41

Freight transport

Units: ton-miles per gallon of petrol equivalent

All railways, 1971—high passenger: freight (see text)	56
All railways, 1971—low passenger: freight (see text)	112
All UK inland and coastal shipping, 1971	99
All road goods vehicles in UK, 1971	27

Sources: See text.

fuel consumption figures shown in Table 3.5. The figure for buses is a slight under-estimate because the energy statistics show fuel consumed by buses, coaches and taxis together, whereas the road transport (passenger-mile) statistics are for buses and coaches only. For private cars, the fuel consumption figure used includes the petrol used by motorcycles, but excludes fuel used by taxis; the passenger-mile statistic excludes both taxis and motorcycles. The achieved efficiency of road freight transport was calculated directly from the published statistics and did not involve any problems of category definition. However, the efficiency figure obtained represents a very wide range of vehicles, from the lightest and least energy-efficient vans to heavy articulated lorries, which are relatively energy-efficient; consequently, this average efficiency is a rather uninformative figure. In all these calculations a small estimated correction was made to allow for the fact that Northern Ireland is included in the energy statistics, but excluded from the traffic statistics.

For rail transport the calculation is very imprecise. The basic reason for this is that British Rail uses many of its locomotives for hauling both passengers and freight and does not keep records which would enable the amounts of fuel used for the two purposes to be identified. Figures for passenger-miles and freight ton-miles were obtained from the Annual Reports of British Rail and London Transport.

In order to calculate energy efficiency, an assumption has to be made about the relative average fuel consumption per train-mile of passenger and freight trains. In Table L we give two estimates, described in the Table as high passenger: freight and low passenger:freight. The former assumes that the average number of train-miles per unit of fuel is three times as high for passenger trains as for freight trains, and the latter assumes that the averages are the same.

An alternative estimate for short-distance stopping passenger train services can be obtained for London Transport alone. A spokesman for London Transport told the Commission that electricity consumed for all purposes is 840–850 GWh per annum. Since we know the annual passenger mileage, the achieved efficiency can be calculated. This estimate is low, because not all the electricity is used to drive trains; it serves also lighting, escalators, workshops, bus depots, and so on.

For inland and coastal shipping, the achieved efficiency is readily calculated from the energy and freight transport statistics.

For domestic air transport, an estimate can be obtained for the relevant subsidiaries of British Airways, using the fuel consumption figure previously calculated (A2.2 above) and the passenger-miles carried, which are published in the Annual Reports of British Airways.

REFERENCES

[1] Dawson, R. F. F.: *Cost of road accidents in Great Britain.* Transport and Road Research Laboratory Report LR 396, 1967.
[2] Dawson, R. L. L.: *Current cost of road accidents in Great Britain,* Transport and Road Research Laboratory Report LR 396, 1971.
[3] *Road Accidents in Great Britain 1970.* HMSO, 1971.
[4] Leach, G., and Slesser, M.: *Energy equivalents of network inputs to food producing processes.* Strathclyde University, Glasgow, 1973.

Appendix to Chapter 4: Other Costs of Transport

A3.1 ACCIDENTS

Table M: Transport deaths and injuries per thousand million passenger-miles travelled

Year	Road Deaths	Serious injuries	Rail Deaths	Serious injuries
1953	48·2	535	16·2	33·3
1954	46·0	525	12·3	27·9
1955	47·9	538	15·6	33·2
1956	45·4	520	12·4	27·9
1957	47·9	550	17·4	34·4
1958	47·7	553	11·8	31·2
1959	48·4	599	11·6	26·1
1960	49·7	602	11·8	29·2
1961	46·8	576	13·0	33·1
1962	42·2	553	12·5	30·0
1963	42·7	542	11·1	26·3
1964	44·1	538	10·3	26·7
1965	42·2	520	10·2	21·8
1966	40·5	506	7·8	21·4
1967	35·1	450	12·6	20·8
1968	31·4	408	8·9	17·8
1969	33·0	406	9·4	15·0
1970	32·2	401	10·0	13·2
1971	31·0	367	8·6	12·4

Sources: See text.

Death and injury rates for road and rail transport are shown in Table M. The rates for road were calculated for each year by taking as numerator the total deaths and injuries on the roads and as denominator the passenger-miles given in Table 2.1. These passenger-miles exclude the distance travelled by drivers of goods and commercial vehicles, for which there is no estimate available. Consequently, the calculated rates are slightly higher than the true rates.

They are, however, on a comparable basis to the rail figures. Rail passenger-miles exclude the mileage travelled by train crews. Both passenger-miles and casualties are for British Rail and London Transport railways. The numbers of deaths and injuries include all passengers, and railway staff involved in accidents with trains or moving railway vehicles (each year about twice as many railway staff as passengers are killed or seriously injured—workers on the

Table N: Deaths and serious injuries on the roads by age

| | Deaths and serious injuries combined | | | Total | |
Year	Age 0–14	15–19	20 and over	Deaths	Serious injuries
1938				6648	50,782
.					
.					
.					
1946				5062	36,588
1947				4881	35,697
1948				4513	33,067
1949				4773	43,410
1950				5012	48,652
1951	9,902	6,199	41,518	5250	52,369
1952	9,334	5,957	39,766	4706	50,351
1953	10,486	6,750	44,406	5090	56,552
1954	10,032	7,112	45,067	5010	57,201
1955	10,715	8,184	48,733	5526	62,106
1956	10,309	8,145	48,368	5367	61,455
1957	9,929	9,242	50,085	5550	63,706
1958	11,048	10,551	53,537	5970	69,166
1959	11,587	14,232	61,373	6520	80,672
1960	12,604	15,462	63,347	6970	84,443
1961	13,150	16,600	62,094	6908	84,936
1962	12,947	17,244	60,433	6709	83,915
1963	13,235	18,799	62,664	6922	86,776
1964	14,467	22,858	65,955	7820	95,460
1965	14,865	23,176	67,776	7952	97,865
1966	15,661	23,208	68,954	7985	99,838
1967	16,067	21,014	63,995	7319	93,757
1968	16,587	19,702	59,084	6810	88,563
1969	16,253	19,214	62,617	7365	90,719
1970	16,604	19,543	64,851	7499	93,499
1971	16,274	18,773	63,520	7699	90,868

Sources: Road Accidents in Great Britain, HMSO.
Annual Abstracts of Statistics, HMSO.

track are particularly at risk). Trespassers on railway tracks comprise over one third of the deaths. The large numbers of suicides and attempted suicides are excluded.

The definitions of serious injuries used in compiling road and railway accident statistics differ slightly, but the difference is not so important as to invalidate comparisons between the two sets of rates.

Table N shows the trend in numbers of children, adolescents and adults killed and seriously injured on the roads in Britain since 1951. It is not possible to separate deaths from serious injuries, because for a number of years the published accident statistics combined the two categories in showing breakdown by age of victim.

A3.2 NOISE

The measurement of noise

Loudness or sound pressure itself is measured in decibels (dB). This is a logarithmic unit which enables the very wide sensitivity range of the human ear to be conveniently encompassed. Since the loudness of a particular sound as perceived by the ear depends not only on the sound pressure level but also on the frequency of the sound, loudness is usually measured on a weighted decibel scale that attaches different weights to different frequencies in the same way as the ear. Sound level meters measure loudness according to this weighted scale; the scale most commonly used is the A-scale, and the units of loudness are decibels on the A-scale (dB(A)). These are normally used for all important sources of noise except aircraft, for which a perceived noise level scale is used. The units of this are PNdB.

The indices used to measure noise annoyance from road traffic and aircraft, respectively L_{10} and NNI, are based on the measurement of loudness in dB. L_{10} is defined as the level of noise in dB(A) exceeded for just 10% of the time. For the measurement and prediction of traffic noise, the average of L_{10} values for each hour between 6.00 a.m. and midnight is the recommended measure. NNI is defined by the formula $\overline{PNdB} + 15\log_{10}N - 80$, where N is the number of aircraft heard making a noise louder than 80 PNdB and $\overline{PNdB}$ is the mean loudness of these aircraft. For the purposes of comparison NNI is normally calculated on the basis of an average busy summer day.

The numbers affected by noise

In para. 4.26 we mention the numbers affected by road and aircraft noise. The complete figures, from which those quoted in the text were taken, are shown in Tables O and P.

Table O: Numbers of residents in Great Britain exposed to road traffic noise in 1970
Unit: million people

Noise level	Urban	Rural	Total
L_{10} of 70dB(A) or more	8·5	1·2	9·7
L_{10} of 65 to 70dB(A)	12·5	1·7	14·2
L_{10} of less than 65dB(A)	24·3	6·2	30·5
Total	45·3	9·1	54·4

Source: TRRL report LR 357, Transport & Road Research Laboratory, 1970.

Table P: Numbers of residents affected by aircraft noise of over 35 NNI in 1970–71

Airport	Residents affected
Heathrow	2,310,000
Manchester	206,000
Gatwick	62,000
Luton	34,000
Total	2,612,000

Source: Noise Advisory Council.

The cost of noise at Heathrow

The Third London Airport (Roskill) Commission Research Team estimated the cost of noise annoyance to people living in the neighbourhood of each of the four alternative sites which were investigated. The average costs per household in the 35–45 NNI noise zone were between £120 and £315, depending on the site (all costs at 1970 prices) [1]. If we take the number of people estimated to be exposed to noise above 35 NNI at Heathrow in 1971 (2,310,000), and assume that there was an average of 3 people per household (higher than the national average), we can make a very rough estimate of the cost of noise annoyance at Heathrow according to the Roskill Research Team model. This will be a lower estimate than would actually be given by the model if it were applied to Heathrow, because the fact that the cost is higher for people living in areas where the noise is above 45 NNI has been disregarded. The estimated cost is between £93 and £245 million, for a cost per household between £120 and £315. It is now generally agreed that the Roskill Research model puts a low cost on noise annoyance compared with other costs and benefits used in cost-benefit analyses; the Roskill Commission itself in its report placed a higher value on noise annoyance than the Research Team had done.

Possible future reductions in aircraft noise

Richards has estimated that when the new quieter aircraft entirely replace older aircraft, the effect will be a reduction of "the noise climate by up to 10 NNI and the number of people seriously annoyed to about a third" [2]. Flowerdew has calculated the effects at Heathrow in 1985 with unrestrained growth of traffic at present rates and with traffic growth restrained according to the most recent forecasts of the Civil Aviation Authority, which envisage considerable diversion to Maplin [3]. The mix of aircraft types accords with CAA forecast. The results are shown in Table Q. These

Table Q: *Noise at Heathrow in 1985 on two different forecasts*

	1972	1985 unrestrained growth	1985 CAA forecast
Net reduction in NNI compared with 1972	—	8·1	11·3
Number of people in the 35–45 NNI zone	2,200,000	450,000	250,000
Number of people in the over 45 NNI zone	300,000	50,000	28,000

figures suggest that the reduction in numbers annoyed, corresponding to a 10 point reduction in NNI, is rather greater than the figure of one third given by Richards. All these calculations were made before the announcement by the Government in December 1973 of regulations to hasten the introduction of quieter aircraft, which should have the effect of bringing forward by several years the date of achieving the 10 point NNI reduction. All these predictions are based on the assumption that the growth of air traffic will not be restrained by the cost or availability of fuel. It is likely that the numbers of aircraft movements will in fact be less than has been assumed in these calculations, and the noise annoyance will be correspondingly less.

The cost of reducing aircraft noise

An example of the costs involved in four approaches to reducing the noise from one type of aircraft, the DC-8-50, has been given by the McDonnell-Douglas Corporation [4]. The calculations, which are shown in Table R, are for costs in 1975, when the DC-8-50 is expected to have seven years of remaining life.

Table R: Noise reduction costs and benefits for a DC8-50

	Fit hush-kit	Fit new fans	Fit new engines	Replace aircraft by DC10-30
Noise reduction (PNdB)—				
Take-off	5	10	15	13
Approach	12	15	17	15
% reduction of area affected by 100 PNdB noise	54	73	87	73
Cost per aircraft, 1972 US$	560,000	1,700,000	6,200,000	1,700,000
Average cost increase per ticket, 1972 US$	1	4·5	16	2·5

REFERENCES

[1] Third London Airport Commission: *Papers and Proceedings*, Vol. 7, Part 2. HMSO, 1970.
[2] Richards, E. J.: *The cost of aircraft noise*, Environment and Change, September 1973, p. 53–54.
[3] Flowerdew, A. D. J.: *Financial Times*, 13 June 1973.
[4] *Flight*, 12 July, 1973.

A Summary of the Positions Concerning Transport of the Three Major Political Parties[1]

This summary is based on the brochures and papers published by the parties after their conferences in the autumn of 1973.[2] It consists of two parts: first a comparison of the policy aims for transport now and in the future, and secondly a summary of proposals for various aspects of transport—roads, railways, energy, etc.

I—*General Policy Aims*

Each party clearly emphasises its conception of the key issue around which transport policy should evolve. For the Labour Party it is "to improve necessary personal mobility for the *majority* of people"; for the Liberals it is that "individuals or groups should be *free* to choose which form of transport they wish to use"; the Conservatives present *"three crucial aspects"* of concern—"social need, safety and the environment". Accordingly, the parties take different approaches to the subject of management and finance. The Conservative policy is described in general terms as "combining freedom of movement, freedom of competition and freedom of choice", and was specifically translated into the following resolution (carried by an overwhelming majority) at the last conference: "That this conference accepts the necessity for the provision of an adequate system of public transport which may have to be financed in part out of

---

[1] This summary was prepared before the political parties published their manifestoes for the General Election in January 1974.

[2] To date the Liberal Party has not been able to supply us with an up-to-date brochure from the 1973 conference, although it has sent along copies of the most important resolutions passed. Therefore, quotations concerning its approach have been taken from the 1970 *Candidates' Handbook* supplied by the party until such time as they can send a more recent pamphlet.

public funds, but it reaffirms its belief in the duty of H.M. Government and local authorities to make adequate provision for the motor car in urban areas and rejects the proposition that motorists are an anti-social section of the community from whom facilities should be withdrawn".

Labour, on the other hand, regards public transport as a "social service rather than as a purely commercial undertaking", and therefore encourages the following approach: "To ensure that the financial aspects of transport policy—charging policies and allowable expenses for tax purposes, and the benefits and disbenefits of investment—work in a progressive rather than a regressive manner". This is specifically translated into a proposal for a national policy towards "promoting public transport and discouraging the use of cars for the journey to work in city areas", and the statement that with "the provision of adequate subsidies to help contain increases in fares, Labour will promote experiments in free public transport within our major conurbations". "We do not accept the outdated proposition that public transport must 'pay its way' . . . subsidised public transport, including transport on waterways, can create incalculable savings in terms of pollution, of time lost and, we hope, in terms of reduced accidents".

Thus the Conservative and Labour parties take opposing and predictable views concerning the management and finance of transport, which are in accord with their general philosophies. The Liberals take a slightly different approach to reach their objective: that everyone should have freedom of choice concerning the "form of transport they wish to use". They propose "placing the real costs of different kinds of transport on the users of the services concerned"; furthermore these costs include "both the market price and social obligations—such as safety, noise, air pollution and parking or driving in congested areas". More specifically they propose that the private car be restricted in certain designated areas of towns and cities with the provision of "a frequent, convenient and fares-free public transport service within the designated areas". Moreover, they propose that the major responsibility for transport planning and administration should go to "democratic *regional* councils" with "through services provided nationally". This emphasis on regional responsibility for transport appears to be a key objective for the Liberals; at the Edinburgh Assembly in 1968 the party endorsed a plan of basic reforms in the field of transport "because it believed that Britain had a transport system which is mismanaged and, in large measure, inefficient, dangerous and congested". Top priority was given to "establishing Regional Transport Authorities to determine priorities of investment in all forms of transport in the regions; co-ordinate long term planning of main roads, ports, airports, railways and inland waterways; exercise most of the administrative powers currently centralised in the Ministry of Transport". The only transport issues which the Liberals proposed should be handled at national level were planning and maintaining of motorways, accident enquiries, and basic research.

From the brochures and handouts it would appear that the Labour Party is the only party to include social justice issues as part of its general policy approach to transport. In a section entitled "broad aims" it encourages a policy which would "pay particular attention to the needs of the old, the disabled and the poor who may otherwise be cut off from broader relationships and job opportunities"; "It must be remembered that about half the people in this country do not own, nor have the regular use of, a car." Furthermore transport policy should "work within a general planning context to save the character of our cities and countryside— not merely the showpieces and beauty spots—so long as this does not mean perpetuating poor living conditions; and to maintain, in new developments, a sympathetic scale for human living".

II—*Specific proposals concerning various aspects of transport*

Urban transport receives most attention in the various manifestos published by the parties. While Labour proposes to discourage private cars in urban areas, the Conservatives feel that adequate provision should be made for them, while the Liberals come out between the two, proposing restrictions in certain designated areas of towns and cities rather than a broad policy of discouragement in towns. How do the parties see urban transport problems solved more specifically?:

The Liberals want "as many traffic-free shopping precincts as possible, and also to encourage the more rapid introduction of traffic-free streets in the centres of our older cities. Many such streets have been converted from existing thoroughfares on the Continent and all of them have been a considerable success". On public *vs.* private transport, they advocate cutting down on private transport by either "raising charges for motorists more rapidly than fares on railways, the underground and buses, or in reducing public transport fares", the latter involving "public subsidy". Thus the Liberals tend to stand for the preservation of public transport at all costs. This was evidenced by a resolution adopted by the Margate Assembly in 1972, "to preserve transport for the continuity of our communities. Where operators threaten to withdraw services Liberals will campaign to encourage local residents to form ad hoc committees to run local services where necessary, and fight to maintain existing services".

The "new grant system" to be introduced with the reorganisation of local government is seen by the Conservatives as offering the new counties the opportunity "to study their transport problems comprehensively and to develop policies which will take account of the interaction between roads and public and private transport". While they state as a major objective "providing further for the private car in urban areas", no proposals are put forward to further this end; on the contrary, John Peyton stated at the recent party conference when referring to public transport: "We have given unprecedented support to infrastructure transport projects in urban areas ... We have been giving increasing support to the railways, £140 million in 1972, and it will be considerably more this year".

The Labour proposals call for more experiments with free public transport in conurbations and propose that registered taxis be treated as public service vehicles, that is, that the fares be kept "within reason and that taxis be exempt from V.A.T." It is further proposed that "as regards old-age pensioners, the blind or partially sighted, and those suffering from disabilities, we pledge ourselves to introduce a country-wide system of fares-free transport". The Labour policy is opposed to the grant system because a "local authority is free to pick from a very limited range of options ... We feel that while different conurbations have different physical configurations and dissimilar transport histories and traditions, the main transport problems in all of them are surprisingly similar. In other words, a national policy is possible as well as desirable, even though there will be need for variations in its detailed implementation."

Freight

All the parties advocate the increased use of rail services. Mr. Peyton stated at the recent Blackpool conference: "I am currently reviewing the possibilities of getting more identified traffic back on to rail." This bore special reference to the "Channel Tunnel which will afford to British Rail very substantial new opportunities for long haul." But at the same conference he pointed out that "90% of freight journeys are less than 100 miles" and the average is 30 miles; "therefore neither the land nor the distance is suitable for railways". The Liberals proposed that both rail and waterways be encouraged for freight use and that both Boards be prevented from either closing down or allowing deterioration of any railway lines or waterways. The Labour Party brochure gives more details of railway proposals: "Unless traffic moves between rail-connected sidings there will be a road journey at the beginning or the end and, with the present location of rail terminals, the road journey will often be through an urban area. . . . We may well need to take measures to encourage private sidings; we need to investigate the feasibility of cross-city freight lines and we need to extend the ability of skilled, publicly owned transport agents to provide a door-to-door service using rail transport wherever possible". Labour further recommends that coastwise shipping should play a bigger part in long haul freight, especially in the light of containerisation, and thus "there is an even greater need for the shipping industry to be closely integrated with road, rail and port transport . . . The inland waterways should be exploited to the maximum rather than the minimum". Neither the Conservative nor the Liberal Party mentions the waterways and coastwise shipping in reference to the moving of freight, although the Liberals, again promoting regional rule, recommend that the control and planning of the docks should pass to the provinces so that they can overcome "bad labour relations, restrictive practices, poor management, bad forecasting and, above all, an inability to view the ports and their surroundings as a whole, thus leaving them without adequate access". This they propose so that industry should profit from more efficient port service, especially for exports.

Both the Conservatives and the Liberals have an anti-juggernaut proposal; they are against "any significant increase in permitted axle loading".

Railways

Both the Liberals and Labour come down strongly against the Conservative Government for "contemplating a reduction in railway route mileage" (Labour). Labour goes on to say that it would "halt this process. This is necessary to show that we are serious about maintaining a national system, and to give a measure of confidence to workers in the industry, to passengers and to customers". They further suggest that the railway system cannot be "reduced to some mythically 'profitable core' " and therefore that there is "an urgent need for a general examination of the financial structure of the railways". The Liberals, in addition to wanting to encourage freight back on to the railways, state in their 1972 Council Resolution that commuters should be persuaded to use rail services, which should be "recognised as a social service particularly in rural areas, and be subsidised accordingly; that the *true* cost of rail services be used in assessing their feasibility, including environmental factors, social necessity, etc., but not capital outlay".

Without being specific, the Conservatives merely state that they "do not consider 'Draconian cuts' in the railway network are the answer to the industry's or the nation's problems" and that later in 1973 proposals will be announced for the future of the railroads.

Road building and motorways

The Conservative Government had to postpone its trunk road programme announced in June 1971, which laid particular emphasis on the trunk road scheme "especially as regards access to the major ports and provision of by-passes to relieve towns and villages from long distance lorry traffic". Looking to the future Mr. Peyton at the 1973 conference said: "The number of motor vehicles which has grown from $4\frac{1}{2}$ million in 1950 to 16 million now is expected to reach 22 million by 1980, and people would expect to be able to make some use of these motor vehicles . . . We should be able to accommodate them, but we have to do so in a balanced way".

With its commitment to public transport the Labour party does not present a road or motorway programme. Rather it states: "All trunk and principal road schemes of urban road building which have not reached the exchange of contract stage should be re-examined". In its other pamphlet published in 1973, *The Politics of Environment*, Labour expands on its rationale, while supporting subsidised public transport: "It is unacceptable to go on talking about 'the loss' which Britsh Rail makes when no accounts are produced to show how much the roads 'lose'. With motorways costing well over a million pounds a mile to build nobody can say the roads 'pay' on any basis of calculation." The only reference to motorways from the Liberals is in their 1970 *Candidates' Handbook*, in which they propose more city-linking motorways or trunk roads: "Roads linking different parts of the country do not suffer from the same kind of congestion as traffic within cities. The cost per mile of motorways to link cities, to by-pass urban areas and to link them with ports and airports is much less than the cost per mile of urban motorways" (which they are against because of the nuisance to people living next to them). They feel that Britain lags behind other industrial countries "in terms of spending on road building per head of the population"; they go on to point out that inter-city motorways would benefit the country as a whole "in terms of reduced industrial costs, reduced export prices and better export delivery dates".

Rural transport

Both the Liberals and Labour devote sections of their conference reports to rural transport problems. Labour states: "We cannot expect these services to pay their way," and points out that insufficient use is made by the local authorities of their opportunity to recoup losses from loss-making rural bus services from the Exchequer. While also supporting the subsidising of loss-making rail services in rural areas (as well as loss-making commuter services), the party concludes that "greater local authority control over rural services" may be necessary.

311

The Liberals take the view that, since there will be 17 million more people by the year 2000 and our cities are already "bursting at the seams", there will undoubtedly be more new towns in areas at present undeveloped. Therefore the closing down of currently underused rail services is a short-sighted view: "We cannot possibly accept a plan for transport which has no regard to the question of where people are going to live, work and play in the Britain of the future." As a result of an experiment in North Devon a number of proposals were adopted by the Liberal Advisory Panel on Transport. They all concern bus services; minibuses for passengers and mail, fare-paying passengers on school buses, more flexible buses without timetable or set routes and ready to carry passengers to and from certain destinations to be agreed locally. In general they would like to disband the National Bus Company and replace it by county council or contract private owners, create locally elected rural bus committees where all can make their needs known, and "relax regulations that forbid delivery services being merged with bus operations" (Assembly, 1971).

While the Conservatives make no mention of rural transport, they pledge themselves to preserve the countryside from the ill effects of lorries.

Airports—Maplin

A 1971 Council resolution by the Liberals declared: "This Council of the Liberal Party calls on Her Majesty's Government to examine the present siting and use of international airports in the United Kingdom and future needs for such airports. It deplores the short-sightedness of assessing airport needs simply in relation to London and urges that expansion of international airport facilities should be concentrated outside South-East England. It affirms that, wherever possible, future major airports should be sited away from populated areas so as to minimise damage to the environment." General policy statements were not provided by the other parties. All the parties have very particular attitudes towards Maplin; as would be expected, the Conservative Government feels that it is a programme Britain cannot afford to abandon because there will be "an extra 20 million passengers a year to Heathrow by the mid-1980s", which would mean doubling the M4, providing a rail link as well, removing a large sewage works there and increasing Stansted traffic fivefold.

On the other hand, Labour claims that recent studies by the Civil Aviation Authority "have tended to show lower demand figures for London area passenger air transport movements, and in view of the movement of population and the introduction of air buses and jumbos this is scarcely surprising". They consider Maplin to be an environmental mistake because of the loss of homes, coastline and rare wild-life; further it will divert resources away from the development of regional airports and will ultimately have no effect on noise levels at Heathrow, since the development of quieter aircraft will be the deciding factor.

The 1973 Council Resolution from the Liberal Party conveys the same attitude as the Labour view, with more detailed objections to the plan: "The use of the mouth of the Thames by fleets of large tankers will create unacceptable dangers and pollution hazards"; "the shortage of fossil fuels will become more acute within a few years of the projected operational date of the Airport, putting in serious question the volume of air travel which it is designed to accommodate". It proposes a rethinking of the future of air traffic, the design of aircraft, the use of existing airports and the need for a deep water port.

In anticipation of the environmental concern the Conservatives passed a resolution at the last conference which "calls upon Her Majesty's Government to ensure that these projects (Maplin and the Channel Tunnel) are planned not only to prevent any deleterious effect upon the environment in their immediate neighbourhood but also to improve the quality of life of the whole country by making certain that adequate road and rail links are built, thus diminishing heavy traffic on unsuitable roads and restoring a measure of peace to those communities which are adversely affected".

Channel Tunnel

The Conservative Government supports the Channel Tunnel on two grounds: "to generate traffic and trade with Europe", and to save money on road building and port expansion: "Without the Tunnel more traffic would have to go by road. Dover and other South-east ports would have to be expanded at considerable cost, including back-up facilities." On environmental grounds it points out that more road building would involve "greater demolition of houses, to make way for the new road pattern that would be necessary", than would the building of Maplin. The Liberals call for more information so that "an informed choice" can be made between alternatives "with due regard to environmental and developmental considerations". They propose to ensure that only freight would be carried by through rail services between Britain and the continent. The information received from the Labour Party contained no references to the Tunnel.

Environmental issues—pollution, noise and energy

In August 1972 the Conservatives announced a phased programme to reduce the lead content of petrol by cutting the maximum level by almost a half over a period of three years. The Labour party promises to set up "progressive programmes for cleaning up our environment, containing completion dates and timetables"; it makes special reference to "vehicle exhausts", which will "not be allowed to lag behind any imposed schedule".

The Conservatives promise to introduce legislation regarding noise levels, particularly from heavy lorries; the Labour Party promises to introduce "tighter restrictions on noise levels for motor vehicles" and to "implement a ban on supersonic flights over Britain and introduce even tighter controls over general aircraft noise".

Neither of these issues is referred to in the information received from the Liberal Party. The Liberals passed a special resolution regarding energy at the 1973 Assembly in which they proposed, on account of the world energy crisis, that a permanent Energy Commission be set up to advise the government; that there be introduced "immediate measures to promote more economical use of energy in transport, power generation," etc.; that explicit assumptions about price availability of energy be stated for all projects— Maplin, motorways, etc.; that Britain's dependence on imported energy be reduced, and that alternative modes of energy be developed. The Conservatives included nothing on energy in their brochures and Labour made only a general reference to research into substitutes for the "dwindling finite resources".

The Urban Mobility Problems of the Elderly
Jackie Garden

Introduction

A5.1 Although this study is confined to the problems of the elderly in towns, other groups such as the disabled, the poor, the young and housewives without access to a car during the day suffer from similar problems in urban and suburban areas. Taken together the people in these groups form a substantial proportion of the population.

A5.2 The form and location of transport services available for journeys within towns, route patterns, frequency, reliability, the cost of fares and the design of the vehicles used all create problems for the elderly. Much of the information drawn upon here was collected from different parts of the country; it is evident that the same problems recur in many areas. Sources for this study are the *Age Concern report on Transport*; a joint report issued by four Age Concern groups entitled *The Northern Forum*; and additional information from many contacts and much correspondence with elderly people.

A5.3 Why do the elderly travel? Although the journey to work seldom figures among the transport needs of the elderly, they do travel regularly, particularly to visit the Post Office and to shop. Other trips are made in order to visit friends and relatives, either in their homes or in hospital, and for social activities, for example to attend old people's clubs and day centres. In many cases, deteriorating health will also require regular visits to the doctor, clinics and hospitals. The great majority of elderly people do not have the use of a car, and indeed 85% of those over 65 do not hold a driving licence. The problems of urban mobility discussed below refer either to public transport (usually buses) or to walking.

A5.4 Difficulties encountered with shopping trips are related both to the particular circumstances of pensioners and to more general problems of location.

A5.5 Frequent shopping trips are necessary because many old people do not own refrigerators, lack storage space, and have insufficient means to buy in large quantities. Others may be too frail to carry heavy loads of shopping, particularly if they live some distance from the shops. "Rather a long walk from the shops, so have to do a little shopping each day—but find roads and pavements very bad when one has a painful knee. Cannot carry too much at a time." And from another: "I have to make extra journeys because I cannot carry everything I require at once." To be able to do one's own shopping is a basic principle. With increasing age, however, it can only be managed if the distances involved are short. For people suffering from arthritis, shortness of breath or unsteady legs, carrying shopping bags makes journeys slow, painful and ultimately impossible. Developments in the last twenty years have increased these difficulties for the elderly.

A5.6 In many towns there has been considerable urban renewal which has caused the destruction of old communities. The former residents find themselves dispersed and, as a result of economic pressures, are often rehoused at some distance from the city centre. The new developments and estates no longer support the close street structure of the corner shop, the local butcher, the Post Office and the pub. It would appear that the increasing closure of small shops is causing much concern to old people. For those who, because of their restricted mobility, depended on small local shops the anxiety can be acute: "All the stalls clear off at 1 p.m. and some shops close down Mondays and Thursdays. Lots of shops have closed down completely and more are going. How are disabled people like me going to get food?"

A5.7 Removal and relocation of the elderly give rise to many difficulties. This is particularly so when they are called upon to change their patterns of travel, using services which are ill adapted to their needs. The fear of isolation and the need to maintain communication is consistently referred to.

"Owing to a large amount of development in the area elderly people have been rehoused in areas where they have no family or friends. If they cannot afford to take the bus then they become isolated."

A5.8 Physical location is also a problem for those who have to walk. "On my return from the shops with the goods I have bought, I have to walk up a big hill before getting to my bungalow ... and it is very exhausting, especially in winter. These pensioners' bungalows are very nice, but why they had to build them up a hill like this, I really don't know." These problems are not always directly caused by local authorities, for many pensioners retire to new areas by choice at a time when they are fit and well. They then suffer from isolation because of the loss of a partner (usually the husband) and also, in some cases, because of the distance at which they now live from family and friends, and through lack of public transport. "Apart from the council rented property there are many elderly living $1\frac{1}{2}$ miles from the town on estates; these people come to retire here. Unfortunately, after a few years the husband dies and their transport goes with him; they also find great difficulty getting into town for shopping."

The elderly pedestrian

A5.9 The problem of the elderly pedestrian is two-fold: traffic today is markedly worse than it was twenty years ago and walking is more difficult for old people. Many find today's traffic both dangerous and frightening, and crossing main roads and the town High Street is a particular problem. "Main road too busy with vehicles—have to make detour down back roads" is a typical comment. Another remark often made is "Walking for us is too slow, difficult and wearisome." In addition to having to cope with the speed and increased volume of traffic on the roads, elderly people have slower reactions to the approach of danger. They also walk more slowly, often with a stick or a frame, and they find that insufficient time is allowed for crossing at busy intersections. The lack of an auditory signal at lights-controlled crossings, and steep kerbs, are additional hazards for those whose eyesight is poor.

A5.10 Elderly people in towns, most of whom are pedestrians from necessity, therefore have the worst of both worlds. They bear the social cost of busier roads, higher vehicle exhaust levels and deteriorating conditions for the pedestrian generally, at a time when physically they find walking increasingly difficult. Their need for a cheap, reliable, sensibly routed public transport service is therefore even greater than that of other non-car owners. Unfortunately these requirements are seldom met.

High costs of travel and the social life of the elderly

A5.11 A popular social activity among the elderly is attendance at old people's clubs and day centres. These supply a great variety of facilities, and many find in them friends and recreation, often with hot meals and all-day warmth. For old people they provide a social activity that is central to their lives. Travel to these clubs is very important, and the many reports of transport difficulties and consequent curtailment of recreational activities are disturbing. Although the clubs mostly draw on a local membership there will often be members who have been rehoused some distance away and who need to travel back to maintain old friendships. Some of the larger day centres have a much wider catchment area, and the cost of making good deficient public transport by offering specialised transport for the old and the disabled can be a costly burden on local authorities. Volunteers often help to provide transport, but it would seem that there are many old people who cannot attend such centres as regularly as they wish because of high fares. "A Veterans' Club, open every day, and drawing members from a wide area, was finding that members were having to come less often. Another club reported that some bowling fixtures were being cancelled as members could not afford the bus fares." This kind of remark is often made both by the elderly themselves and by club leaders. "Some of the members attend a club once a week only, instead of twice, due to the cost of travel." "We are having difficulty with some of our members who, owing to the increased fares, cannot afford to come to the club every week and are now having to come about every second week. This they do not like." These activities matter a great deal to old people and particularly to those who live alone, for they may well provide the only time during the week when they have other people to talk to. One club leader said: "I could quote any number of instances where

318

lonely people, who need the companionship of the centre, can now only come in three times a week instead of six or seven owing to the cost of the bus fare".

A5.12 In addition to attendance at clubs and day centres, regular contact with friends and relations is vital in maintaining the reassuring continuity of relationships. This does not necessarily mean that old people wish simply to receive visits. For many, performing a useful service such as baby-sitting or visiting friends and relatives in hospital is a means of establishing that they still have an active, independent role in society. The elderly often dislike having to accept help from younger people and delight in continuing to perform useful service for others. For this reason travel limitations can create hardship, since they may bring the need to accept a more passive role. "There is general hardship involving old people visiting their relatives in hospital, as we have no large hospital in this district and it means travelling to C . . . . . or R . . . . . by bus. The increased fare makes it very costly."

A5.13 For some old people it becomes necessary to trade off one form of journey against another because of financial hardship. "Seven members come to the club from a suburb and find it very heavy on their purses to come into town for shopping and other various functions which they say if they have to give up they will soon become housebound. Others find the bus fares too high and they have to cut vital visits to other members of the family and friends and neighbours in hospital." One old lady was spending on travel instead of food in order to make some trips: "Have to go without lunch if I go to town. Fares much too high for an O.A.P."

A5.14 Those not living on a fixed income or a pension may not appreciate how delicately balanced a pensioner's budget can be and the relative importance of a fare increase is not always realised. "Even an increase from 3p to 4p on a single local fare presents a problem to a pensioner." Although many areas have now adopted a free or concessionary fares policy, this is by no means universally accepted and indeed raises problems of equity among pensioners with different mobility needs. Cost, however, is only one of the factors that contribute to the transport problems of old people.

Inconvenient services

A5.15 For the elderly, as for other users of public transport, convenience is clearly associated with the frequency, reliability and routeing of services. Long waits of 30 to 40 minutes at an unsheltered bus stop without anywhere to sit are tiresome enough for a normally fit person, but for the elderly they can mean painful hardship and are likely to become a positive deterrent to regular journeys. When scheduled services fail to arrive, as they do, all too often as a result of staff shortages, this can cause much distress to someone who has timed his journey to fit, for example, hospital visiting hours.

A5.16 Other difficulties arise from changes in routes and services, the implications of which have not always been investigated in advance. An established network is something to which the elderly become accustomed, and changes can be extremely disturbing. The following example is characteristic: "A number of services were changed in a reorganisation. Complaints about services were mostly linked with those changes as some inter-suburban journeys became less convenient. Residents in one suburb in the east side lost a direct bus link with some parts of the west side where many appeared to have relatives. In another district a direct bus link to an adjoining area with a concentration of doctors' surgeries, chiropodists, hairdressers, etc., was lost."

A5.17 No traveller likes to have his journey broken by changing vehicles, and the elderly are no exception. Changing buses is expensive, because it involves two fares, and is time-consuming and tiring because additional waiting is required. "The main present difficulty is that it is not possible to travel from one district to another without going to the centre first and transferring to another bus to complete the journey". Slow complex journeys of this kind can make regular visiting, which means a great deal to the people involved, a real nightmare. "Journeys to hospital and back are alarming. All we need is a little help to make these necessary trips not such a worry."

A5.18 The problems are exacerbated both by less frequent evening services (often the time when visiting takes place) and also by reduced and sometimes non-existent Sunday services. Car-owning relatives and neighbours cannot always be relied upon to fill these gaps. Constant regular visiting, perhaps between a husband and wife, can often be a harrowing experience over a considerable period of time. Infrequent and unreliable services, combined with perhaps ill-considered changes of route, can cause a great deal of hardship and must, in many cases, deter elderly people from making journeys which they would have made under better conditions.

Design and operation of vehicles

A5.19 The design of public transport vehicles is unlikely in itself to deter the elderly from using them, but there is considerable evidence that many elderly people do encounter serious difficulties. With increasing age and fragility old people are likely to be easily discouraged.

A5.20 Many see the process of boarding and riding on a bus as a series of obstacles and hazards which have to be overcome. Beginning with the point of entry, it is an effort to climb on to the bus for most, and a painful process for those with bad legs. The height of the steps is one of the most frequently mentioned problems. "Steps are too high on all buses, especially for those suffering from arthritis in hips and legs. One-man buses cannot help the elderly ones off buses." This problem of high steps is often compounded by buses not pulling right into the kerb, so that the height is even greater. Parked cars and traffic congestion are usually responsible for this. One-man buses, which are increasingly being used, are disliked not only because there is no conductor to help, but because of the need to pay the fare while standing up, carrying shopping and perhaps a stick. All too frequently the bus will jerk into motion before there is time to secure a seat. The elderly dislike asking for help and yet feel guilty because they are holding up other passengers.

A5.21 Additional problems are raised by the seating arrangements; the long bench seats near the entrance are unpopular because they are often too high and there is nothing to hold on to when the bus is braking or going round a corner. Some people, particularly those less steady on their feet, experience great difficulty in reaching the bell and walking down the aisle to the door while the bus is in motion. Yet those who are slower-moving are often fearful of being either shut in the doors or taken on beyond their stop. On very crowded buses drivers cannot always see the exit doors clearly.

Conclusion

A5.22 It is impossible to tell how many old people, including those in relatively good health, give up using public transport because of the deficiencies described above. When this does happen they become dependent on their ability to walk (often in unpleasant traffic conditions) and, for longer recreational trips, on relatives or friends with cars. They may have to resort to taxis for some essential trips. The elderly thus begin to lose their much-valued independence and, depending on the location of their homes and the different facilities they require, they become practically housebound. A5.23 It is a matter of social concern that the elderly should not be forced off public transport, and it is in the interest of the whole community that they should continue to travel for as long as they wish and are able, thus maintaining their independence and their social life. Urban transport planners and operators should be aware of the consequences of pedestrian hazards and defects in public transport on the well-being of many elderly people.

Sources:
Age Concern: *Age Concern on Transport* (1971)
Age Concern: *Northern Forum on Transport*
Age Concern: *Shopping for Food*

The Impact on Rural Life of Declining Public Transport Services for Communities and Individuals

by Lois Pulling and Colin Speakman

A6.1 Between half and a third of country people in many rural areas now suffer an isolation unprecedented since the age of the stagecoach. For some of them scarcely any means of transport now remain, and the basic needs of life are in jeopardy unless they rely upon the charity of voluntary organisations, the WRVS, or kind neighbours. We make the claim in full knowledge that it clashes with official accounts, but we are counting not households—the favourite unit of official researchers—but people, each to count for one. If our attitude to the situation is at odds with that of some other observers, it is partly for this reason and partly because we find it paradoxical that an affluent society, which has everywhere else tried to reduce people's dependence upon charity, should set such store by it in the field of rural transport. It is not just that, as one respondent said, "No one likes to be beholden". It is also that total dependence upon charity (a) has certain dangers we shall discuss and (b) can solve only a small part of the rural transport problem (while it may well make the rest of the problems even more intractable by further undermining the economics of remaining public transport services).

A6.2 If there have been few general studies of the effects of the withdrawal or reduction of public transport services on individuals and communities, there have been even fewer systematic studies of the problem in a rural context. Any studies that we have seen have tended to take a relatively superficial view of what rural transport deprivation really means. No study we have seen was compiled or written by people who were actually dependent on the rural bus or train services they were describing. Nonetheless, the studies that we know do confirm certain clear and general patterns. It seems that the people who suffer in rural areas when services are reduced or withdrawn are, as always, the old, the poor, the disabled, the young, and womenfolk. Taken together these represent a substantial number of the rural population needing or seeking transport. But the difference between town and country is not just a question of degree. Facilities in rural areas are more scattered and at far longer distances from people's homes. For many people in the country the ownership of a car is therefore as necessary as food or the roof over their heads. This explains why car ownership is significantly higher in the countryside than in towns. It suggests that a significantly higher percentage of personal incomes in the countryside has to be diverted, whether willingly or not, into the owning and running of a motor vehicle or vehicles.

A6.3 Two of the most influential studies of rural transport produced in recent years were the reports commissioned by the Department of the Environment for Devon and West Suffolk [1], [2]. These studies were published in 1971 and have had a considerable effect on official thinking on rural transport questions, and are in some ways a useful step forward in helping government and local authorities to recognise the complexity of the problem.

A6.4 The studies are incomplete, however, in certain respects. Problems are not always seen in their full complexity, nor are wider environmental and social factors taken into account. But the chief failure of both reports lies in their inexplicit assumption that the rural transport problem is essentially the problem of a small residue of non-car owners. The message of these reports is that, with co-operation and voluntary effort, the problem arising within these areas can be easily solved.

A6.5 That view is misleading. Rural transport problems are more far-reaching than the reports seem to recognise, and the limited solutions they suggest overlook the fundamental nature of the difficulty. We examine the Devon study [1] to substantiate these claims.

324

Study of rural transport in Devon

A6.6 The Devon Steering Group consisted of nine members
—the Transport Co ordinating Officer of Devon County
Council, three officials of the Department of the Environment (one of whom served as the Group's secretary,
another as its chairman); two county councillors, one former
Deputy Chairman of the Executive Board of the National
Bus Company, and one chartered surveyor. Only one
member, County Alderman Mrs. Perkins, was a woman.
Given the structure of the Steering Group, which consisted
in the main of local authority officers and did not include
any members of the general public, we think it would have
been surprising if they had been able to see the problem in
the same light as housewives, teenagers or poorer agricultural workers and pensioners. The greatest weakness of the
report lies in its inability to explore properly the deprivation
of the less fortunate—the group described by Hillman [3] as
experiencing "mobility deprivation". This is compensated to
some extent in both the Suffolk and Devon Reports by
appendices prepared from the findings of the British Market
Research Bureau.

A6.7 The changes that the Steering Committee records
arise in the first instance from a rapid increase in car ownership. In comparing results from a previous survey in the
Crediton district, the report notes that households owning
cars increased from 44% in 1963 to 72% in 1971. (The latter
figure is lower than the average of 74% noted for the study
area as a whole.) There had been a corresponding decline in
the number of public transport services offered. Between
1961 and 1971 210 miles of railway line had been closed,
together with 82 stations and halts; a mere 191 miles and
51 stations were left, and many of them were under sentence
of closure at the time the report was being written. The
report concludes that "railways no longer play any significant part in the rural transport scene in Devon" (para. 3.7)
—a questionable assumption on any view, unless it is supposed that surviving transport services do not or cannot or
should not provide connecting services to existing railheads.

A6.8 Bus services had also declined—less dramatically than
rail services, but the report was written before the National
Bus Company's draconian cuts in rural bus services. Before

325

this happened, and between 1955 and 1970, there had been a 25% reduction in road passenger mileage along the Western National routes, and a 50% reduction in passenger mileage. No figures for the smaller, independent operators (which numbered 26 in the county) were supplied. The report simply takes it for granted that this process will continue (para. 3.16), and that the forces which created this situation—including the familiar cost–fares spiral—will continue.

A6.9 The Devon and Suffolk studies were regarded as case studies with wider national implications, but it was shown in Appendix A of the reports that 20% of the respondents were from AB social classifications (professional and managerial grades), the national average being 12·5%. Together with certain other evidence in the Devon report, this suggests that the study is less typical than the Minister has assumed. In Devon it seems there are more prosperous households and more motor cars than in other regions of Britain, such as Scotland, Wales or the Pennine regions.

A6.10 But even in Devon, the BMRB survey notes "the availability of a car is strongly related to sex (men more than twice as likely as women), to social grade (AB about three times as likely as DE) and to age (25–44 nearly three times as likely as those over 65)." A substantial part of the population must be without the immediate use of a car.

A6.11 That there will always be a substantial number of people without the use of a car is accepted by the report; but, curiously, it confuses actual behaviour (section 4) with "demand". In order to discover what is likely to be future "demand", four main headings are devised— *Work Journeys*, (mostly supplied by private car, including lifts, and some contract buses), *School Transport* (using both stage services and contract hire; out-of-school provision is conceded to be "haphazard"); *Shopping and Personal Trips* (mostly private transport, with only 13% of shopping trips and 5% of personal trips by bus); and *Leisure Journeys*. With disarming simplicity the report notes that for these purposes "buses are only used if available." Which is only to say that if there is no public transport people without cars have nothing else to depend on than the casual charity of lifts.

A6.12 The weakness of the report is exposed when the authors examine a village totally without public transport—

the village of Spreyton. Here, as elsewhere in the report, where people are deprived of transport, they are praised for their "adaptability". But even in prosperous Spreyton, where almost every household has a car and lifts are offered freely, it is conceded that there is a problem—"chiefly among housewives whose husbands drove to work in the family car". What the problem means to this group is not indicated, except by the observation that a fifth and only a fifth of the people in the village (i.e. 60 people) thought they would make one or more trips a week if a bus service were to be provided. "Clearly people have adapted to the absence of a bus; those who could not, presumably left some time ago. Those who have moved in, including retired people, have cars" (para. 4.31). The report does not speculate about the social character of a rural community recruited or maintained in this fashion.

A6.13 The Steering Committee has many positive and useful recommendations to make about using the subsidy provisions of Section 34 of the 1968 Transport Act to maintain basic services, and using school, works, postal and dual purpose (local carriers') vehicles more intelligently to get a better standard of co-ordinated service; but its overall solution lies in simply recognising ever greater car ownership and using "lifts" and voluntary services to replace communal enterprise. The broader implications of rising car ownership, including the trend towards two and three-car families in country areas, the resulting congestion and demand for car parking in neighbouring country towns, and the long-term social and ecological implications, are all ignored. Equally, the morality of casual charity replacing a public service and the danger of encouraging young people, especially girls and women, to depend on the lift offered by a total stranger who may be criminally inclined, is not considered.

A6.14 The assumption that people have "adapted" to low levels of public transport is not supported by the evidence that 36% of the respondents of the survey in Appendix A of the report reported that they were unable to make journeys they would have liked to make. Of these, 45% suggested that this happened one day a week or more often, leisure being the main source of deprivation. Most people felt that public transport was unsatisfactory. One third noted that "they had relatives or friends unable to visit them because of deficiencies in public transport." The real meaning of the deprivation is indicated by the fact that 47% of the carless reported that it was either "not very easy" or "not at all easy" to obtain lifts.

Study of rural problems in Lincolnshire and
East Nottingham

A6.15 A more recent study [4], published by the Open University and written by the Lincolnshire Geographical Research Group (Joan Garlick, Bill Goodhand and John Molyneux), with a study on the economics of rural bus services in Lincolnshire by Mark Evans of Hull University, has a different emphasis and focus from those of the DoE Devon study. It recognises that the problem of rural transport is broader and more complex than is often assumed— it is "a key problem in rural geography". Unfortunately, comparative statistics for car ownership figures are not available, but car ownership would seem to be lower than in rural Devon. There is still much dependence on public transport.

A6.16 The report looks at six Rural Districts (Caistor, Louth, Horncastle, Neward and East and West Kesteven) in some detail, and notes that it is impossible to make a complete distinction between rural and urban services. For instance, when tougher parking measures were introduced in the city of Nottingham, local operators noticed improvements in passenger mileage ratios on their bus services because passengers were discouraged from using cars on trips into the town. This suggests that the more radical measures introduced in Nottingham in 1973 may help public transport in the surrounding areas. The report suggests that attitudes towards public transport are changing and that the immediate goal should be to sustain existing public transport services until there are new appraisals and new initiatives.

A6.17 As in Devon, railway services have been severely pruned. As recently as 1971 the East Lincolnshire line was closed, and surviving lines such as the Grimsby–Lincoln–London line have lost their local stations. Villages in the Lincolnshire wolds have been left entirely without rail or bus services. The Nottingham–Lincoln line still has local trains and unstaffed halts served on a paytrain basis. Market Rasen station on the Lincoln–Grimsby line has become the railhead for the surrounding districts and has more trains than before.

A6.18 The Lincolnshire Road Car Company operates bus services on the main arterial roads. The authors of the Report comment on the company's unresponsiveness to the needs of local communities. These needs are better satisfied by small local operators. Because they have lower overheads, because they can operate within the community they serve rather than from some distant garage, and because they cross-subsidise from lucrative private hire and contract work, these concerns can often run a stage carriage service at lower fares and with greater flexibility than the LRC. Mark Evans, who contributes the section of the paper on the economics of rural bus operation in Lincolnshire, speaks of the advantages of a complex "fabric" of interdependent rural transport services, with the LRC providing the inter-urban services while smaller operators provide complementary services. So far from this being the declining industry usually supposed, Evans suggests that there is a substantial market for public transport at economic rates. He does however concede that stage services, because they have to run throughout the year, are usually a financial risk for any operator, and must often require grant aid and some protection from market forces. The refusal of Lindsey County Council to make grants under Section 34 of the 1968 Transport Act has already meant withdrawals, because of the policy adopted by the National Bus Company since 1970. Evans notes a contradiction here. Lindsey County Council had given grants for "social car services" run by the Lindsey and Holland Rural Community Council and the WRVS for essential purposes, but had refused grants for equally essential LRCC or independent bus services.

A6.19 Mark Evans' solution is to establish a Rural Passenger Transport Authority for the county—rather on the pattern of urban Passenger Transport Authorities—with powers to co-ordinate the overall pattern of services and make grants where necessary to support essential services and promote the best use of contract, works and schools services, postal buses and local delivery services. It would determine the levels of service essential for the well-being of the community as a whole.

A6.20 Thus when, as Joan Garlick reports, "lack of daily transport in North Kelsey is preventing young people from taking advantage of available jobs in the towns", or, as Dennis Mills notes, the village of South Clifton in Newark RDC has lost its bus service and now has several empty houses (Lincolnshire not enjoying the same attraction for car-owning, retired couples as Spreyton, Devon), it would be for the RPTA to determine the scale of the problem and investigate the level of service required to remedy matters. Integration of road, rail and postal services on the Swiss pattern would also be encouraged by an authority able to use the financial incentive of grants to mould transport to the most efficient and economical pattern for both community and operator. The needs of the community must come first, and with the funds at its disposal the RTPA should ensure that they do.

A6.21 The perceptions of the compilers of the Lincolnshire study are well encapsulated in the following quotation from John Molyneux's essay on East and West Kesteven:

"Field work in this area suggests that the rural public transport pattern is not critical in terms of the occupation of the head of the household, who usually has a car or access to one to achieve the journey to work if necessary. Much more important is the impact on the other sections of the community, the teenagers whose urban education is catered for, but not their leisure, the mothers of one-car households, the retired and the rural poor who are more vulnerable in many respects than their urban counterparts."

A6.22 Other studies, such as that of Topham on East Yorkshire [5], fully confirm this view. In spite of vastly increased levels of car ownership in the country, it is likely that when public transport is reduced the majority of the population always suffers a reduction in the whole quality of life. The planners' obsession with car ownership *per household* totally obscured the realities of personal mobility. People, not vehicles per household, are what matters.

Deprivation caused by the decline of rural transport

A6.23 We now examine in more detail just some of the problems being experienced by people in rural areas as a result of the reductions in public transport. It is difficult to find a good measure of the degree of "hardship" felt when transport services are reduced. In general we have deemed "hardship" to exist when sufficient numbers of individuals have felt cause to complain or disinterested commentators have reported what they were prepared to call "deprivation".

Hospitals

A6.24 The planners "plan", but much of what they plan fails to match people's fundamental requirements because they do not work together or co-ordinate the planning. Government policies are often inconsistent as a result.

A6.25 At the time of the Beeching Report, the Ministry of Health was proposing the "Ten Year Hospital Plan" [6]. The whole hospital pattern as we then knew it was to alter, and there were to be larger hospitals with centralised comprehensive medical services, serving much wider areas of both rural and urban Britain. The transport implication was increased demand for public transport on the part of patients and their visitors, for whom the widespread withdrawals of Sunday bus services has proved particularly troublesome. In practice, it has turned out that very long journeys need to be made in some parts of the country. For the people of Merioneth in North Wales, for instance, hospitals are situated at Wrexham and Liverpool, both more than 50 miles away. Patients have to be driven by ambulance in winter over icy and rough roads. If they have no car, relatives have to depend on expensive hire-car services or on friends with a car. Bus services are infrequent, and relatives visiting Wrexham by bus are often unable to make the return journey on the same day. It would not be surprising if they wondered whether the Government's left hand knew what its right hand was doing.

A6.26 It would be unfair not to stress that the hardship for both patient and relative is worst in areas of Wales, Scotland and the remoter parts of northern, eastern and western England, and that the longer journey times by such replacements as still exist for withdrawn services bear particularly hard upon these people.

A6.27 Now, ten years after the reorganisation of regional hospitals, another reorganisation of the National Health Services is going to put a further strain on people with transport problems. Centralised health centres and clinics are being developed. How do the planners expect people, who are often from the nature of the case elderly or disabled, to get to them? What we now face is not only diminished public transport, but also a fuel shortage. A bad situation will be an even worse one if private cars and voluntary services have to be more restricted than ever, and the kind neighbour unable to act as a kind neighbour in the future.

A6.28 To help relieve some of the hardships of getting to hospitals in Wales, the Department of Health and Social Security (Welsh Office) has issued a paper *Travelling Expenses and Transport for Hospital Patients and Visitors*, May 1973 [7]. Under the NHS (Expenses in Attending Hospitals) Regulations 1950, patients and visitors may, after an assessment of requirements by the Supplementary Benefits Commission, apply for and receive payment of travelling expenses. Part 3 of the memorandum says: "The problem for some patients and visitors of getting to hospital may be one of transport rather than finance. Because of the reduction in public transport services in rural areas and the growing concentration of hospital services, some patients and visitors who do not have cars, or friends with a car, may find it difficult to get to hospital; the problems of elderly and frail people in these circumstances come particularly to mind. While hospital authorities should not do anything to discourage self-help, various ways of giving assistance with travel, where this is desirable, are set out in this part of the memorandum. It is for hospital authorities in the first place to identify the areas and hospitals where transport difficulties exist, or are expected to arise." This is an inadequate and unco-ordinated response to one part of the larger problem of public transport. Even as an *ad hoc* solution to the hospital difficulty, it makes little if any allowance for the trouble and indignity involved in applying for travelling expenses or for the difficulties of the many people whose income falls just above the maximum eligible for supplementary benefit.

A6.29 The needs of a patient going to hospital are well provided for. Almost all rural areas of Great Britain have adequate transport services paid for by the Department of Health and Social Security and administered by the hospital. The patient will be taken to hospital for treatment or consultation or after-care by ambulance or by the hospital car pool.

A6.30 The hardship that patients now experience, apart from the much greater distance they have to be taken, is their distance from relatives and friends who might visit them. It is difficult to fault the basic reasons for the move towards regional hospitals, covering in many cases very large areas of rural England. They provide specialist treatment and expensive equipment and staffing which could not have been carried by the older and smaller hospitals. Our point relates to the hardship for the relatives and friends of patients, which results from the withdrawal of all public transport in some rural areas and the inadequacy of what remains in others. Public transport requirements and their costs should have been taken into account when these reorganisations were being planned.

A6.31 Another factor which seems to go ignored, is the serious effect on the patients themselves when relatives are unable to visit them. Medical workers tell us that this has a considerable bearing on the mental outlook of a patient, and that lying in a distant hospital without visits often retards recovery. This applies particularly to the elderly, who are frightened by their isolation and their distance from home, but the very young and other age groups are not immune.

The old in rural areas

A6.32 Among the groups mentioned, the plight of old people living in the country seemed to us to be the most serious, and the inability of society to respond generously to relatively modest needs most deplorable. For old people the problem of declining income and higher and higher fares is compounded by their physical inability to walk long distances to a village or market town when bus and rail services have ceased. Waiting at a bus stop in bad weather means a degree of suffering and even physical risk for old people when services are infrequent or irregular. Many are deterred from using what remains.

333

A6.33 Age Concern, the National Old People's Welfare Council, in its report *Age Concern on Transport* [8], summarises the views of 3000 people collected by its local committees from 33 counties and 27 county boroughs during 1971. The reductions and worsening levels of public transport were a problem even for urban areas, but the picture that emerges from rural areas is a stark one. "Elderly people", the report states, "are virtually prisoners to their neighbourhood"; and one county organiser notes bitterly:

"Old people now bear the burdens of the changes of travel fashions made possible by a prosperity for which they laid the foundations."

Shopping trips, visits to doctor and hospital and social trips are among the major needs of old people listed which declining services can no longer adequately supply. It is reported that in Norfolk, for example, there are now 30 villages without a daily bus. Pensioners have to walk very long distances on dangerous roads or resign themselves to impossibly inconvenient services. The following example is from Berkshire:

(i) "This is a hamlet where there is now no post-office or shop of any kind. It is $1\frac{1}{2}$ miles from the nearest village, 4 miles from the nearest town and 8 miles from the nearest large town. It is situated on an intersection between two very busy roads with an immense amount of lorry traffic, and it is quite unsafe for the pensioners to walk to the nearest village, even if they were all capable of doing so. The only bus service is to the large town—8 a.m. there, and return 5.40 p.m., except on Thursday when a bus returns at approximately 10 a.m. This is used by pensioners, but costs them 30p return. Only those who are compelled to go use this service, because it is too expensive apart from being inconvenient. A day in town is too long for them, as to spend time in a town *costs* money."

(ii) Or again from South Staffordshire:
"Members find visiting the doctor's surgery a hardship. There is no convenient return bus, so they have to walk $3\frac{1}{2}$ miles back. This is a situation which has been intensified all over Great Britain with the trend developing for doctors to have group practices and surgeries."

(iii) A committee from Derbyshire reports:
"We have over 200 pensioners in this village who just cannot afford to travel."

To put the notion of "hardship" in a different perspective, the South Staffordshire Branch reports graphically:

(iv) "To visit our old members in hospital costs 70p. This means that their old friends cannot afford to visit them. This is a tragedy; I feel the clasp of a hand means so much more than a letter probably written and read second-hand."

A6.34 Others emphasise that the very people who still rely on public transport are prevented from using it by being priced off the services, which must all have the same subsidies if they are to continue to operate. The *Oxford and Area Rural Bus Services Steering Committee Report* [9] gives a number of verbatim comments by old people:

"I have to choose between my lunch and a trip to town."
"If I go to town, I can't afford to buy anything there."
"It is such a change, and a breath of fresh air, to take a bus ride but on a pension an elderly couple like us cannot manage it."

Municipalities have for some time been operating a system of concessionary fares subsidised by the rates, but in general this has not been introduced in rural areas. The Oxford Committee estimates that bus fares have been rising in recent times at a rate of about 22% per annum.

Women

A6.35 Neville Topham, in a study of East Yorkshire, *Rural Transport in the East Riding of Yorkshire* [5], and David St. John Thomas in his study of the Lake District, Northumberland and Devon in *The Rural Transport Problem* [10], both noted that the effects of the reduction in rural transport fell most heavily on women and girls in the community. Not only was the wife more likely to be house-bound during the daytime, but if there was a car in the household she was more likely to be a non-driver, and thus not to have the use of the vehicle in the evenings or week-ends for her own leisure

335

or shopping. Teenage boys find it easier than girls to acquire a scooter, motorcycle or old car to attend evening classes or to go to a club. It is also more difficult and more markedly dangerous for girls to depend on casual lifts offered by strangers.

A6.36 We would refer anyone with an interest in these matters to a survey undertaken for the Commission by the National Council of Women of Great Britain [11] in 1973, which describes the acute difficulties people experience in rural areas in reaching hospitals and doctors, and making shopping and social trips. We record below, from the NCW surveys and also from letters collected by the NCW, some of the difficulties noted, especially those experienced by women.

Purpose of journey: Medical

A6.37 (a) A woman living in *Clitheroe* who needed to attend Blackburn Infirmary over a period of time found public transport useless. Not being a driver of a car, she attended clinics by various means, including hitch-hiking. At one point she was reduced to using (what may have been safer) milk floats and farm tractors.

(b) *Cottingham, East Yorks.* It takes five hours to visit a patient in Sutton Annex Hospital, Hull, from the suburb of Cottingham, including travelling out and home.

(c) *Canterbury District.* Buses do not fit in for visiting from several villages. To get to Margate, Canterbury or Ramsgate two changes are necessary. People in the village of St. Nicholas have to go 4 miles to Birchington, then in a second bus (which goes every 1½ hours in winter, every 40 minutes in the summer) 4 miles to Minster Geriatric Hospital, which is 4 miles from St. Nicholas.

(d) *Reigate and District.* A number of rural bus services have been cut down without warning. Most of the Sunday services have been cut out altogether, including the only bus going to Smallfield Hospital and village. This means that no one can visit patients on Sunday without private transport.

(e) *Malvern and Worcester District.* For hospital visiting and visits to their doctors people without their own transport have to rely solely on neighbours or friends with cars.

Purpose of journey: Shopping

A6.38 Very few villages in remote rural areas have more than
the sub-post office-cum-village general store. In some cases
this may be rather inadequate, but it is also worth saying
that in a well-to-do district this one shop may be stocked
like a miniature Harrods grocery department. Very often
there is also a butcher's shop serving a large number of
surrounding villages. For the average village in rural areas,
however, one must come down to earth and realise that in
most cases country folk *are very dependent on a train or bus*
to reach the nearest town for the minimum needs of daily
existence. Before the first world war and to some extent
between the wars, the village carrier did a good trade and
helped people to overcome their isolation by taking orders
into the nearest big town and bringing back the goods. But
as buses gradually began to serve the rural areas the day of
the carrier was no more, and the bus service took over.
Today these same villages find themselves *without bus or
train or carrier's cart*. In some areas, such as Langley on the
outskirts of Eastbourne, where a very large industrial
housing estate is springing up, supermarkets like Sainsbury
and Tesco have taken over in a large shopping precinct,
together with essential shops. This is a trend which will be
difficult to resist. Splendid though the arrangements are for
parking cars and shopping in unhurried comfort, they are
only for car owners, or the people of the surrounding
housing estate. They are not the answer for country people,
for in most cases these estates are either on no bus route or
on no direct bus route from the surrounding villages.

A6.40 We give here a selection of reports and letters which
could be multiplied indefinitely from villages everywhere.

(a) *Miss Stratford writes from King's Lynn:* "My members
(NCW) felt that the more marked change was not the disappearance of village shops but the prosperity of suburban
stores, caused by the strangulation of town centres by cars.
The ring of prosperity seems to be moving steadily outwards
from the centre, chased by the ring of decay as planners
"plan" the centre, completing its destruction; the shops in
small towns flourish, and we feel that there is little reason
other than character of the owner, for shops in villages do
not do well. Many of them remain the centres of village life."

337

(b) *East Dean, nr. Chichester, West Sussex.* This is reported as one example of conditions generally. The 1.30 bus from Chichester to East Dean, returning from East Dean at 2.30, has been taken off. This was an exceedingly useful bus; many people caught the midday bus into Chichester and returned on it. Now nobody can get into Chichester for shopping or social activities after midday until the 4.30 p.m. bus, unless by walking two miles to Singleton, where there is a reasonable bus service to Chichester. It is now impossible to get to Petworth by public transport.

(c) *Easton village and similar small villages in Suffolk.* People with cars assist those who have no transport to visit towns for shopping. The bus services have worsened in these small villages, even though Wickham Market on the A12 and places on this route from Ipswich have had an improvement.

(d) *Henley/Reading area of Berkshire and Oxfordshire.* Some buses to Reading, which take in the villages on the route, occasionally turn round a quarter or half way there without prior notice, and do not complete the journey to Reading. Passengers have to wait for the next bus.

Purpose of journey: Social

A6.41 From the letters and reports collected by the National Council of Women, it is clear that nobody who does not own a car can carry on social activities independently in rural areas where there is little or no public transport. Even if there is a limited service, there are countless difficulties and much waste of time, or the problem of a bus one way and having to rely on a good neighbour for the return journey. Many afternoon meetings are arranged on the one day a bus service is running, but even here uncertainties are ever present. This is said to be having a serious effect on cultural life, and on the theatres and cinemas of even such large towns as Oxford, where people used to pour in from the surrounding areas. Television is sometimes blamed for this, but one has only to meet and talk to rural dwellers today to realise how far this is from the whole truth. They feel themselves to be isolated and deprived. They have no choice but to accept their loss of one more simple pleasure. In most rural areas today social activities outside the village have to be a community affair, with a mini-bus or a coach hired for the occasion. This naturally makes outings of this sort very few and far between. An example is *Woodstock*, 8 *miles from Oxford*, a sizeable little royal borough compared with the villages around. It still has a limited but quite reasonable bus service because it is also on a direct route from other Cotswold towns. Even so, the last bus from Oxford now leaves too early in the evening to allow people without their own transport to enjoy a full evening's entertainment or social activity. But by ordinary standards Woodstock is extremely fortunate.

Schools

A6.42 Parents are finding getting their children to school in the rural areas more and more difficult; apart from the lack of public transport, the criteria for school buses are unsatisfactory. The system functions reasonably well in straightforward cases where a child is over eight years old and lives more than three miles from the school, or where he is between five and seven and lives more than two miles from it. Otherwise parents are responsible for arranging transport if they consider it unsuitable for the child to walk to school. If they are within the catchment areas of two schools and they choose the further of the two (and if it is also not the normal choice for most children of that area) then again they are responsible for transport to school. School bus services are usually provided for official school outings, trips to sports contests, swimming lessons and other occasions. Inside the three-mile and two-mile limits, it is still very often necessary for parents to send their children to school by some form of transport, for some of the following reasons:

(i) *dangerous roads* due to the considerable increase in traffic.

(ii) *weather* is often unsuitable for children to walk to school, especially in severe winter weather: they arrive soaking wet in clothes which they then have to sit in all day.

(iii) *physical unfitness:* some people question whether five and six year-olds should be expected to walk two miles each way to school.

(iv) *equipment:* the amount which has to be carried nowadays is sometimes considerable. Since the rise in the cost of school meals, many children take their own lunches, in addition to school equipment.

A6.43 The Steering Committee on Oxford and Area Rural Bus Services reports: "One eight-year old has to carry regularly with her, for a journey of two and a half miles to her primary school every Tuesday morning, her satchel of books, her lunch bag, her violin, her music case and bathing things. She could give up music and swimming, but is this a satisfactory solution? Public transport in this case is half a mile from her home and passes nowhere near the school. Her father usually takes her when he goes to work, but this means a wait of half an hour outside the school gates in all winds and weathers."

A6.44 Parents in Cumnor Hill, Berkshire, state that it is not possible for their children to be sure of regularly reaching the direct grant schools in Oxford at which they have won places, because public services habitually run late, are often full, and sometimes fail altogether. Many children have to change buses in Oxford to reach some of the schools. Because the buses at that time of day are very overcrowded, children often find they are not allowed on.

A6.45 It is also reported: "Such difficulties make for an undesirable increase in the number of children who are brought to school by car, resulting in congestion outside the school gates. In some rural areas of Berkshire, as many as a quarter of the children attending have to be brought to school by their parents in cars. Senior or final year students who stay on for extra study or other school activities have to find their own way home, either by public transport, if any, or walk or bicycle."

A6.46 This type of situation repeats itself over and over again in almost every rural area of Great Britain. Reports have come in giving similar stories and examples. In some cases the bus services have been withdrawn altogether; in others buses are not only infrequent but keep poor timing, so that the children cannot be got to school on time by public transport.

A6.47 Evidence from West Ashling District, West Sussex: "Over a period of time the withdrawal of bus services has brought about more and more private cars needed to get workers and children around on time, especially in the winter."

A6.48 From Worcestershire Rural areas around Malvern come reports about the Midland Red Bus Company's withdrawal of country bus services. Parents are concerned by the reshuffle of the education authorities in this area and the closing and alteration in status of some of the schools. This is going to put a large number of children out of the school-bus radius, and there is no public means of transport for them.

A6.49 Part of the trouble seems to be that so many new schools are being built off bus routes. Another general trouble is that parents feel that it is no longer safe for very young children to walk distances alone to school.

The visitor in the countryside

A6.50 The withdrawal of services which has made life difficult for country people has also created problems for the visitor to the countryside. We have now created a situation in which many remote and lovely areas cannot be reached except by private car or coach. A recent study by The Ramblers' Association, *Rural Transport in Crisis* [12], has shown the frustration felt by many people who can no longer reach famous and beautiful areas of the British Isles because transport services have been withdrawn.

A6.51 Examples could be taken from many parts of the country—not only from the remote and mountainous areas of Scotland, Wales, the Northern Pennines and Dartmoor, but also from areas that have traditionally welcomed visitors. The traffic congestion during the summer months which results from thousands of visitors trying to reach the Cornish coast is now notorious. Much of that coastline is no longer accessible for those without their own transport. We end by quoting from a letter by Mr. V. W. A. Conn of London [13] who went, with his wife, to St. Ives early in 1972 to discover that all buses had been withdrawn around the Lands End peninsula:

"These buses gave access to some of the finest coast and moorland country in Cornwall, indeed in the British Isles, and their disappearance is a disaster to walkers and people seeking out the wilder and more remote areas. One could drop off the 515 bus anywhere along the eighteen or so miles of this north Penwith coast and walk down to

341

remote coves like Perthmoor or climb up the moors just inland. There is now no way of reaching, for example, the National Trust headland of Zennor Head or Gurnards Head. The 514 bus turned inland and ran through the Try Valley, convenient for visiting Chysauster Neolithic Settlement on Carnaquidden Downs with the Nine Maidens stone circle, Mulfra Quoit, the Men-an-Tol and other standing stones nearby."

REFERENCES

[1] Department of the Environment: *Study of rural transport in Devon*. 1971.
[2] Department of the Environment: *Study of rural transport in West Suffolk*. 1971.
[3] Hillman and others: *Personal mobility and transport policy*. P.E.P., 1973.
[4] Garlick, Joan, and others: *Rural transport problems in Lincolnshire and East Nottingham*: Open University, East Midlands Region, 1973.
[5] Topham, Neville: *Rural transport in the East Riding of Yorkshire*. 1966.
[6] Ministry of Health: *Hospital Plan for England and Wales* (revision to 1972–3), April 1963.
[7] Department of Health and Social Security and Welsh Office: *Travelling expenses and transport for hospital patients and visitors*. 1973.
[8] Age Concern (National Old People's Welfare Council): *Age Concern on Transport*. 1971.
[9] *Oxford and Area Rural Bus Services Steering Committee Report*. 1973.
[10] Thomas, St John: *The rural transport problem*. 1963.
[11] National Council of Women: *Survey of Rural Transport Problems*, 1973.
[12] Ramblers' Association: *Rural transport in crisis*. 1973.
[13] Conn, V. W. A.: Letter to the Chairman of the Western National Bus Company, 14 April 1972.

Looking at Transport Problems From the Grass Roots

A7.1 Having presented the national trends and predictions concerning transport in rural and urban communities, the Commission felt that the more human face of transport issues might appear to be lacking in this report. Pamela Johnson, an environmentalist with a specific interest in transport, was invited to visit a variety of communities ranging from a small village to an industrial centre to observe how local residents are being affected by increased traffic and problems of personal mobility; to talk to local people and see just how aware they are of the transport problems in their areas, and what they are doing or hoping to do about them; and to get an idea of their general attitudes, feelings, fears and frustrations on the transport decisions with which they have to live. The communities visited included Nutfield on the A25 near Redhill and the neighbouring parish of South Merstham; Lewes in East Sussex; Gloucester; and Glasgow.

A7.2 The first impression on the visitor, and the most frequent complaint of the residents of these communities is the density and frequency of traffic, especially lorry traffic. Compaints in Nutfield vary. Some complain about the "steady stream of traffic" through their village, which is so dense as to be "practically stationary much of the time". Others say that large lorries come through "at the rate of one every four or five seconds' at certain times of the day. In Lewes people complain of the very heavy lorry traffic revving and braking through the hilly town centre; this is further aggravated by the increased holiday traffic en route to the south coast. In the little village of South Merstham a new sand quarry opened two years ago, bringing a constant stream of open tipper lorries to remove the sand and rubbish lorries to bring in fill for the holes. Residents conducted a ten-hour count and found that the lorries for the quarry made up 74% of the traffic, one heavy lorry passing through the village every 78 seconds. With a railway in the town Pamela Johnson wonders why new sidings have not been considered as a way of servicing the quarry; instead, there is now a campaign to reroute the traffic through Nutfield, simply because it is on a trunk route and "the people are used to such traffic".

A7.3 Furthermore, residents in these communities feel that they cannot physically accommodate the large lorries in their towns and villages. People in Lewes explained: "I'm scared that the lorries will brush past me and knock over my shopping basket"; "I keep my children on the inside of the pavement and I teach them never to walk on the curb because I'm scared of lorries mounting the pavement". Nutfield residents pointed out that their roads were so narrow that "lorries and buses seem to overhang the pavement". One woman antique dealer in Lewes surely must be given top marks for tolerance; the porch of her 18th century house has been hit thirteen times by lorries, although they have to mount the pavement to do so.

A7.4 Fears of lorries mounting the pavement or swiping pedestrians are just one of the many stresses caused by the current transport in these communities. In Nutfield a pedestrian count was conducted by the authorities which apparently failed to show adequate need for a pedestrian crossing, since none has been provided; people cannot cross the street in time to catch buses to work or to the shops, and mothers are afraid to let their children cross the road alone to go to school. Residents maintain that the wrong section of the street was chosen for the count, since there is clearly a need for a pedestrian crossing, just as there is a need to revitalise the deteriorating bus service and the neglected footpaths of Nutfield. The lack of a pedestrian crossing at the Phoenix Causeway, a new bridge over the Ouse in Lewes, causes concern to parents who have to accompany children to and from school. One mother had finally and reluctantly allowed her eleven-year-old son to cycle in this area after he had been able to ride for six years—"You have to let him have some freedom. You can't say no to everything for ever".

A7.5 The one-way system in Lewes allows the increased

volume of traffic to flow significantly faster, thus cutting off neighbours by isolating them on their own sides of the street and "destroying community feeling". The increased volume of traffic has made Lewes residents aware of the way in which "cars cut folk off from the places they drive through in them". Motorists do not react to the people of Lewes as individuals, but as obstacles to their journey—"Car drivers get bad tempered with us pedestrians when they meet us car-to-person in the street". The indifference of the motorists who use Lewes as a "go-between" is further aggravated by the increased noise of so many cars and lorries revving up and braking in the hilly, narrow streets of this 11th century town dominated by its Norman castle. One family in Lewes moves every summer to a hut at the bottom of the garden to get some quiet and enjoy fresh air. On the most heavily trafficked streets, where there is a let-up only from 12.30 a.m. to 5 a.m., people live mostly at the backs of their houses; adults were not to be seen talking in the High Street; children were yelling in each other's ears; and shopkeepers tended to keep their doors and windows shut. Traffic brings not only noise but dirt and pollution; one house-proud woman had given up keeping window boxes because the struggle to keep the flowers alive was just too much. Another resigned citizen of Lewes commented: "I expect we'll get cancer with all these fumes, whether we give up smoking or not".

A7.6 Current traffic is not the only source of stress for residents in these communities. Road building and future road building plans bring hardship to many individuals and destroy community life; one family living near the construction of the M23 near Nutfield reports the severe stress suffered by the wife: "My wife teeters on the edge of a nervous breakdown when she has to go to the village. It is a sort of physical fear. She was in London during the blitz, and I don't think she was as frightened as she is today with earth-movers outside the door. Once they came through the fence and she was frightened to death; it goes into your subconscious and you become a frightened person". In Lewes residents reported how a number of listed houses on a *likely* route were destroyed *before* it was decided whether to build an inner relief road; other buildings were evacuated simply to provide better road access. In South Merstham the people want their lorry traffic diverted through Nutfield; the people in Nutfield to say the least are not pleased with their neighbouring village—"If you must attack do so on a broad front, don't just close a useful little side road so that you and your parishioners can sleep in peace". In Nutfield the same family plagued by the building of the M23 report that stress from traffic and new roads contaminates community life—"You react to your neighbours with fear and violence. People at a public meeting fight with each other because, although they are all against the traffic, they are divided over its solution."

A7.7 If this is the plight of these towns and villages in Britain today, what of larger cities where town planners are using the knowledge and know-how of other large megalopolises around the world? What will the future be like when current plans are fulfilled? Glasgow is a good example of a city with a plan which is to provide twice as many motorway miles per head of population as in London, while at the same time providing half as many public transport miles per head of population as in London, in a city where car ownership is half that of London. This approach has already had dramatic effects on the life of people in Glasgow; it encourages people to move out of the city and to commute to work, with the result that within the city trams have been scrapped and much of the underground system has been destroyed or is disused. There is in general a rundown of the public transport system. As Colin Buchanan was recently quoted in the *New Glasgow Society News*—"Most cities would give their right arm to have a network of disused railway tunnels like Glasgow's". Clearly Glasgow is going the direction of a motorway city; for example, two flanks of the inner ring road have been completed. There is however some considerable controversy about the remainder, at least among architects:

"This east flank is aligned up Glasgow High Street, removing from its path two Adams buildings, a 1751 chapel and Charles Rennie MacIntosh's Martyrs School. As it crosses the Clyde at a height of 60 feet, it will overshadow the Justiciary Courts (Starke, 1806), ruin the views and scale of St. Andrew's Square and make a nonsense of the 17th century Tolbooth and Merchant's

House Steeples: at its upper end it will cut off the cathedral from the city to which it gave birth. This eastern flank joins the M74, which has been aligned through Glasgow Green at the heart of the old city. Here a motorway interchange is planned, virtually annihilating Britain's oldest civic park and increasing polarisation between east and west." (C. and J. M. McKean, *The Architect's Journal*, 27 October 1971).

A7.8 A different approach has been taken in Gloucester, where the principal decision is to keep commerce alive within the city and not to construct shopping centres outside the town. However, the result has been that mass retailing establishments have been built on the site of ancient buildings to cater for car shoppers; and a 60% increase in car ownership has been allowed for in the provision of parking facilities in the town centre, with the result that there are now car parks on two sides of the cathedral and high multi-storey car parks which link shopping centres at roof level, so that cars can circulate from building to building off the street. While these centres allow for large potentially attractive pedestrian precincts, the flat, uniform roof line created by the car parks will give the city a "hard, horizontal, unserrated skyline", according to one architect. Add to this the visual tediousness of the many concrete ramps, stairs and lifts which accompany a multi-storey car park, and the reshaping of a fine cathedral city would seem inevitable. Since there is currently a plan for an inner ring road to encircle the very centre of the city, downtown Gloucester will soon be a tight little hypermarket island.

A7.9 Every community in the country will have its own tale to tell; will it be so very different from that of Nutfield, South Merstham, Lewes, Gloucester and Glasgow? Is there anywhere a successful, happy, stressless marriage between man and motor vehicle?

Scotland and Transport

John Francis

A8.1 While it is essential to achieve a fully integrated transport network for the whole of the United Kingdom, transport decisions cannot be easily isolated from other elements of regional policy. This is certainly true in many parts of the country including the North of England, Wales and in particular Scotland, where some difficult investment choices must soon be resolved. In Scotland the problems of regional development are all too familiar, set as they are against a backcloth of declining employment in traditional heavy industries such as steel and shipbuilding. This is reflected in the reduced dependence on transport systems geared to serve the principal centres of industry. Since 1963, the route mileage of railways in Scotland has been cut down by over one third to the present level of 2,000 miles, while at the same time the number of men and women employed on the Scottish Region of British Rail has been almost halved from 43,000 to 22,000. The progressive erosion of a substantial fixed investment such as the rail network in a country of 20 million acres, and with a population of just over 5 million, can only mean one thing, namely a loss of mobility for a large fraction of the population. The situation is further complicated by the division of financial responsibility for transport in Scotland between the Department of the Environment (railways) and the Scottish Office (roads, airports, shipping); this all too often appears to lead to an inadequate planning response when new industrial initiatives are being taken.

A8.2 This latter dilemma has obviously been recognised in the recent report of the Royal Commission on the Constitution under the chairmanship of Lord Kilbrandon [1]. In the section of the report favouring a scheme of legislative devolution for Scotland, it is suggested that responsibility would generally be transferred for whole subject areas, although these would be mainly those for which the Secretary of State or the Lord Advocate now has executive responsibility. It is significant that among the general range of matters considered to be suitable for transfer are listed roads (including the construction, use and licensing of vehicles), road passenger transport and harbours, and environmental services such as prevention of pollution. In the case of the Scottish Assembly, sea transport might also be considered as a matter for transfer; but in addition the Assembly might also have limited powers in relation to some aspects of railways, road freight and civil aviation. Couched in general terms, it is possible to see this as an open acknowledgement of present difficulties in forward planning of Scotland's transport requirements.

A8.3 This concern is further echoed in another important document relating to future growth strategy for Scotland [2]. It is argued that because of the large geographical area and difficult terrain, particularly in the Highlands, Scotland must be treated as a special case in order to expedite economic development and to capture the new opportunities emanating either from the North Sea oil and gas industries or from the rising tide of tourism. Through the agency of the Scottish Council (Development and Industry), this report has recommended "a co-ordinated transport policy for all modes of transport in Scotland under the control of a new body such as the executive assembly proposed by Kilbrandon." Nobody with any feeling for policy-making at a regional level would doubt that this is a most necessary correction of the administrative machinery, provided that it will lead to a proper revaluation of transport needs and a more balanced appraisal of each sector. Despite this recommendation, it is a foregone conclusion that priority will be given to the improvement of roads to Hunterston, Inverness and Aberdeen, now widely recognised as the new regional growth centres. The evidence for this long-term commitment to road transport can be found in the pages of the 1972 report of the Scottish Development Department [3]:

"The highest priority is being given to reconstructing the Perth–Inverness–Invergordon road largely on entirely new alignment. It will be built as a high standard single carriageway road, with lengths of dual carriageway where these are desirable, and will be designed so as to facilitate the provision of a second carriageway if, at a future date, this becomes necessary. . . . The total cost of the reconstruction, which will include new crossings of the Beauly and Cromarty Firths, is expected to be of the order of £60 million at 1972 prices."

A8.4 It has been Government policy in recent years to regard road improvement schemes as a primary instrument of regional policy, although the benefits of massive projects planned ahead of demand have often failed to materialise, e.g. the Erskine bridge is under-utilised [4]. The proposed investment in the A9 is seen to be compatible with the anticipated scale of industrial development along the Cromarty Firth resulting from the emergence of the North Sea as the world's leading centre for offshore oil and gas. In the euphoria of the moment, and with a recent history of economic depression only slowly fading, it is hardly surprising that a streamlined system of communications must be guaranteed before the confidence begins to wane. After all, in the case of offshore oil and gas, the planners are likely to be dealing with a highly cyclical industry which may frequently by-pass the difficulties of bulk distribution by passing products down a pipeline. On the other hand, process industries including refineries and gas separation or liquefaction plant may be closely related to the more favoured landfalls from the offshore fields. The uncertainties in this evolving situation are, of course, considerable, and it is not surprising that the principal agency involved, the Scottish Development Department, should have declared its intentions at the earliest possible moment in order to escape public criticism. Nevertheless, it is surprising that, at a time when a country such as Sweden is considering proposals to ban road transport of heavy goods over 250 kilometres (160 miles) for reasons other than a shortage of fuel, a Government agency in one region of this country can declare itself to be still effectively committed to a "roads only" approach. It is for just this kind of reason that the Scottish Association for Public Transport (SAPT) is prepared to challenge the assumptions and the implications of the A9 decision, on the grounds that a more balanced solution could be found to the regional transport problem if the unexpected surge of industrial activity in the north and north east were coupled with a willingness on the part of the Government to invest in public transport in a new growth area [5].

A8.5 Presented as a case study, the circumstances surrounding the A9 programme will serve as an illustration of the major disturbance that can be caused by a failure to co-ordinate the pattern of investment in road and rail systems at a time when there is an increasing demand on financial resources to seed housing schemes and other vital community-based projects. It is argued that, instead of the proposed expenditure on the A9, a smaller and more balanced programme of transport improvement should be undertaken in association with other forms of regional aid more directly related to employment.

Focus on the A9

A8.6 Even before the great surge of development caused by oil, the attractions of the Northern Highlands have generated a need for improved access: during the summer peak the small towns and villages along the route have counted the environmental cost of tourist cars and caravans. While the occupants of these vehicles have themselves become increasingly frustrated in their struggle to find the countryside, there has been added in to this already one-sided equation the inevitable sign of rising prosperity in any region—the slow-moving lorry. It is perfectly understandable, therefore, that in order to achieve a traffic flow on this road the planners were faced with the almost inevitable task of upgrading the route or of finding some equally viable solution to their problem. Within the U.K., it seems extremely doubtful whether there is a better example of the relative factors determining road freight versus rail freight prices, since, for the bulk of heavy goods moved via Perth to and from the Inverness–Invergordon area, this represents an uninterrupted single haul of more than 150 miles.

A8.7 The traffic density is fairly thin by most of the standards applied elsewhere in the country, with flows ranging from only 1,000 vehicles per day in winter to 5,500 at the summer peak; the average daily flow in 1973 is estimated at

2,500 vehicles, corresponding to an annual total of 900,000. The breakdown of investment costs, allowing £17 million for the new "Bridges Route" between Inverness and Invergordon, would indicate £43 million expenditure on the route south of Inverness during the planned construction period 1974–77. According to traffic estimates published by SAPT [5], the number of vehicles using the A9 in 1979 is unlikely to exceed 1·3 million. Given the expected level of capital expenditure at 1972 prices, and assuming a notional capital charge of 10%, this would be equivalent to an annual social grant to the road of £4·3 million, or approximately *fourteen times* the present rail social grant. In any case, if the parallel rail route was to continue in existence, this would at the present level of funding necessitate cumulative annual rail grants of £5 to £10 million over the next twenty years, which would have to be added in under the umbrella of the road investment programme.

A8.8 It is not as if the present systems of handling freight and passenger traffic were radically out of balance at the present time. SAPT estimates of annual freight tonnage on the A9 come out at around 500,000 tons, compared with rail traffic which is currently approaching 450,000 tons (according to British Rail sources, the predominant flow in 1972 was 400,000 tons northward in support of the platform fabrication and pipe-coating yards). However, the A9 probably carried 2·25 million passengers a year (excluding lorry, van and bus drivers) compared with 375,000 by rail, thus further emphasising the significance of the summer peaks. From these figures it should be clear that, whatever the investment priorities may have been at the point of assessment, there is no single form of transport that can be expected to adapt to these demands on the time scale that is now envisaged.

An alternative strategy for investment

A8.9 In a recent edition of the *Scottish Economic Bulletin* [6] British Rail was commended for its response to the activity generated by oil developments, whether by improvement of passenger services or by the incorporation of rail links with some of the new installations along the north-east coast. The rapid construction (*in one week*) of a quarter-mile spur from the Inverness-to-Wick/Thurso line to serve the pipe-coating yard of M. K. Shand Ltd, at Invergordon, and the re-opening of the passenger station at Alness (closed since 1960), were cited as examples of a more flexible style of operation. This contribution, taken together with the railways' potential for protection of the environment, e.g. by handling the bulk movement of timber to the pulp mill at Fort William or of aluminium from the smelter at Invergordon, cannot be discounted lightly. Yet, at the point of decision concerning an arterial linkage between Perth and Inverness, these factors are far too easily disregarded. In the context of this appendix, it is important to understand the way in which measures to restore the balance between road and rail investment, such as the suggested rail freight subsidy, would have an immediate bearing in Scotland. The A9 case perfectly illustrates the dilemma whereby substantial volumes of traffic, which could be handled by rail at lower environmental cost and without any significant increase in track costs, are positively encouraged to take to the road. A number of alternatives have been clearly identified by the SAPT [5] in its memorandum to the Commission as follows:

1. *Priority use of the trunk railway between Perth and Inverness.* Traffic should be attracted to rail *by reducing the level of charges*, provided that marginal costs are still covered, and *by constructing railway sidings to the major industrial sites*. Since the marginal social cost of freight transport by heavy road vehicles is in most situations higher than by alternative means, this should be recognised through compensatory payments to alternative modes of transport. [The case for a bonus of 0·5p per extra ton-mile of freight carried by rail or water has already been introduced in the main body of this report.] No major capital expenditure would be involved in the spur rail links to connect the platform fabrication yards at Nigg Bay and at Ardesier with the principal rail network, but some additional financial incentive may be necessary if the user is not prepared to absorb the initial installation costs. These measures would act in favour of immediate relief of heavy vehicle congestion of the A9, while utilising the spare capacity of the railway for bulk freight movements.

353

2. *Conventional modernisation of the rail route to Inverness*. The first option for the medium-term future would be an investment appraisal of the route with a view to restoring passing places, resignalling and the replacement of ageing diesel locomotives through electrification. Although this programme would involve some major items of expenditure during the period 1974–79, these would go a long way towards restoring confidence in the railways as a contributory factor in the development of the Scottish economy. It must be apparent that British Rail has chosen to invest very little in the modernisation of the railway system north of Edinburgh and Glasgow. There are understandable anomalies which have dramatically cut across the accepted guidelines of regional development policy, notably the fact that the bulk of Government assistance for railway investment has been *directed* towards south east England. With industrial complexes springing up in remote and largely unexpected corners (as far as direct road communications are concerned), there should be a ready demonstration of the flexibility of the installed rail system to respond to new markets and to remain competitive, while fighting off the challenge from large-scale highway construction programmes in the Highlands. At least the struggle should be engaged on equal terms. In the absence of a co-ordinating transport authority, as already implied, the Scottish Development Department is able to plan the road network alone in accordance with the developing needs of the Scottish economy. It is surely reasonable to propose that the same criteria should be applied to the circumstances surrounding investment in railways, particularly at the present time.

3. *Dual purpose modernisation to include the "ferry train"*. If there is a serious possibility of revising the investment strategy for the A9, it is worth while to extend the analysis beyond conventional modernisation to a concept that is far more compatible with the longer-term future. There would seem to be a peculiar irony in talking about fuel shortages, particularly in Scotland today with its vast oil and gas reserves offshore; but it is conceivable that in the not-too-distant future the holiday motorist or long-distance haulier will be better disposed towards fuel

conservation. In that likely event, the ability to exercise freedom at the periphery will be a direct function of options at the centre of the transport network. The SAPT [5] indicates that "the best ratio of cost to benefit might be achieved by double tracking some of the Perth–Inverness railway and by heightening the loading gauge (simultaneously with electrification) to permit the carriage of lorries and buses as well as cars, vans and caravans on frequent 'ferry trains' ". Rolling stock would be similar to that designed for use in the Channel Tunnel, and again the siting of the terminals would be a key factor in deciding the financial viability of the project. This level of innovation might necessitate some double-track working and a significant level of expenditure over and above that associated with conventional modernisation as discussed in the previous section. The total freight tonnage carried on the track might be expected to double if this facility was available, together with a corresponding increase in passenger traffic. The anticipated cash flow would suggest that within three years from the start of the "ferry train" service all movement costs would be effectively covered, and a suitable rate of return on investment should be calculable past that point.

It is interesting to note that a Motorail service is to be introduced during 1974 between Stirling and Inverness to assist the business traveller who wants to avoid the inevitable congestion and delays during improvements to the A9 over the next four years. British Rail have taken the line that this is a "roadworks diversionary service"—the first of its kind to be prompted by roadworks in the U.K. With fares of £8 for a driver and any size of car, and supplementary fares of £2 and £1 for adult and child passengers, the 151-mile Motorail tie-up would seem to constitute already a sufficiently attractive economic baseline from which to plan a more extensive "ferry train" operation for the future.

There is almost inevitably a reciprocal problem connected with the piggy-back principle of rail haulage, as this new connection with Stirling will allow travellers from Inverness to take their cars by rail as far south as Newton Abbot, i.e. a total distance of 649 miles. Although the potential exists, it does not follow that utilisation will be high.

The regional policy incentive

A8.10 It is often observed that regional factors clearly play in important part in road investment strategy. The forward planning strategy of the Scottish Development Department has already been cited as an example. There is certainly no lack of statutory power at the disposal of the Government if it decided to distribute the available resources in a more balanced way, particularly in the case of the competition between road and rail that has now emerged in connection with the route between Perth and Inverness. If this is considered to be too localised an example it would not be difficult, under the terms of the Transport Act 1968 (S.56) or of the Local Employment Act 1972 (S.7), to find other schemes elsewhere in Scotland where investment in railway infrastructure would make a positive contribution to regional development. There is an immediate concern that if this course of action is delayed any further the opportunity will be lost beneath the weight of EEC regulations on regional aid to which the UK Government will be obliged to respond in the interests of harmonisation of economic policy throughout the Community.

A8.11 While the principle of a social rate of return, whether estimated as a saving of users' time or as the more indirect benefits of reduced congestion, is embodied in S.56 of the Transport Act 1968, this principle has so far been little exercised on railway projects based in Scotland. Major capital grants at 75% of the total cost have been achieved for rolling stock, station improvements, resignalling schemes, track and electrification in other parts of the country, notably the South East. During the period June 1970 to December 1972, a total of £180 million was allocated to London Transport and British Rail for capital projects in South-East England under the provisions of the Act. In Scotland during the same period the only major scheme to benefit has been the £1·5 million Hamilton Circle railway electrification—and Scotland has one-tenth of the UK population.

A8.12 Another fundamental weakness in the criteria governing the balance between road and rail investment has been the provision of roads ahead of demand for reasons of regional development. This has already been identified in

356

the A9 study, but the same is true essentially elsewhere, e.g.
in North East Scotland road construction programmes
have been accorded higher priority than housing or other
essential community services. It would be ludicrous to argue
for a complete moratorium when road improvements can,
with judicious management, expedite the health of a regional
economy. The solution should not depend on a mutually
exclusive policy of roads rather than railways, or even of
roads in competition with other forms of essential community expenditure. However, it is particularly disturbing
that it is the quality of the decisions themselves which
suggests that, despite the lessons of the recent past, the flow
of investment has been dominated by the road programme.
A8.13 Across-the-board estimates of expenditure on major
technological improvements, such as electrification, can be
misleading, since these are usually carefully phased to match
expanding markets. If the railways, in particular, have been
under-funded in Scotland during the post-Beeching era,
there is no time like the present to discriminate between the
various opportunities for investment that still exist. Although
west and east coast main line electrification is now well in
hand, Scottish internal services continue to be neglected.
According to SAPT sources, a sum of £25m–£35m at current
prices would be required to provide Scotland with an
electrified internal rail system which could be easily incorporated over 5 to 6 years. The reluctance of the Scottish
Development Department to declare a national indicative
strategy for the new oil-related industries currently being
attracted to Scotland is therefore reflected at every nodal
point in the transport network. If this really is the economic
event of the century for Scotland, it would be as well to
generate the appropriate planning response now that the
distribution of the incoming industry has been reasonably
well established.
A8.14 Meantime, in the absence of effective co-ordination,
a cohesive transport policy for the region is nowhere in
prospect. Aviation interests debate the logic or otherwise of
a Central Scottish Airport at the same time as large schemes
for the extension of airport facilities at Glasgow, Edinburgh,
Aberdeen and Inverness go rolling forward. The advantages
of the Clyde as a natural deepwater anchorage for the next
generation of super-carriers is hotly advocated at the same

time as the Government primes harbour development at the £1–2 million level in a number of east coast ports and as far north as the Shetland Islands. The sea-borne ferry services between the islands and their links with the mainland services are a constant source of dispute, and so on. It is because Scotland has a number of special transport requirements that it is not possible to conclude even a short statement without some reference to this latter problem.

Freight transport to the Scottish Islands

A8.15 In April 1972 the Secretary of State for Scotland introduced a revision of financial assistance available for shipping services to the Islands in no uncertain terms: "The fullest possible exploitation of roll-on/roll-off vessels operating from purpose-built terminals on the shortest practicable crossings." With the gradual disappearance of traditional passenger and loose-cargo freight vessels, goods previously consigned by sea from the Clyde to the Hebrides are now sent by road through the Highlands. The island communities have themselves come to regard the ferry services as extensions of the arterial road system and to insist that the provision and maintenance of vessels should be a central charge rather than an additional cost to be carried by specific users. This attitude seems to stem from the usual spectrum of uncertainty arising out of road-building and road-pricing policies. As a direct result of this policy change, there will be an increase in the demand for grant aid from the Department of the Environment for rail services previously carrying freight for onward shipment by sea. Although there is no stated policy for complete closure of railway lines in the Highlands, this trend will only serve to further undermine their viability. Again, in connection with the rapidly expanding North Sea oil industry, there has been a substantial increase in passenger traffic between the mainland and the outer islands, which has been largely absorbed by improved air services. Air freight cannot be expected to meet the continuing demands of this industry, apart from rapid transit of small and highly specialised components. It is accepted that road haulage is the only immediately practicable form for the island part of the journey; but it does not follow that on the mainland haulage to and from the ferry ports should be exclusively by road.

The transfer of containers (of ISO size or smaller) between rail and road at mainland ports or suitable railheads would enable the advantages of roll-on/roll-off operation to be achieved without the disadvantages of long-distance road haulage; this would be in accordance with the freight integration policy outlined in the Transport Act 1968.

A8.16 It should be remembered that the pattern and distribution of oil-related development throughout the Highlands is already extensive, while exploratory drilling in many parts of the North Sea has yet to reach a peak of activity. Since the British Government is now committed to maximum rates of exploitation of oil and gas reserves on the shortest possible time scale, it is inevitable that in the light of present trends both islander and mainlander alike will be subjected to increases in the size and weight of lorries. As developments spread in the direction of the Western Highlands, with long stretches of narrow road and the problem of peak tourist traffic, the implications are particularly serious, both for the environment and for the effects on other road users. Full utilisation of the rail network in places must therefore be put at a premium if it is to serve the needs of an oil industry with a 40 year commitment to Scotland and the island communities that must survive without the continuing wealth from the sea.

REFERENCES

[1] *Royal Commission on the Constitution, 1969–73, Report.* Cmnd 5460, HMSO, 1973.
[2] *A Future for Scotland.* Scottish Council (Development & Industry), October 1973.
[3] *Scottish Development Department—Report for 1972*, Cmnd 5274, HMSO, 1972.
[4] *Eighth Report of the Public Accounts Committee*, Session 1972–73, HC 385, Comments on Erskine Bridge, pp 34–37.
[5] *Communications to the Moray Firth: Expenditure Priorities 1974–79.* Scottish Association for Public Transport, November 1973.
[6] Scottish Economic Bulletin: *North Sea Oil.* HMSO, March 1973.

Acknowledgements

The Commission has been helped in its work by a large number of individuals and public and private organisations. We are particularly grateful to the writers of position papers whose names and papers appear in the next section. As well as providing us with much useful information they answered many subsequent queries for us. We acknowledge also the help of the following individuals:

Dr. Eric Albone (University of Bristol), Mr. Terence Bendixson, Mr. David Bevan (Oxford University), Mr. Reginald Bottini (National Union of Agricultural and Allied Workers), Mr. Roger Calvert (National Council on Inland Transport), Mr. R. W. Canvin (University of Exeter), Mr. G. A. Carter (Environmental Consulting Office), Mr. D. M. Caton, Mr. Geoffrey Chandler, Mr. Eric Claxton, OBE, Mrs. Daphne Cloke, Mrs. Irene Coates (Conservation Society), Mr. Nicholas Cole (British Cycling Bureau), Mr. J. S. Dodgson (University of Liverpool), Miss Madge Dugdale, Dr. Martin Elton (Joint Unit for Planning Research, University College London), Mr. Gerard Fiennes, Mr. Christopher Foster (London School of Economics), Mr. Harry Frost, Professor Olaf Gunnarson (Göteborg), Mr. Charles Hadfield, Mr. Christopher Hall, Mrs. E. Hazlewood (National Union of Townswomen's Guilds), Mr. John Hillier, Mr. Peter Hills (University of Leeds), Mr. Gerald Hoinville, Mrs. Ann Holmes, Mr. John Hough (British Council of Churches), Dr. P. C. Humphreys (School of Environmental Studies, University College London), Mr Graham Jenkins, Mrs. Pamela Johnson, Sir Henry Jones, CBE, Professor P. J. Lawther (MRC Air Pollution Unit) Mr. R. B. Lenthall (Stevenage Development Corporation), Mr. J. R. Lucas (Merton College, Oxford), Mr. Peter Mansbridge (Transport and the Environment Group), Dr. K. Meyer, Dr. Dennis Mills (Open University), Professor

Norman Morris (West London Hospital), Mr. Christopher Nash (Southampton University), Mr. David Pearce (Southampton University), Dr. Raymond Plant (Manchester University), Mr. O. H. Prosser, Dr. M. C. Reed (Scottish Association for Public Transport), Mr. E. Relton (Light Railway Transport League), Mrs. Alison Sander (Women's Group on Public Welfare), Mr. A. Sapsford, Professor R. J. Smeed (University College, London), Dr. David Streeter (University of Sussex), Dr. Michael Tainsh (University of Aston in Birmingham), Dr. Leonard Taitz (Conservation Society), Mr. Ray Thomas (Open University), Mr. G. R. Tolliday, Mr. Ed. Turner, Professor P. H. Venables (Birkbeck College), Dr. Bernard Warner, Mr. L. Warner (Cyclists' Touring Club), Mr. Robin Whittaker, Mr. Peter White (Polytechnic of Central London), Mr Geoffrey Williams, Mr. Arthur Wiltshire (A41 Trunk Road Action Committee), Mr. Christopher Wood (University of Manchester).

We also wish to record our thanks to representatives of the following organisations, in particular the Department of the Environment, British Rail and the Transport and Road Research Laboratory:

A25 Villages Association, Aeroport de Paris, Age Concern, Association of River Authorities, Automobile Association, Bath Corporation, Brighton Corporation, British Association of Removers, British Broadcasting Corporation, British Road Federation, British Vehicle Rental and Leasing Association, British Waterways Board, Central Statistical Office, Chamber of Shipping of the United Kingdom, Civic Trust, the Conservative Party, Cornwall County Council Planning Department, Council for the Protection of Rural England, Countryside Commission, City of Coventry Transport Study Group, Daniels Marketing Research Ltd., Disabled Living Foundation, Edinburgh Corporation, Evening Standard, Ministère de l'Aménagement du Territoire, de l'Equipment, du Logement et du Tourisme, France, Freight Transport Association, Gallup, GLC Department of Planning and Transportation, Heathrow Association for the Control of Aircraft Noise, Institute of Community Studies, Institution of Chemical Engineers, Isle of Wight County Council, Joint Committee on Mobility for the Disabled, the Labour Party, Lancashire and Western Sea Fisheries Joint Committee, the Liberal Party, County Council of Lincoln—

Parts of Lindsey, Location of Offices Bureau, London Transport Executive, Market and Opinion Research International, National Bus Company, National Ports Council, National Economic Development Office, National Society for Clean Air, Netherlands—Economisch Bureau Voor Het Wagen Waterverfoer, Noise Advisory Council, NOP Market Research Ltd., Opinion Research Centre, Pedestrians' Association for Road Safety, Post Office Telecommunications Headquarters, Ramblers Association, Road Haulage Association, Royal Society for the Prevention of Accidents, Sand and Gravel Association, Scottish Economic Planning Department, Shell Mex & B.P. Ltd., Social and Community Planning Research, Social Science Research Council, J. Walter Thompson Co., Department of Trade and Industry, Thames Television, Traffic Research Centre, United Kingdom Atomic Energy Authority (Culham Laboratory), Wasey Prichard, Wood & Quadrant, Westminster Reference Library.

Independent Commission on Transport

List of position papers written at the request of the Commission

Scale of transport activity—Barbara J. Mostyn (social psychologist)

Regional planning—Roy Gazzard, Department of Geography, Durham University, (urban geographer, town planner and development consultant)

Railways—Richard Hope (editor, *Railway Gazette International*)

Organisation of the road passenger and freight transport industries—John Hibbs (Principal Lecturer in Transport and Business Studies, City of Birmingham Polytechnic)

Roads—their administration, planning and finance—Geoffrey P. Crow, Department of Civil Engineering, Imperial College of Science and Technology

Transport and resources—Gerald Leach (Visiting Fellow, Science Policy Research Unit, Sussex University; formerly Science Correspondent, The Observer)

Vehicle population—Ian P. Priban (strategic planning counsellor)

Road improvements and accidents—J. J. Leeming (accident studies consultant)

Why Mobility?—Gerald Foley (Energy and Physical Planning Research Group, Architectural Association)

Economic concepts, human values and the rationality of social policy—Raymond Plant (Lecturer in Philosophy, Manchester University)

Social justice and transport—Mayer Hillman (Senior Research Fellow, PEP)

Aesthetics and transport—Father Cyril Barrett, Department of Philosophy, University of Warwick

Urban position paper—W. J. Tyson (Lecturer in Economics, University of Manchester)

New forms of urban transport—Roland Graham, Department of Applied Mathematics, University of Liverpool

Inland waterways—Frederic Doerflinger (Chairman, Inland Shipping Group, Inland Waterways Association)

Coastal shipping—Victor Thorne (freelance journalist)

Pipelines—current applications and possible future developments as a contribution to the transport problems of the UK—H. I. Evans, MBE, and J. J. Johnson (consulting engineer)

Inter-urban roads—criteria and methods of study—Eamonn Judge, Institute for Transport Studies, Leeds University and Ken Button, Department of Economics, Loughborough University of Technology

The position of people living in the country—John S. Gilks (Assistant Secretary of the Rural District Councils Association)

The impact of transport on the countryside—H. P. White (Professor of Geography, University of Salford)

Public opinion of transportation today—Barbara J. Mostyn (social psychologist)

Tailpiece

MEDITATION ON THE A30

by Sir John Betjeman

A man on his own in a car
Is revenging himself on his wife;
He opens the throttle and bubbles with dottle
And puffs at his pitiful life.

"She's losing her looks very fast,
She loses her temper all day;
That lorry won't let me get past,
That Mini is blocking my way.

"Why can't you step on it and shift her!
I can't go on crawling like this!
At breakfast she said that she wished I was dead—
Thank heavens we don't have to kiss.

"I'd like a nice blonde on my knee
And one who won't argue or nag.
Who dares to come hooting at *me*?
I only give way to a Jag.

"You're barmy or plastered, I'll pay you, you bastard—
I *will* overtake you. I *will*!"
As he clenches his pipe, his moment is ripe
And the corner's accepting its kill.

HERE ARE THREE MORE TOPICAL
AND INFORMATIVE CORONET TITLES

HELP YOURSELF
MAVIS NICHOLSON

Who has the right to march into your home uninvited?

How evil or useful are credit cards?

How do you set about making a will?

Why one bank rather than any of the others?

How do you change doctors?

Who might be interested in your old furniture?

This pocket-sized dictionary of self-help deals with a myriad of topics under such headings as Marriage, Money, Work, Death, Leisure, Pets and Home; a reservoir of sensible advice and original suggestions on everyday problems.

INSIDE AUSTRALIA AND NEW ZEALAND
JOHN GUNTHER

Inside Australia And New Zealand is the ninth and last of the famous *Inside* series

Completed by William Forbis after John Gunther's death in 1970, the book provides a vivid picture of Australia and New Zealand in uniquely readable form, bridging the gap between history and contemporary events.

The *Inside* series has achieved considerable success, establishing the author's reputation by selling several million copies in over twenty languages.

THE SOVEREIGN STATE
The secret history of ITT
ANTHONY SAMPSON

Here in devastating detail are revealed the secret workings of a multi-national conglomerate.

'A lucidly written and very readable account of ITT. Mr Sampson's book is likely to be widely read'   *Sunday Telegraph*

'An original, topical, sensational, truly significant book'
                                            Evening Standard

'A very good book'   J. K. Galbraith in *The Sunday Times*

'Reads with the pace of a thriller'   *Yorkshire Post*

LEADING CORONET NON-FICTION TITLES

Mavis Nicholson
☐ 18631 3   Help Yourself   50p

John Gunther
☐ 18299 7   Inside Australia And New Zealand   60p

Anthony Sampson
☐ 18284 9   The Sovereign State
             (The Secret History of ITT)   40p

Kenneth Allsop
☐ 18637 2   In The Country   40p

Fred Archer
☐ 17863 9   The Distant Scene   35p
☐ 17864 7   Under The Parish Lantern   35p
☐ 17865 5   The Secrets Of Bredon Hill   35p

Leslie Frewin
☐ 18662 3   Dietrich   50p

Robert Heller
☐ 17876 0   The Naked Manager   40p

John Arlott
☐ 18105 2   Fred   40p
             (*Fred Trueman's life story*)

All these books are available at your bookshop or newsagent, or can be ordered direct from the publisher. Just tick the titles you want and fill in the form below.

CORONET BOOKS, P.O. Box 11, Falmouth, Cornwall.

Please send cheque or postal order. No currency, and allow the following for postage and packing:

1 book—10p, 2 books—15p, 3 books—20p, 4–5 books—25p, 6–9 books—4p per copy, 10–15 books—2½p per copy, 16–30 books—2p per copy, over 30 books free within the U.K.

Overseas—please allow 10p for the first book and 5p per copy for each additional book.

Name..

Address...